COLLEGE ARGUMENTS

UNDERSTANDING THE GENRES

D0473030

Irene L. Clark

with

Emmanuel Sabaiz-Birdsill

SECOND EDITION

Kendall Hunt
publishing company

Cover image © Shutterstock, Inc.
Image on p. x ©Valua Vitaly/Shutterstock.com
Chapter image ©Planner/Shutterstock.com

Kendall Hunt
publishing company

www.kendallhunt.com
Send all inquiries to:
4050 Westmark Drive
Dubuque, IA 52004-1840

Copyright © 2010, 2016 by Kendall Hunt Publishing Company

ISBN 978-1-4652-7734-3

All rights reserved. No part of this publication may be reproduced,
stored in a retrieval system, or transmitted, in any form or by any means,
electronic, mechanical, photocopying, recording, or otherwise,
without the prior written permission of the copyright owner.

Printed in the United States of America

CONTENTS

PREFACE

College Arguments: Understanding the Genres, 2nd edition aims to help students approach college writing assignments with greater insight, focusing on two significant terms: *argument* and *genre*. The first edition of this book used both terms in a singular form and focused primarily on a type of essay that many teachers and scholars refer to as "academic argument." In the second edition, both terms appear in plural, because we now recognize that there are a number of writing **genres** assigned in college classes and that students are often asked to write **arguments** of different types. As Yancey, Robertson, and Taczak point out in a recent book, "the academic argumentative writing that so influenced the teaching of composition is now regarded as only one variety of writing" (1). This realization, however, does not mean that "academic argument," as it was defined in the first edition of *College Argument: Understanding the Genre*, is not important. In fact, based on our work with writing tasks assigned across the curriculum, we still think that this type of writing is expected in many college classes and professional settings and that it is an important genre for students to understand and be able to produce. However, we also acknowledge that other types of essays are being assigned—reports, literacy narratives, multimodal essays—and therefore, this second edition, while retaining its focus on academic argument, utilizes a genre approach to other types of college writing as well. It has therefore expanded the use of the word "argument" to refer to any essay that is intended to persuade someone that an idea or perspective is worth considering or important to think about.

The use of the plural in the word "genre," is based on our recognition that the type of "argument" assigned in college classes varies considerably. Some writing assignments may require students to "argue" a position on a debatable issue, such as the morality of assisted suicide, the requirement that all children be vaccinated, the legal age at which a person should be permitted to drink alcohol, or whether schools should require students to wear school uniforms. However, other types of essays may also be assigned that are less obviously "argumentative"—a literacy narrative, which discusses a student's struggle with learning English as a second or subsequent language, an essay based on an ethnographic exploration of a children's toy store in the context of investigating gender stereotypes, a discussion of the role of the media on various aspects of modern life, a review of a film, or the analysis of a character in a literary work. All of these topics may result in essays that can be considered a form of "argument" because they all are focused around a main idea, point, or persuasive goal, although not necessarily a debatable pro/con issue.

A "GENRE" APPROACH TO COLLEGE WRITING

Although the word "genre," in the past, has been used to refer to a particular literary "form," such as a poem, short story, or play, recent scholarship suggests that the term pertains equally well to non-literary, "real-world" texts and that genres come into existence because they effectively fulfill a particular function. For example, a wedding invitation is a genre that has the function of inviting guests to a ceremony and celebration, and a grant proposal has the function of justifying a request for funds for a particular project. Non-literary genres thus address particular needs and are strongly connected with the concept of "rhetoric"— which was defined a long time ago as referring to how a writer locates ways of persuading an audience. We now understand that persuasion varies among cultures and contexts, and we now refer to different "rhetorics" such as feminist rhetorics or Native American rhetorics that vary according to differing purposes and populations. Approaching writing assignments rhetorically means looking at an essay in terms of its purpose and audience, insight that will foster understanding of other features of a text—the representation of the writer within the text, the choice of topic, the approach taken to the topic, the type of support and evidence presented, as well as conventions associated with form and style. Deriving from discussions of genre theory over the past thirty years, the book is based on the following concepts:

1. Most writing assigned in college classes requires students to develop an argument of some kind—that is to support a main idea in order to persuade an audience that this idea is worth considering or at least thinking about. Although each academic discipline may define argument in different ways and utilize particular approaches, devices, and patterns, a number of elements pertain across disciplines and fields.

2. Many arguments written in college courses are intended to address a "rhetorical situation"—that is, a problem, situation, or need that can be impacted or changed in some way through writing. A rhetorical situation is generated by an exigence, which means a defect, an obstacle, a question, or something that is not as it ought to be or about which there can be disagreement or at least is not obvious or generally acknowledged.

3. An important characteristic of argument often involves the "problematizing" of a topic— that is, in developing a position or thesis for an argumentative writing assignment, the writer identifies a specific problem, assumption, idea, view, or situation that requires some form of reevaluation or reexamination that can be addressed in writing. Problematization is an important strategy to generate ideas for college writing.

4. The genre of college argument can be defined not primarily in terms of form but rather in terms of rhetorical and social situations that invite written response. These situations construct the role of the writer and determine the writer's conception of audience.

5. College argument is intended to move readers to consider what is being said, think about the reasons and evidence presented, acknowledge that the argument is compelling, and then, perhaps reevaluate and modify its point of view.

6. Writing a compelling argument supported by convincing evidence involves the ability to critically evaluate published material and incorporate outside information into a text.

THE RECONCEPTUALIZATION OF GENRE: BACKGROUND

Traditionally, the word *genre* has been associated with notions of form and classifications of text, in particular with describing the formal features of a literary work. In a pedagogical context, this way of looking at genre has frequently suggested an emphasis on form and, to a certain extent, on form for form's sake. The most problematic application of this view completely separates form from content, an example being the use of formulaic slots into which students are instructed to apply content. A notorious example of this approach is the five-paragraph essay, which many students apply indiscriminately to any writing task they are asked to complete, without questioning why there should be five, rather than four or six paragraphs, or examining the relationship of one paragraph to another.

Recently, however, the concept of genre has been reconceptualized in terms of **function**. While recognizing that genres can be characterized by regularities in textual form and substance, current thinking about genre looks at these regularities as surface manifestations of a more fundamental kind of regularity. The work of Devitt, Freedman and Medway, and Swales, among others, recognizes that although genres can be characterized by regularities in textual form, such regularity represents "typical ways of engaging rhetorically with recurring situations" (Freedman and Medway 2) and that similarities in textual form and feature derive from an effective response to situations that "writers encounter repeatedly" (Devitt 576). Because genres arise because writers respond appropriately to recurring rhetorical situations, the new concept of genre perceives generic conventions as deriving from suitability and effectiveness rather than from arbitrary traditions and conventions.

To a great extent, this reconceptualized concept of genre builds on other theories that have impacted the teaching of writing, particularly those that emphasize the functionality of text and the role of context in determining text effectiveness. Genre theory is consistent with rhetorical approaches, which focus attention on context, audience, and occasion and which view writing as a way of responding to a specific reader (or readers) within a specific context on a specific occasion (Freedman and Medway 5). Genre theory is also compatible with social constructionist theory, which recognizes that the act of composing draws on previous interactions with others and with speech act theory, which emphasizes the function of language as a way of acting in the world and the importance of context in creating meaning.

In accord with this emphasis on context, John Swales defines the concept of genre primarily by its common communicative purposes. Swales maintains that these purposes and the role of the genre within its environment have generated specific textual features and he advocates a genre-centered approach to teaching as a means of enabling students to understand why a particular genre has acquired characteristic features.

PEDAGOGICAL APPLICATIONS OF GENRE THEORY

An important idea that informs this book is not to teach text form and formula as ends in and of themselves. The goal, rather, is to help students acquire genre knowledge or genre *awareness* so that they will be able to engage with a variety of writing assignments more effectively. The idea of genre *awareness* involves fostering students' understanding of what motivates the production of different types of texts so that they will be able to develop appropriate response strategies. This position maintains that being able to produce an example of a genre is a matter not just of generating a text that adheres to certain formal characteristics, but that insight into how genres come to exist and the factors that make a genre what it is will enable students to apply generic conventions in a multiplicity of contexts.

A genre approach to college writing and especially to argument can have a significant impact on students throughout their university careers, because a great deal of the writing students are required to do at the university, the sort of writing that is frequently referred to as "academic discourse," is really a form of argumentation, whether or not it is specifically labeled as such. Most college writing assignments, from the Freshman essay to the content area research paper, are actually *arguments* in the sense that they require students to establish and support a clearly stated thesis or position concerned with a substantive and frequently controversial topic, to problematize that topic in order to establish an argumentative context for that thesis, and to establish a credentialed persona through the use of citation and acknowledgment of a counter argument. However, this is the type of writing that students often have the most difficulty with, not only because they are unfamiliar with it as a genre, but also because the requirements of the assignment are often presented solely in terms of form rather than purpose. As a result, students confuse argumentation with exposition, and the papers they write may consist of a linear sequencing of unprocessed material in the body of the essay with evaluative comment, if it exists at all, postponed to the concluding paragraph.

Irene Clark first became interested in applying genre analysis to argumentation when she was teaching at the University of Utrecht in the Netherlands, working with Ph.D. candidates in Geography who wished to write social science articles in English. These students were all high achievers within their field; yet most of them were unsuccessful in writing articles in English, not because of poor language skills, but because they were unfamiliar with the purpose—that is, the "genre" of scholarly articles in the social sciences. She taught in Utrecht on two occasions, and during the second, she developed several class lessons based on John M. Swales' concept of genre analysis. Like many native English speaking students, the Dutch students were unaware of the necessity of problematizing a topic, did not understand what constitutes convincing evidence, and had not analyzed the role of writer and audience in constructing an effective argument. Once they understood the importance of formulating an argumentative purpose, their writing improved impressively and she then began to use this approach with composition students in the United States, and encourage writing instructors with whom she worked to use this approach in their own teaching. As an experienced college instructor, Emmanuel Sabaiz-Birdsill found this approach extremely useful in teaching a variety of college writing courses, including courses in business writing, critical thinking, and queer studies. By utilizing the many different approaches to specific genres, he has been able to develop a curriculum that allows his students to understand the importance of genre awareness. *College Arguments: Understanding the Genres* thus represents Clark and Sabaiz-Birdsill's adaptation of this approach to college writing.

OTHER ADDITIONS TO THE SECOND EDITION

The second edition retains and expands the emphasis on genre and argument that characterized the first edition. But we have added several components that are new to this edition:

- a discussion of deliberative imitation as an invention strategy, both in terms of form, style, and process;
- additional material concerned with the interrelationship between writing and reading;
- an incorporation of material concerned with transnational rhetorics;
- an updated chapter on visual rhetoric and multimodal writing;
- a new chapter that focuses on narrative.

We hope that these additions will help students gain additional awareness of both genre and argument, enabling them to approach college writing tasks with greater insight and ultimately to continue to improve as writers.

ACKNOWLEDGMENTS

There are a number of people whose insights and suggestions have affected this book and whom we would like to thank: Stephanie Jones, Kristin Kaz, Eric Kufs, and Sharon Lim, who worked over a hot Los Angeles summer to help us develop the new material that is included in this new edition.

WORKS CITED

Devitt, Amy J. "Generalizing About Genre: New Conceptions of an Old Concept." *College Composition and Communication 44* (1993): 573–586.

Freedman, Aviva, and Peter Medway. Eds. *Learning and Teaching Genre*. Portsmouth, New Hampshire: Boynton/Cook Publishers, 1994. Print.

Graff, Gerald. *Clueless in Academe: How Schooling Obscures the Life of the Mind*. New Haven, CT: Yale University Press, 2003. Print.

Swales, John. *Genre Analysis*. Cambridge: Cambridge University Press, 1990. Print.

HIBISCUS HAZE

Hibiscus Haze is Number 1 for beautiful, natural skin. If you haven't used it, ask someone who has, and you will understand.

MADE WITH NATURAL INGREDIENTS.
FOR BEAUTIFUL SKIN, THE NATURAL SKIN YOU
WERE BORN WITH, TRY **HIBISCUS HAZE**.
THEN YOU WILL KNOW.

CHAPTER 1

College Writing Genres and the Rhetorical Situation

The picture that opens this chapter is of a beautiful young woman with lovely skin, wearing a hibiscus in her hair. She looks peaceful and serene, with little or no makeup, because she doesn't need it. Her skin is naturally beautiful without any additional aids. The text written above her head says that "Hibiscus Haze is Number 1 for beautiful, natural skin. If you haven't used it, ask someone who has, and you will understand." Below the picture is a statement that tells us that the product is made with "natural ingredients." It then states, "For beautiful skin, the natural skin you were born with, try Hibiscus Haze. Then you will know."

You can easily recognize this picture as an advertisement. The picture and the statement are familiar to you because you are acquainted with the **genre** of advertising. You understand the need and purpose of this ad—to advertise and ultimately sell Hibiscus Haze—and you are aware of how its various **components** create its **form** and make it different from other types of writing.

Because familiarity with a genre is essential for anyone who wishes to reproduce it, this book aims to familiarize you with the **genres** that are assigned in your college classes, in particular the genre of argument. Argumentative writing is an important component of most college classes in courses throughout the disciplines, as well as in composition courses and business writing. When professors assign writing, they usually expect students to produce a genre of writing that establishes, or *argues*, a central point, idea, thesis, or position—often the essay addresses a complex or problematic topic. Moreover, they usually expect that this central point, thesis, or position is founded on a thoughtful, thorough, and open-minded investigation of a topic and is supported through logic-based evidence.

Actually, an advertisement can also have a thesis or central point—in fact, most advertisements do. However, the evidence cited in most advertisements is not always based on logic or an open-minded investigation of a topic. For example, the ad for Hibiscus Haze has the following thesis: Hibiscus Haze will make your skin beautiful, and you should buy Hibiscus Haze. The following ideas support it:

> Hibiscus Haze is Number 1.
> Hibiscus Haze creates beautiful, natural skin.
> Hibiscus Haze is made with natural ingredients.
> People who have tried Hibiscus Haze think it is effective.

Unlike the writing genres usually assigned in college classes, however, none of these supporting ideas is based on logical evidence. The statement that "Hibiscus Haze is Number 1 for beautiful, natural skin" sounds promising. But what is natural skin? What authority on skin has done research to support this claim? And what evidence is presented that this statement is true?

The fact that Hibiscus Haze is number 1 also sounds promising. But number 1 among what group of other products? And where is the evidence that Hibiscus Haze is indeed number 1? Similarly, the statement that asking someone who has used it will enable you to "know" that it is effective sounds convincing. But who is that someone? How many people have actually used this product? How old were these people and under what circumstances did they use it? What are natural ingredients? What is meant by "the natural skin you were born with?" Where is the evidence for any of these claims?

Of course, this lack of logical evidence does not mean that the ad is ineffective, because an important goal of an ad is **not** to make a logical argument but to promote the "name" of a product. Someone who is looking for a skin product, browsing through the aisles of a pharmacy, might recognize the name "Hibiscus Haze" and decide to try it simply because he or she recalls having seen the ad.

College writing, then, particularly argumentative writing, is quite different from an ad in terms of the topics it addresses and the way in which ideas are presented and supported. Although argument is not the only type of writing you will encounter in college and although each discipline may view argument in a special way, the expectation that you can construct an argument based on reason and evidence pertains in many courses, even if the professor does not specifically use the word *argument* or *argumentation*. In fact, it is often the quality of the argument that most significantly influences the grade a paper will receive. In fact, in a collection of student writing from the University of Michigan, the essays consisted primarily of argumentative essays, reports, or research papers, with few exceptions, and a careful look at the reports and research papers indicates that these too, were arguments. Many reports and research papers addressed a debatable issue and even those that did not, had a central focus that needed to be explored and were supported by logic-based evidence.

Students, however, may be unfamiliar with college argument and misunderstand its purpose. Sometimes they think of argument as a disagreement or dispute, as in, "I had an argument with my roommate last night." Or they think of it as more difficult than other types of writing, such as narrative writing, which tells a story, or expository writing, which presents information and, in fact, is also a type of argument. But once students become aware of what argument is, they can write their essays more easily.

By approaching argument as a *genre, College Arguments: Understanding the Genres* aims to take the mystery out of college writing. In this chapter, we will explain several terms that are important to understand in the context of writing an essay; in particular, *rhetoric, exigence, rhetorical situation, audience,* and *identity.* These are terms that will be used throughout the book. We will also show what a typical argument essay usually looks like in terms of its *structure* or *form.* The premise of this book is that the better you understand how various features of argumentative writing help achieve its purpose, the more successfully you will be able to write essays in your college classes.

RHETORIC, EXIGENCE, AND THE RHETORICAL SITUATION

The term *rhetoric* in the context of college writing refers to the effective use of language to persuade, inform, or educate. Although people sometimes use the term *rhetoric* to mean words that mean nothing, as in "that is just rhetoric," ancient Greek philosophers considered it a serious form of writing and speaking that is oriented toward influencing an audience— finding approaches and strategies that are likely to be convincing to those for whom an essay is intended. Several years ago, a scholar named Lloyd Bitzer wrote an article with the title "The Rhetorical Situation," in which he used the expression "rhetorical situation" to mean a problem, situation, or need that can be impacted or changed in some way through writing. Bitzer used the word *exigence* to refer to a defect, an obstacle, or "something that is other than it should be," and if you are a student who is in the process of finding a topic for an essay, you might ask yourself, "WHERE'S THE EXIGENCE?"

Just as there are many kinds of genres and many kinds of argument, there are also many kinds of exigencies. But a rhetorical exigence exists when something can be done about it through writing, if only to impact how people think about it. To help you understand the idea of exigence, imagine that administrators on a college campus had decided to change the evening curfew from midnight to 10:00 p.m. during the week, a policy to which many students object. The exigence in this scenario, the situation that is "other than it should be," was the early curfew, and in order to convince administrators to make the curfew later, the students decided to draft a letter to the dean arguing against it, along with a petition signed by a majority of students.

Exigence is an important component of a rhetorical situation. Other equally important elements are the **writer**, the **audience**, the **context**, the **occasion**, and the **purpose**. In the example of the 10:00 p.m. curfew, the rhetorical situation, which is connected to the context and occasion, is the dissatisfaction students feel about the curfew, which they hope to change. The **writer** consists of the student writers who object to the curfew and the **audience** is administrators who instituted the curfew. The **purpose** of the letter, which addresses the rhetorical situation, is to convince the administrators that the curfew should be made later.

FOR THINKING, DISCUSSION, AND WRITING

1. In the hypothetical situation concerning the curfew, students decided to write a letter and a petition. Why did they choose this genre rather than an ad? Do you think they could have accomplished their purpose with a different genre?

2. Select an ad from a magazine. In small groups discuss the following questions:

    What is the purpose of this ad?

    What features of this ad are similar to those associated with the genre of argument?

    What features in this ad are different from those associated with the genre of argument?

    What is the thesis of this ad? Could this ad be written as an essay?

    Why or why not?

3. Examine a magazine or newspaper and note the "exigence" and rhetorical situation addressed in an article or editorial. Bring the article or editorial to class and discuss the following questions:

    What is the purpose of this article or editorial?

    What exigence does it address?

    What is the thesis of this article or editorial?

    How is this thesis supported?

    How is the structure used to further the purpose of this article or editorial?

COLLEGE ARGUMENTS AND THE RHETORICAL SITUATION

Understanding the concept of exigence and the rhetorical situation will help you write more effectively in college because the purpose of a college argument is to respond to a rhetorical situation. This purpose helps determine its other features, such as:

- the *writer* as he or she appears in the essay,
- the *audience* for whom the essay is intended,
- the *topic* selected,
- the *approach* to the topic,
- the type of *support* and evidence used to develop the main point (also called the claim or thesis), and
- the **assumptions** underlying the main claim or thesis

Moreover, the purpose of an argument essay affects not only the conceptual features of a text; it also affects its structure and style.

AN IDEA WORTH CONSIDERING

Although people sometimes think of an argument as a heated verbal interchange or quarrel characterized by intense emotions and angry words, argument as a genre of writing assigned in college classes is characterized by reason, logic, and careful, often analytical thinking, rather than by emotional excess, although the writer may feel quite strongly about the topic. Its purpose is to convince its audience or readers of the worth of an idea, not to bulldoze them into surrender. Most essays, whether written in college or elsewhere, are unlikely to cause readers to change their minds completely, particularly if the topic is complex and if people already have strong feelings about it. When you read an essay, how often do you say, *"Wow! That essay has completely changed my mind!"* Probably not very often, and to aim for a response like this is unrealistic.

The goal of an argument essay in a college class, then, is not to change people's minds completely, although that does happen sometimes. What you hope to do is influence your readers to *consider* your thesis or claim, *think* about the reasons and evidence, *acknowledge* that the thesis has merit, and then perhaps to reevaluate and modify their point of view somewhat. After a thoughtful reader has read a well-written essay, he or she should say, *"That is an idea worth considering."* We suggest that you write that statement on a sticky note and attach it to your computer screen. You will then be able to keep this goal in mind as you write essays for your college classes.

FEATURES OF ARGUMENTATION AFFECTED BY ITS PURPOSE

The Writer: How Does the Purpose of Academic Argument Affect the Writer?

All of us are more likely to accept another person's ideas if we think of that person as knowledgeable, trustworthy, logical, and fair as opposed to ignorant, untrustworthy, illogical, and biased. In order to convince an audience that their ideas are worth considering, writers of argument-based college essays thus aim to present themselves as people of intelligence, moral integrity, and good intentions. *Ethos,* or credibility, is created when writers present themselves in the following ways:

1. The writer must convince the audience that he or she is knowledgeable about the subject.

To become knowledgeable about the subject of the argumentative essay, the writer needs to research the topic and learn as much about it as possible within the time limits of the assignment. For example, if you are writing an essay arguing that children in public schools should be required to wear school uniforms, you should indicate to your reader that you know a lot about the controversy concerned with school uniforms. You, yourself, may have worn a uniform, and your experience is certainly relevant to your essay. But you would probably want to include other types of information written by those who have studied the issue, such as educators or psychologists. Otherwise, your reader may not accept your ideas.

2. *The writer must indicate awareness and understanding of the ideas of others by presenting a balanced perspective on the topic.*

The writer of an effective argumentative essay has examined multiple ideas about an issue or topic and indicates to the reader that he or she has done so. For example, if you are writing about the controversy concerning school uniforms, you should indicate that you are familiar with several perspectives on the topic—that some people feel that uniforms stifle self-expression and individual freedom while others feel that uniforms actually promote self-expression and freedom because children can focus on learning rather than on clothing.

3. *The writer should base his or her claims on the evidence that is most likely to convince the intended audience.*

The credibility of evidence varies according to the audience for whom the essay is intended, and sometimes a personal narrative may serve as adequate evidence. Usually, though, argument-based college essays are written for readers who value logic and reason, readers who expect convincing evidence rather than empty assertions. If you are writing about the controversy concerning school uniforms, you can include your own experience, but you should probably be able to cite authorities who have had experience with the effect of uniforms on children's behavior and performance in school. You might also wish to cite statistics about crimes committed in schools when children fight over brand name clothing or with reports of gang-related incidents when children are mistaken for gang members as a result of their clothing. Simply making an assertion that uniforms are better (or worse) or saying that you liked or didn't like wearing a uniform when you were in school, is inadequate support for a claim within the genre of argument. You must be prepared to say "why" uniforms are better or worse and provide sound evidence for your ideas.

4. *The writer must use language in such a way as to appear truthful and fair.*

A college essay written in the genre of argument is written for a community that values truth and rational thinking, however these concepts are defined within that community. Such a community will not accept the ideas of a writer who appears biased or hysterical, or a writer who uses language to inflame rather than convince. Although you may feel strongly about your subject (and it's good to have strong feelings about topics you write about), you should aim for a tone that suggests that you are a careful person who thinks seriously about the statements you write. Overblown statements such as "school uniforms are a form of fascism," or "if students do not wear uniforms, they will never learn anything in school" are unlikely to convince a thoughtful audience.

The Audience: For Whom Are Argument-Based College Essays Written?

When students write essays for their college classes, they often assume that they are writing exclusively for their teachers. This is not an unreasonable assumption, because certainly your teacher is likely to be **one** of your readers—and the one who is going to assign a grade! However, an argument-based college essay is not usually intended for only one person. Rather, it is oriented toward a broader audience or readership consisting of educated people who tend to be convinced by reason and supported claims rather than by empty statements and inflammatory assertions. Your teacher, then, is a *representative* of this audience, not the only audience the writer should consider. Although this audience may not be completely knowledgeable about the topic being discussed, writers of academic arguments presume an audience that is familiar with the purpose and conventions of argument and will be able to understand what is being written if adequate context, background, and explanation are provided. This perspective on audience would help when dealing with intercultural/transnational audiences who will need that background information to understand your arguments.

Students who think they are writing only for their teachers may leave out important information about the background or context that people other than the teacher would not know. For example, we recently read an essay that began with the following sentences: "This essay will discuss an article assigned in class about the pros and cons of lowering the drinking age." A teacher who has assigned this topic would know what article the essay is referring to, but someone else would not.

In considering the audience or readership for your college writing assignments, imagine that you have left a copy of your essay on a table in the college library. If you have explained and supported your position adequately and included sufficient background and context for the topic, a person who finds your essay in the library should be able to understand its central point, even if he or she is not thoroughly familiar with the topic or the assigned writing task.

The Topic: What Sort of Topics Are Suitable for College Argument? How Much Background Should the Writer Provide?

Argument-based college writing is usually concerned with topics that are problematic, unresolved, and complex. Suitable topics do not address questions of fact or taste; rather, they focus on questions on which more than one perspective is possible or topics about which most people do not have a great deal of general information. An important characteristic of argument is that it deals with a problem or difficulty within a topic—that is, the writer identifies a specific problem, assumption, idea, view, or situation that requires some form of reevaluation, additional understanding, exploration, or reexamination that can be addressed in writing. For example, a problem associated with the topic of school uniforms concerns the controversy over what effect uniforms have on individual creativity or the question of whether or not schools have the right to dictate what students must wear. In establishing a context for an argumentative essay, the writer must present sufficient background information so that readers understand the situation, but not so much information that they become overwhelmed or confused.

Moreover, in deciding what information to include, it is also important to think about what may be considered "new" as opposed to "common" knowledge. *New* knowledge, such as a discussion of a little-known scientific term, or, in the case of school uniforms, a study showing the impact of uniforms on students' performance in school, must be explained and the source of new information must be acknowledged by a citation. *Common* knowledge, such as the fact that George Washington was the first president of the United States, is presumed familiar and requires no special acknowledgment or citation.

Approach to the Topic: What Kind of Approach Is Appropriate in Argument-Based College Writing?

Because argumentative writing is concerned with complex, unresolved, or problematic topics, thoughtful writers of academic argument understand that their thesis or claim that expresses their ideas is rarely true 100% of the time. Therefore, a great deal of academic writing is characterized by a careful or *qualified* approach to a topic, and an effective thesis statement reflects that qualified approach. Writers may predict consequences or present an analysis of particular conditions or events, but they may also acknowledge that their statements are true only under certain conditions, discuss alternative points of view, or indicate the tentativeness of their observations by using qualifying words such as "seems," "suggests," "indicates," "to some degree," or "to a certain extent." For the topic of school uniforms, an appropriate statement might be that school uniforms are *likely* to enhance academic performance or that they are *likely* to minimize gang-related incidents.

The appropriateness of using a qualified approach to a potentially controversial topic is in accord with the way most people react to a perspective that might be different from their own—in fact, it was mentioned in Ben Franklin's autobiography, which was published 1791. In the section recounting how Franklin learned to write, Franklin maintains the value of a "modest" or "diffident" tone as more convincing to a potentially resistant audience, and notes that "when advanced any thing that may possibly be disputed," he never uses words such as *certainly, undoubtedly,* or any others that give the "air of positiveness to an opinion." Rather, Franklin maintains, he tends to say

> *I conceive* or *apprehend* a thing to be so and so; *It appears to me,* or *I should not think it, so* or *so, for such and such reasons*; or, *I imagine it to be so; or It is so, if I am not mistaken.* This habit, I believe, has been of great advantage to me when I have had occasion to inculcate my opinions and persuade men into measures that I have been from time to time engaged in promoting. And as the chief ends of conversation are to *inform* or to be *informed,* to *please* or to *persuade,* I wish well-meaning and sensible men would not lessen their power of doing

good by a positive assuming manner that seldom fails to disgust, tends to create opposition, and to defeat every one of those purposes for which speech was given to us. In fact if you wish to instruct others, a positive dogmatic manner in advancing your sentiments may occasion opposition and prevent a candid attention. If you desire instruction and improvement from others, you should not at the same time express yourself fixed in your present opinions. (Franklin, Benjamin. *The Autobiography of Benjamin Franklin. 1868*. New York: Barnes & Noble, 2008.)

Support: What Kind of Support and Evidence Are Used in Argument-Based College Writing?

A main point, thesis, or claim in argument-based college writing is usually supported by logic and reason not by emotional rhetoric. The evidence cited should be from a reliable source and may take the form of appropriate examples, valid analogies, statements from credible authorities, and information from reputable published works. In using evidence obtained from statistics, the writer must consider how, where, when, and why the data was collected and examine carefully how it pertains to the claim being established. For the topic of school uniforms, appropriate evidence might consist of statements from school authorities or educators who have studied their effect on student performance.

Assumptions: What Is the Role of Underlying Assumptions in Academic Argument?

Although adequate support is necessary in order for a rational audience to accept a writer's claim, no thesis or claim will be convincing unless the writer and the audience share assumptions, beliefs, or principles that can serve as a common ground between them. For example, a mother might say to a teenager, "You should take a summer math class, because it will help you become a better student." But because this claim is based on the assumption that being a good student is desirable, it will only be convincing if both the teenager and the mother share this belief. The teenager would then say, "Good idea, Mom. It's important for me to become a better student. I definitely want to take that math class." Other assumptions are also implicit in this claim—the idea that extra work in the present will have benefit in the future, or that summers should be used for educational enrichment, to name two.

The teenager, however, might not share his mother's assumptions (teenagers often don't) and therefore he might say, "I don't care about being a good student. I want to spend time playing volleyball at the beach so I can have a toned, tanned body. My body is what is important to me." For a teenager, the future may seem far in the distance—too far to worry about when the sun is shining and the waves are splashing onto the shore. The teenager may conceive of summer as a time for relaxing, playing sports, or working on a tan, not for improving math skills. Therefore, the mother's argument about the importance of taking the math class would not be convincing to the teenager.

THE ROLE OF STRUCTURE

The features discussed above are important for argument-based college writing. However, if you are unfamiliar with what a college essay looks like, you will need to read one—in fact, many—so that you can understand how these features are incorporated into the text. A very useful strategy to use when you are not sure what sort of essay you are expected to write is to find an example and begin your writing process by **imitating its structure**. The final section of this chapter will discuss the structure that a college essay often takes and includes some illustrative examples. In Chapter 7, which is concerned with form, we will suggest some imitative strategies that can help you begin your writing process.

What Does an Argument-Based College Essay Look Like? A Qualification About Structure

Argument-based college essays often conform to a particular structure that reflects the purposes and goals of argumentation, although this structure, like any other, is also a matter of convention and all conventions are arbitrary, at least to some extent. This means that the goals of argumentation might be realized through a number of different essay forms, and indeed, writers wishing to exercise their creativity might attempt to experiment with different ways of presenting their ideas. Nevertheless, because this structure continues to dominate most academic writing and because many college professors expect assigned essays to appear in this form, you will want to become familiar with it, understand how it functions within the genre of argument, and incorporate that understanding into your writing.

Before we examine the components of this structure, discuss its purpose, or suggest strategies for using it or varying it, though, we would like to emphasize the importance of **questioning** how the formal features of any text help writers accomplish their purpose, because mechanical adherence to any form stifles creative thought and results in a boring, ineffective essay. The structure of the essays you write should reflect careful thinking about the relationship of form to function.

For example, many students in high school are taught the form known as "the five paragraph essay," which consists of an introduction, three body paragraphs, and a conclusion. The problem with the five paragraph essay is that once students have been using it for several years, some of them then believe that *all* essays are required to have five paragraphs, no matter what subject is being discussed. Unaware that the value of any pattern is determined solely by whether or not it fulfills the writer's purpose, these students maintain a mechanical, uncritical perspective on their writing assignments, producing essays that are usually simplistic and boring. Form must follow content, not the other way around, so whatever essay form you use, it is important to think about how form contributes to the purpose of argumentation—that is, to establish an adequately supported thesis or claim that will influence a reader to say, "That is an idea worth considering."

Having made this qualification, we will now talk about the central components of an argumentative essay.

THE CLASSICAL FORM OF ARGUMENTATION

The classical argumentative structure consists of an introduction, which states the thesis or claim; a body, which supports that claim and addresses the opposing viewpoint; and a conclusion, which sums up the main ideas and perhaps restates the thesis. The components of this form, which are probably familiar to you, can be summarized as follows:

1. Introduction

In this section, which may consist of only one or two paragraphs, the writer indicates the topic, narrows the topic, briefly explains the exigence, and presents the thesis or claim. The introduction may also include relevant background material. In some instances, it might summarize a viewpoint that the body of the essay will refute or support.

2. The Body

The body of the essay consists of the following components:

The Rhetorical Situation

This further explains the situation, conflict, or problem and summarizes various viewpoints as a way of indicating that the writer understands the complexity of the topic and has researched the topic thoroughly. This component might also define important key terms and can include personal experience that is relevant to the topic.

Support for the Thesis

This is usually the longest and most substantive section of the essay. It supports the thesis with compelling reasons and evidence that might include facts, statistics, data, statements by authorities, and illustrative examples. It may also establish common ground between the writer and the intended readers of the essay.

Anticipation and Refutation of Opposing Viewpoints

In this section, the writer indicates areas where an opponent will probably disagree with the thesis. Discussing an opposing viewpoint adds strength to an essay, because by indicating awareness of an opponent's point of view, the writer can then argue against it, showing how the ideas in the essay are superior.

3. Conclusion

This section provides a sense of closure by summarizing the writer's main argument. It may also suggest what action, if any, the readers ought to take or postulate potential implications or consequences.

These are the various "parts" of an argumentative essay in terms of the classical structure. In subsequent chapters in this book, we will discuss each of these parts in more detail and also suggest alternative ways you may wish to structure your essay.

USE OF OUTSIDE SOURCES IN AN ARGUMENT-BASED COLLEGE ESSAY

Although some essay topics may ask you to write from personal experience, many college writing assignments will require you to support your thesis with information from books and articles from the library or electronic data sources. When you include outside information in your essay, it is important to indicate to your reader the source from which you obtained it. To do so, conventions associated with argumentation require you to cite your source within the body of your essay and then compile a "Works Cited" or "References" page at the end of the essay that provides complete bibliographic information. Chapter 10 will discuss strategies for locating information from published works. The Appendix will discuss citation conventions.

ANALYZING AN ARGUMENTATIVE ESSAY

The essay reproduction that follows exemplifies the conceptual features, structure, and citation conventions associated with an argument-based college essay. It was written in response to an assignment concerned with the topic of political correctness, which asked students to examine the extent to which policies mandating what can and cannot be said on college campuses are likely to cause benefit or harm to the university community. Examining this essay and its annotations can help you understand more fully how the conceptual features of argumentation help fulfill its purpose. It will also give you a more complete picture of what an argumentative essay usually looks like in terms of form and structure.

JOHN'S ESSAY

Political Repression: The Reality of PC

(The title provides insight into the main idea in the essay)

INTRODUCTION

(The Introduction establishes the exigence and discusses its background.
It also presents the thesis.)

Although the United States prides itself on its tolerance for people of all races, ethnic origins, and sexual preference, a great deal of prejudice and mistrust of people considered "different" still exists. Many people continue to hold racist, sexist, and homophobic perspectives, as is indicated by sexist, racist, or homophobic comments made by politicians. Fear of violence associated with prejudiced views has moved officials at colleges and universities to mandate what can and cannot be said on campus. This idea that students should modify their speech and writing on campus has come to be known as Political Correctness or PC. <u>However, although Political Correctness is intended to benefit society by preventing hurtful speech against minorities, homosexuals, and women, in actuality it serves to undercut one of the most important values of our educational system—the free exchange of ideas. Instead of fostering an environment conducive to understanding and learning as its proponents maintain, PC suppresses discussion and meaningful interchange between students.</u> **(The underlined sentence explains the exigence and the rhetorical situation. It also establishes the thesis of the essay.)** Such suppression allows misconceptions of others to fester in secret. **(This sentence expands on the thesis and indicates why it is important.)**

THE BODY

(The body of this essay begins with the opposing viewpoint, a useful strategy for beginning an argumentative essay. The writer indicates that he understands the opposing viewpoint, but then he shows why he disagrees with it.)

Supporters of PC maintain that their goal is to assist marginalized groups such as racial minorities, women, gays, and lesbians by creating an environment that "affirms the uniqueness and worth of each person" (Siegel 34). While there is nothing wrong with this statement— indeed it is an admirable one—the way in which PC groups assert themselves to maintain this goal is where the danger lies. In order to succeed in creating such an environment, proponents of PC have established a climate in which people fear expressing themselves for fear of penalties or consequences, a restriction that affects both liberals and conservatives.

Unfortunately, attempts to restrict what one may or may not say frequently become a slippery slope. **(This is a main supporting point.)** Once one begins to forbid certain words to be said, other words also become forbidden, ultimately destroying any hope for an environment dedicated to the pursuit of knowledge and free inquiry. Even without speech codes, the necessity of being PC has been so drilled in to students that some avoid even talking about controversial topics—topics such as affirmative action or abortion (Hentoff 372)—for fear of saying something that might be misinterpreted. Moreover, schools with speech codes face another problem: The fine line between freedom of thought and thought control. In the words of Stanford president, Donald Kennedy, once you start telling people what they can't say, you will end up telling them what they can't think (Hentoff 371). **(The writer cites an authority to lend credibility to his supporting point.)**

In some instances, restrictions on speech, even when a statement is intended as a joke, have gone to the extreme. **(The writer cites an example to support his thesis.)** One Asian American student at Southport University was actually thrown out of school for displaying her homemade poster that read, "bimbos should be shot on sight" before the ruling was overturned in a federal district court (Emerson 18). The joke was obviously in bad taste, but still, the consequence of being thrown out of school was a bit extreme. And suppose a student expresses an opinion that is not politically correct? Should that student be thrown out of school? It is dangerous when a person cannot voice their beliefs or views without being subject to abuse or harassment. But it is especially troubling when such speech codes do nothing to change the misunderstandings that perpetuate racism and sexism.

Advocates of speech codes argue that racist or sexist slurs create a climate of fear on campus, damaging students' feelings of self-worth and interfering with their ability to learn. **(The writer cites an opposing viewpoint and then argues against it.)** However, it can also be argued that students must learn to face these so-called "non-politically correct" words so that they can deal more effectively with them at a later time when they are out in the world. During a debate about speech codes at Harvard Law School, a white student got up and said "that the codes are necessary because without them, black students would be driven away from colleges and thereby deprived of the equal opportunity to get an education" (Hentoff 372). However, a black student then countered this remark by saying that the white student had "a hell of a nerve to assume that he—in the face of racist speech—would pack up his books and go home. He'd been familiar with that kind of speech all his life and he had never felt the need to run away from it" (Hentoff 372). **(This example further supports the thesis and lends authority to the author's point of view.)**

Moreover, speech codes do little to create a better environment for minorities because they do not influence people's ideas, and in that sense, they are actually dangerous. **(This is**

another supporting point.) People are not going to stop thinking, even if they are restricted from expressing their ideas, and thoughts of racism and sexism aren't going to disappear simply because an administration decides to restrict what people can and cannot say. Instead, by preventing the free exchange of ideas, PC restrictions may prejudice people more, leaving a facade of tolerance that hides the anger and suspicion that lie beneath the surface. As the National Association of Scholars points out, "Tolerance is a core value of academic life, as is civility. College authorities should ensure that these values prevail. But tolerance involves a willingness not to suppress, but to allow divergent opinions" (401). **(This is another statement from an authority that adds credibility to the writer's main point.)**

Moreover, as Richard Perry and Patricia Williams point out, PC rules do not "prevent racist or sexist thought in private" (Perry and Williams 66). To believe that restricting speech will eliminate intolerance of others is an oversimplified solution to a complex problem.

THE CONCLUSION

(The conclusion summarizes the writer's main point and indicates that the topic is
important to think about because it has widespread societal impact.)

Freedom of expression is the essence of a democratic society, and by stifling free speech, the Political Correctness Movement will ultimately harm our society. Campuses are no longer centers of intellectual discussion, but rather schools of indoctrination, hiding potentially serious problems festering under an externally imposed facade. Prejudice in our society can be eliminated only through the understanding and mutual acceptance that comes from the free exchange of ideas, not by externally imposed rules about what one can and cannot say.

Works Cited

(The works cited section lists the sources referred to in the text.
This essay cites sources using MLA citation form.)

D'Souza, Dinesh. "The Visogoths in Tweed." *Writing About Diversity: An Argument Reader and Guide.* Ed. Irene L. Clark. Fort Worth: Harcourt Brace, 1998. 361–369. Print.

Emerson, Ken. "Only Correct." *The New Republic* 18 Feb. 1991. 18–19. Print.

Hentoff, Nat. "Speech Codes and Free Speech." *Writing About Diversity: An Argument Reader and Guide.* Ed. Irene L. Clark. Fort Worth: Harcourt Brace. 1998. 370–375. Print.

Perry, Richard, and Patricia Williams. "Freedom of Hate Speech." *Writing About Diversity: An Argument Reader and Guide.* Ed. Irene L. Clark. Fort Worth: Harcourt Brace. 1998. 398–401. Print.

Siegel, Fred. "The Cult of Multiculturalism." *The New Republic* 18 Feb. 1991: 34–36. Print.

QUESTIONS

1. What is the exigence in this essay?
2. What is the purpose of this essay?
3. What strategies does John use to support his thesis?
4. How does John's essay use the structure associated with academic argument?

TIM'S ESSAY

In Tim's essay that follows, which is also concerned with the topic of political correctness, we have marked instances that indicate that he did not fully understand the requirements of the genre of argument. Read Tim's essay and the comments that are inserted. Then examine the analysis that follows.

PC is Ridiculous!

(This title does not indicate the seriousness of the topic.)

INTRODUCTION

(This introduction introduces the topic through a definition.
However, it does not lead smoothly into a thesis statement, as did John's essay.)

A debate has scourged the United States for several decades regarding the issue of "PC." The abbreviation is often confused with several different meanings, such as Personal Computer and President's Choice, but instead I am addressing the coined term "Political Correctness." **(The abbreviation and mistakes one might make in understanding are not really relevant to the main point of the essay.)** Every day the debate about PC becomes a more prominent topic in the classroom, the newspapers, and casual conversation, and people are getting sick of it. **(This last sentence uses an overly conversational expression that is inappropriate for a college argument. Moreover, it does not establish an exigence.)**

THE BODY

(The body of this essay lacks cogent arguments with supporting points.
It also does not indicate awareness of audience.)

The truth of the matter is actually simple. **(Actually, the matter is complex. If it were simple, it wouldn't be a suitable topic for college argument.)** No matter what Stanley Fish **(the writer does not identify the reference to Stanley Fish)** might claim, political correctness stifles free speech and will ultimately lead to a completely repressive society. Even now, students are afraid to open their mouths **(this is a slang expression that is inappropriate for college argument)** and say what they really think because they are afraid of being labeled "racist," "sexist," or "homophobic." Is this what education is about? Isn't it time we stopped being afraid of telling the truth? **(This is an exaggerated statement that is inappropriate for college argument.)**

Political correctness has been taken to an extreme. People can't say that someone is "short" anymore. They have to say they are "vertically challenged." It is now considered insulting to refer to a female person as a "girl" because we now have to say "woman." **(This is a trivial example that does not address the more important issues associated with the topic.)** This is just ridiculous! **(Simply saying that something is ridiculous is an inflammatory assertion.)** Anyone who gets insulted from such trivial statements can't be very intelligent. **(This is an exaggerated statement that is more likely to insult the audience than serve as a convincing argument.)**

CONCLUSION

**(The hysterical tone and extreme statements in this conclusion
detract from the writer's credibility.)**

Our country was founded on the Bill of Rights, and the first amendment to that document guarantees freedom of speech. If the PC people continue to make policy in our colleges and universities, free speech will no longer be a guaranteed right for students. Are students supposed to be considered second citizens? Isn't the university a place where people can speak freely? The PC movement has gotten completely out of hand and all policies concerned with it on campus ought to be eliminated.

ANALYSIS OF TIM'S ESSAY

Below is an analysis of Tim's essay in terms of the conceptual features of academic argument discussed in this chapter.

The Writer

As a writer, Tim does not appear to be trustworthy, objective, logical, or fair. He presents only a limited perspective on the topic and uses a strident tone; moreover, he does not seem to have done much reading or research, nor does he indicate awareness and understanding of the ideas of others. Tim simply states his opinion without acknowledging that some people might disagree with his ideas. Phrases such as "This is just ridiculous!" and "Anyone who gets insulted from such trivial statements can't be very intelligent." characterize a personal shouting match, not a thoughtful examination of a complex issue. Moreover, several statements in Tim's conclusion are exaggerated and not supported by careful evidence. Tim does not therefore present himself as a writer who is familiar with the purpose and conventions of the genre of argument.

The Audience

Tim does not seem to have considered his audience very much at all. He does not define PC, assuming that his audience already knows what he is referring to, nor does he explain his reference to Stanley Fish. A reader who is not familiar with Tim's topic might well ask, "Who is Stanley Fish?", and why is Tim arguing with him? Moreover, Tim's tone indicates that he has not thought about how stridency and exaggerated claims will affect a reader. Few of us are likely to be convinced by a statement such as "Anyone who gets insulted from such trivial statements can't be very intelligent." In fact, most people would find a statement such as this quite insulting.

The Topic and the Context

Tim has chosen a topic that is appropriate for college argument, but he has not adequately defined the exigence, nor did he provide sufficient background information. By not acknowledging an opposing position, Tim's stance in this essay appears one-sided.

Approach to the Topic

Tim approaches this topic as if he is having an emotionally heated interchange with an opponent. His language is inappropriate to the genre of argument because he relies on unsupported assertions and unanswered questions.

Support

Tim does not provide compelling support for his statements. His essay consists of unsupported claims and rhetorical questions.

Assumptions

Tim does not establish that he shares assumptions with his intended audience. He seems inclined to attack his opposition rather than establish a basis for understanding.

You will also note that Tim does not incorporate information from outside sources, and so, of course, he cannot include a "Works Cited" section.

FOR THINKING, DISCUSSION, AND WRITING

Consider the following scenario in the context of a rhetorical situation:

After many years of ruthless pursuit, your mortal enemy, agent 008, has finally tracked you down to the edge of the Grand Canyon. You hang over a cliff, clutching a rope desperately, about to fall to your death. Agent 008 looks down at you with a cruel grin, ready to cut the rope with a Swiss army knife. It is almost over for you. But—aha! You see a flicker of doubt in his/her eyes, and you take that moment to persuade him/her that you should live. How can you be most persuasive? Consider the following elements:

- Tone: Do you use a 1) loud, aggressive voice, 2) a calm voice, or 3) a soft-spoken voice? Why? Explain.
- Identification: How can you make him/her relate to you and get him/her to step into your shoes? Why is this important? Explain.
- Authority figure(s): Mr. Oz is your (anonymous) boss and a very important man in the spy world. Can you convince 008 that Mr. Oz is important enough to get him/her anything he/she might want? What are Mr. Oz's credentials?
- Reasoning: What are some good reasons why you should live and not die? For example, what do you have left to accomplish and how would 008 benefit from letting you live? Convince 008.

(This exercise was developed by Cesar Soto.)

FOR THINKING, DISCUSSION, AND WRITING

A critical feature of argument is that it usually deals with an exigence, a problem or situation that might be improved through reexamination, reevaluation, or change. For example, a problem associated with the topic of legalizing marijuana, at least according to some people, is that restrictions imposed on it make it difficult to use it for medical purposes. These people also claim that enforcing the law against it costs a great deal of money. Opponents of this position claim that marijuana is a dangerous drug and that a dangerous drug should not be made easily available.

To gain practice in finding problems within a topic, think about the topics that follow and try to locate a problem that might lend itself to argumentative writing. This exercise can be done either on your own or in small groups in class.

1. Required courses in undergraduate education
2. Athletics on campus
3. Living in the residence halls on campus
4. Short answer exams
5. Animal rights
6. Quotas in employment or educational settings
7. Child care centers in the workplace
8. Part-time jobs for students
9. School uniforms

After locating a problem within these topics, choose one and see if you can formulate a position on it.

WORKING WITH READINGS

In some chapters in this book, we have included readings; in others, we will provide you with titles and Internet addresses so that you can locate the readings online. Of course, you can also find other readings on your own. In working with readings, it is useful to review the features of argument-based writing discussed in this chapter. You can also discuss readings in small groups.

In examining a reading, please consider the following questions:

1. What is the purpose of the reading?
2. Does the reading establish an exigence?
3. Does it address a controversial or complex topic?
4. Does it explore an idea that needs explanation?
5. What is the thesis or claim made in this reading? Can you locate it?
6. Does the writer indicate awareness of multiple perspectives? Can you list at least two viewpoints on this topic?
7. Does the writer qualify any of the statements made in the reading?
8. Does the writer indicate awareness of audience? How and where?
9. What sort of tone characterizes this reading? Does the tone contribute to or detract from the credibility of the writer?
10. Examine the structure of the reading. How is it similar to and different from the classical argumentative structure discussed in this chapter?
11. Is this reading an example of the genre of argument? Why or why not?

— Obama's Inaugural Address: 20th January 2009

OBAMA'S INAUGURAL ADDRESS

My fellow citizens: I stand here today humbled by the task before us, grateful for the trust you've bestowed, mindful of the sacrifices borne by our ancestors.

I thank President Bush for his service to our nation—(applause)—as well as the generosity and cooperation he has shown throughout this transition.

Forty-four Americans have now taken the presidential oath. The words have been spoken during rising tides of prosperity and the still waters of peace. Yet, every so often, the oath is taken amidst gathering clouds and raging storms. At these moments, America has carried on not simply because of the skill or vision of those in high office, but because we, the people, have remained faithful to the ideals of our forebears and true to our founding documents.

So it has been; so it must be with this generation of reading Americans.

That we are in the midst of crisis is now well understood. Our nation is at war against a far-reaching network of violence and hatred. Our economy is badly weakened, a consequence of greed and irresponsibility on the part of some, but also our collective failure to make hard choices and prepare the nation for a new age. Homes have been lost, jobs shed, businesses shuttered. Our health care is too costly, our schools fail too many—and each day brings further evidence that the ways we use energy strengthen our adversaries and threaten our planet.

These are the indicators of crisis, subject to data and statistics. Less measurable, but no less profound, is a sapping of confidence across our land; a nagging fear that America's decline is inevitable, that the next generation must lower its sights.

Today I say to you that the challenges we face are real. They are serious and they are many. They will not be met easily or in a short span of time. But know this America: They will be met. (Applause.)

On this day, we gather because we have chosen hope over fear, unity of purpose over conflict and discord. On this day, we come to proclaim an end to the petty grievances and false promises, the recriminations and worn-out dogmas that for far too long have strangled our politics. We remain a young nation. But in the words of Scripture, the time has come to set aside childish things. The time has come to reaffirm our enduring spirit; to choose our better history; to carry forward that precious gift, that noble idea passed on from generation to generation: the God-given promise that all are equal, all are free, and all deserve a chance to pursue their full measure of happiness. (Applause.)

In reaffirming the greatness of our nation we understand that greatness is never a given. It must be earned. Our journey has never been one of short-cuts or settling for less. It has not been the path for the faint-hearted, for those that prefer leisure over work, or seek only the pleasures of riches and fame. Rather, it has been the risk-takers, the doers, the makers of things—some celebrated, but more often men and women obscure in their labor—who have carried us up the long rugged path towards prosperity and freedom.

For us, they packed up their few worldly possessions and traveled across oceans in search of a new life. For us, they toiled in sweatshops, and settled the West, endured the lash of the whip, and plowed the hard earth. For us, they fought and died in places like Concord and Gettysburg, Normandy and Khe Sahn.

Time and again these men and women struggled and sacrificed and worked till their hands were raw so that we might live a better life. They saw America as bigger than the sum of our individual ambitions, greater than all the differences of birth or wealth or faction.

This is the journey we continue today. We remain the most prosperous, powerful nation on Earth. Our workers are no less productive than when this crisis began. Our minds are no less inventive, our goods and services no less needed than they were last week, or last month, or last year. Our capacity remains undiminished. But our time of standing pat, of protecting narrow interests and putting off unpleasant decisions—that time has surely passed. Starting today, we must pick ourselves up, dust ourselves off, and begin again the work of remaking America. (Applause.)

For everywhere we look, there is work to be done. The state of our economy calls for action, bold and swift. And we will act, not only to create new jobs, but to lay a new foundation for growth. We will build the roads and bridges, the electric grids and digital lines that feed our commerce and bind us together. We'll restore science to its rightful place, and wield technology's wonders to raise health care's quality and lower its cost. We will harness the sun and the winds and the soil to fuel our cars and run our factories. And we will transform our schools and colleges and universities to meet the demands of a new age. All this we can do. All this we will do.

Now, there are some who question the scale of our ambitions, who suggest that our system cannot tolerate too many big plans. Their memories are short, for they have forgotten what this country has already done, what free men and women can achieve when imagination is joined to common purpose, and necessity to courage. What the cynics fail to understand is that the ground has shifted beneath them, that the stale political arguments that have consumed us for so long no longer apply.

The question we ask today is not whether our government is too big or too small, but whether it works—whether it helps families find jobs at a decent wage, care they can afford, a retirement that is dignified. Where the answer is yes, we intend to move forward. Where the answer is no, programs will end. And those of us who manage the public's dollars will be held to account, to spend wisely, reform bad habits, and do our business in the light of day, because only then can we restore the vital trust between a people and their government.

Nor is the question before us whether the market is a force for good or ill. Its power to generate wealth and expand freedom is unmatched. But this crisis has reminded us that without a watchful eye, the market can spin out of control. The nation cannot prosper long when it favors only the prosperous. The success of our economy has always depended not just on the size of our gross domestic product, but on the reach of our prosperity, on the ability to extend opportunity to every willing heart—not out of charity, but because it is the surest route to our common good. (Applause.)

As for our common defense, we reject as false the choice between our safety and our ideals. Our Founding Fathers—(applause)—our Founding Fathers, faced with perils that we can scarcely imagine, drafted a charter to assure the rule of law and the rights of man—a charter expanded by the blood of generations. Those ideals still light the world, and we will not give them up for expedience sake. (Applause.)

And so, to all the other peoples and governments who are watching today, from the grandest capitals to the small village where my father was born, know that America is a friend of each nation, and every man, woman and child who seeks a future of peace and dignity. And we are ready to lead once more. (Applause.)

Recall that earlier generations faced down fascism and communism not just with missiles and tanks, but with the sturdy alliances and enduring convictions. They understood that our power alone cannot protect us, nor does it entitle us to do as we please. Instead they knew that our power grows through its prudent use; our security emanates from the justness of our cause, the force of our example, the tempering qualities of humility and restraint.

We are the keepers of this legacy. Guided by these principles once more we can meet those new threats that demand even greater effort, even greater cooperation and understanding between nations. We will begin to responsibly leave Iraq to its people and forge a hard-earned peace in Afghanistan. With old friends and former foes, we'll work tirelessly to lessen the nuclear threat, and roll back the specter of a warming planet.

We will not apologize for our way of life, nor will we waver in its defense. And for those who seek to advance their aims by inducing terror and slaughtering innocents, we say to you now that our spirit is stronger and cannot be broken—you cannot outlast us, and we will defeat you. (Applause.)

For we know that our patchwork heritage is a strength, not a weakness. We are a nation of Christians and Muslims, Jews and Hindus, and non-believers. We are shaped by every language and culture, drawn from every end of this Earth; and because we have tasted the bitter swill of civil war and segregation, and emerged from that dark chapter stronger and more united, we cannot help but believe that the old hatreds shall someday pass; that the lines of tribe shall soon dissolve;

that as the world grows smaller, our common humanity shall reveal itself; and that America must play its role in ushering in a new era of peace.

To the Muslim world, we seek a new way forward, based on mutual interest and mutual respect. To those leaders around the globe who seek to sow conflict, or blame their society's ills on the West, know that your people will judge you on what you can build, not what you destroy. (Applause.)

To those who cling to power through corruption and deceit and the silencing of dissent, know that you are on the wrong side of history, but that we will extend a hand if you are willing to unclench your fist. (Applause.)

To the people of poor nations, we pledge to work alongside you to make your farms flourish and let clean waters flow; to nourish starved bodies and feed hungry minds. And to those nations like ours that enjoy relative plenty, we say we can no longer afford indifference to the suffering outside our borders, nor can we consume the world's resources without regard to effect. For the world has changed, and we must change with it.

As we consider the role that unfolds before us, we remember with humble gratitude those brave Americans who at this very hour patrol far-off deserts and distant mountains. They have something to tell us, just as the fallen heroes who lie in Arlington whisper through the ages.

We honor them not only because they are the guardians of our liberty, but because they embody the spirit of service—a willingness to find meaning in something greater than themselves.

And yet at this moment, a moment that will define a generation, it is precisely this spirit that must inhabit us all. For as much as government can do, and must do, it is ultimately the faith and determination of the American people upon which this nation relies. It is the kindness to take in a stranger when the levees break, the selflessness of workers who would rather cut their hours than see a friend lose their job which sees us through our darkest hours. It is the firefighter's courage to storm a stairway filled with smoke, but also a parent's willingness to nurture a child that finally decides our fate.

Our challenges may be new. The instruments with which we meet them may be new. But those values upon which our success depends—honesty and hard work, courage and fair play, tolerance and curiosity, loyalty and patriotism—these things are old. These things are true. They have been the quiet force of progress throughout our history.

What is demanded, then, is a return to these truths. What is required of us now is a new era of responsibility—a recognition on the part of every American that we have duties to ourselves, our nation and the world; duties that we do not grudgingly accept, but rather seize gladly, firm in the knowledge that there is nothing so satisfying to the spirit, so defining of our character than giving our all to a difficult task.

This is the price and the promise of citizenship. This is the source of our confidence—the knowledge that God calls on us to shape an uncertain destiny. This is the meaning of our liberty and our creed, why men and women and children of every race and every faith can join in celebration across this magnificent mall; and why a man whose father less than 60 years ago might not have been served in a local restaurant can now stand before you to take a most sacred oath. (Applause.)

So let us mark this day with remembrance of who we are and how far we have traveled. In the year of America's birth, in the coldest of months, a small band of patriots huddled by dying campfires on the shores of an icy river. The capital was abandoned. The enemy was advancing. The snow was stained with blood. At the moment when the outcome of our revolution was most in doubt, the father of our nation ordered these words to be read to the people:

"Let it be told to the future world . . . that in the depth of winter, when nothing but hope and virtue could survive . . . that the city and the country, alarmed at one common danger, came forth to meet [it]."

America: In the face of our common dangers, in this winter of our hardship, let us remember these timeless words. With hope and virtue, let us brave once more the icy currents, and endure what storms may come. Let it be said by our children's children that when we were tested we refused to let this journey end, that we did not turn back nor did we falter; and with eyes fixed on the horizon and God's grace upon us, we carried forth that great gift of freedom and delivered it safely to future generations.

Thank you. God bless you. And God bless the United States of America.

2

CHAPTER

Engaging with Ideas:
A Three-Pass Approach to Critical Reading

At one time, college writing courses focused exclusively on writing, not on reading, because it was assumed that students already knew how to read when they arrived on a college campus. This assumption meant that readings were simply "assigned." The teacher handed out a syllabus that listed the readings for the course and the dates they were due, and students were expected to complete them. What we now understand, however, is that readings assigned in a college course are usually more complex than those assigned in high school and that it is important to help students learn to engage with them meaningfully—that is, to read *critically* and *rhetorically*. Below are several reasons that reading has now become an important component of many writing classes:

Writing assignments are often based on readings.
Reading helps students develop ideas for their own writing.
Support for a thesis or argument is often derived from outside reading.
Readings assigned in a college writing class are often complex and require a focus and **critical** attention that many students have not learned.
Reading and writing are intertwined—both are processes, and both involve **rhetorical moves**.

MISCONCEPTIONS ABOUT READING

Before they come to college, most students have done a great deal of reading in school or elsewhere. But the readings assigned in college classes are not only longer, but may also be more challenging and difficult to understand than those read previously, not only in terms of style and vocabulary, but also because they may refer to unfamiliar concepts. Because of these factors, students often have difficulty with assigned readings, difficulties that may be due to several misconceptions about reading:

- That reading means simply being able to pronounce or "decode" the words on a page;
- That reading always requires the reader to move sequentially through a text, line by line, from beginning to end;
- That good readers read quickly.

The word "decoding" is often used to refer to the ability to pronounce words that appear on a screen or paper, such as "The cat is on the mat," a simple sentence that all literate English language speakers will be able to "read," pronounce, and understand. However, *reading* an academic text, means much more than being able to decode the words. You may be able to pronounce most of the words that appear in articles and books assigned in your college classes, but you may not understand what they are saying or be aware that most academic texts are written in order to respond to some sort of exigence or situation—that is, to enter a conversation. Reading a complex text involves engaging with it in a meaningful way and frequently requires a different reading process than simply beginning at the beginning of the text and proceeding through to the end, as if you were reading a storybook. Reading, like writing, is a process that varies according to the type of text, the challenge it presents in terms of form, style, and language, and a reader's familiarity with the topic. That process often requires becoming aware of the conversation or debate that it addresses, analyzing the author's perspective, and considering its credibility. The Three-Pass Approach to **Critical Reading** discussed below, outlines a process you can use to understand and evaluate many of the texts you read in your college classes.

FOR THINKING, DISCUSSION, AND WRITING

In small groups, discuss the process you use when you are assigned to read an article or section of a book on one of your classes. How do you begin the process? Do you take notes, underline, or use a highlighter? Do you summarize main points or pose questions in the margins? Do you work with a dictionary? Do you read every sentence? How successful have you found this process to be?

READING TO DISCOVER IDEAS

When students are given an assignment to write an essay or research paper, many go immediately to the Internet or library to begin locating sources, and of course, conducting research is often an important component of a college writing assignment. But before you immerse yourself in the ideas of others, it is a good idea to think about what you already may know or think about the topic. The Exploration Questions below may help you discover that you know quite a bit, and become aware of what you DON'T know, so that you can ask your teacher or do some preliminary research.

EXPLORATION QUESTIONS TO THINK ABOUT WHAT YOU ALREADY KNOW

1. Why is this topic important? To whom is it important? Why does it matter?
2. Are there multiple perspectives or controversies associated with this topic? Can you summarize them?
3. Were you brought up to have an opinion on this topic? Did your family or community care about this topic? Why or why not?
4. How did your school experiences influence your conception of the topic? Did your teachers and classmates feel the same way about it as did your family? Were there any points of disagreement?
5. Can you think of at least two people who hold differing ideas about this topic? If so, describe these people and summarize what you believe were their points of view.
6. Has your opinion changed about this topic in any way? Why or why not?

Exploration questions can help you access information about a topic, and if you discover that you know nothing about it at all, we suggest that you consult sources that will provide you with at least an overview. An online encyclopedia or an introductory book on the subject can usually provide you with at least some context and background.

MOVING BEYOND YOUR OWN IDEAS: READING CRITICALLY

After you have become aware of what you already know and think about this topic, you can expand your thinking by reading what others have said about it, and that is when you begin the process of reading possible sources you might be able to use. It is therefore important for you to learn how to evaluate the quality of published materials by reading *critically.*

An important idea to keep in mind as you read is that most published work was written by *someone* who is likely to have a particular perspective, approach, or opinion on the topic and that the goal of any publication is to convince you, the reader, that what is being said is valuable, or at least worth considering. Another important idea to remember as you read is that the publication of a book, article, or online resource does not automatically mean that it is valid or true. All sorts of texts get published, and skillful writers understand how to convince readers of the worth of their ideas. So, if most books, articles, and online resources are written to promote an agenda or opinion, how can you know whether or not to trust a particular source or believe what it is saying?

Given the quantity of available material, there is no simple answer to this question. However, if you develop the skill of *critical reading,* you will become aware of criteria you can use for making an informed decision about the credibility of a book, an article, or an online resource.

CRITICAL READING AND THE ONGOING CONVERSATION

To introduce the idea of critical reading, we would like you to imagine that you had arrived at a party at which a heated discussion was already going on. Wishing to join the conversation, you approach the group and listen for a while, trying to figure out whose point of view you find worthwhile. Suppose, though, that all of the speakers were strangers to you and that you knew nothing about their backgrounds or interests. How would you know whose opinion to take seriously? What criteria would you use to evaluate what was being said? On what basis would you be able to decide?

Reading a published work, whether in the form of a newspaper, magazine article, material from a book, or an online resource is somewhat like entering an ongoing conversation—in fact, the rhetorician, Kenneth Burke, among others, has made exactly that point—moreover, when you are not familiar with the topic, the process of exploring a topic is uncomfortably similar to entering a room full of strangers. We make this comparison because it is important for you to understand that most of the discussions, issues, or controversies you encounter in print have been going on for some time, and that many of those who are writing about them, like the guests at the party, have been involved in the discussion long before you arrived. The comparison also suggests that deciding which points of view are believable will be a challenge for you.

Nevertheless, although it is difficult to assess the value of a published work, becoming aware of what you already know about the subject and using clues from the text will enable you to make an informed judgment. Having answered the Exploration Questions (above), you can then ask yourself the following questions when you begin to read a published work:

1. What do I already know about this topic?
2. What do I know about the writer of the book, article, Website, blog, etc.? Does the text provide information about the author?
3. Can I assess the quality of the argument based on tone, language, and evidence?

WHAT DO I ALREADY KNOW ABOUT THIS TOPIC?

In terms of the conversation at the party, one way you would be able to decide which speaker was credible would be to reflect on how much you already know about the topic being discussed and then to compare what you know with what you hear in the discussion. In fact, without some basic knowledge about the topic, you would not be able to assess anyone's opinion and would first have to acquire some basic information. If, for example, the speakers were debating the merits of various laptop computers, you would be unable to decide whose recommendation to trust if you knew nothing at all about laptop computers, had no idea what computers did, and had never used any sort of computer. The first requirement for participating in the conversation, then, would be that you know at least something about the subject matter.

In terms of the ongoing discussion at the party, the more similar a particular position is to a viewpoint you already hold, the more likely you will be to agree with it. So, if the topic under discussion was the merits of the Zoink laptop computer, and if you yourself had used a Zoink and liked it, knew others who felt the same way, and had read about the merits of the Zoink, you would be likely to agree that the Zoink was the best laptop computer on the market. Under these circumstances, you would be disinclined to change your mind unless you became aware of a new piece of information.

In addition to understanding the topic of the discussion and being aware of your own views on it, you would also be in a better position to evaluate what was being said if you knew something about the reason that the discussion was being held. Had someone requested the name of a reliable, reasonably priced laptop computer, or was the discussion concerned with deciding which computer was the most technologically advanced? Had something happened recently that had sparked the debate (the release of a new model, for example)? Had the topic been raised in the context of a presumed health hazard from laptop computers? Are there any particular groups or organizations associated with a particular perspective on this controversy?

WHAT DO YOU KNOW ABOUT THE WRITER?

In terms of the party metaphor, you would also be able to decide whose opinion to trust if you knew something about the *participants,* in particular about their qualifications for discoursing on this subject and about what their *motives* or *agendas* might be in this discussion. For example, if you discovered that the gentleman in the red jacket happened to be the president of Zoink Computers Inc., you would be somewhat suspicious of his endorsement of this particular model, since he would obviously have a specific motive or agenda to promote. On the other hand, if the man in the blue T-shirt bearing the slogan "Computers Will Destroy Humanity" was yelling that Zoink computers were infected with all sorts of dangerous viruses, causing users to break out in unsightly rashes, yet he provided no specific evidence to support his claim (and, in fact, was a member of the *Delete Computers Society*), you would distrust his position as well. And, finally, if you realized that the gentleman with the large mustache was a notorious liar who enjoyed fueling discussions whether or not he had any real information to contribute, you would not pay too much attention to his viewpoint either. However, if the woman in the gray suit introduced herself as a research consultant whose profession it was to evaluate laptop computers for a well-known public organization, and if she indicated (in measured tones), based on her extensive research and personal experience, that the Zoink was undoubtedly the best model on the market, you would be most likely to trust her opinion rather than those of the other participants in the debate. In fact, even if you already had an opinion on the topic, you might reevaluate your own point of view if you were sufficiently impressed with what she had to say.

CAN YOU ASSESS THE QUALITY OF THE ARGUMENT BASED ON EVIDENCE, LANGUAGE, AND TONE?

Generally, we tend to be convinced by arguments that are supported by clear reasons and use evidence to support their major claims. College argument, in particular, is usually characterized by the use of well-considered ideas that are carefully supported. We also tend to trust writers who appear calm and who speak in measured, rather than in hysterical, tones. In terms of the party metaphor, we would probably be more likely to trust the lady in the gray suit who seems balanced and restrained, rather than the man in the T-shirt who is yelling.

Now, at this point, we must also point out that it is the *quality of the ideas,* not the style of presentation, that you should ultimately focus on in deciding which opinions to trust, since style is something that can be easily distorted. Television commercials, for example, tend to use people who *seem* calm and knowledgeable, and viewers find themselves trusting what they have to say, even when they know that they are simply actors who are being paid to endorse a particular product. On the other hand, if someone is hysterical, it does not necessarily mean that his or her opinion is not worthwhile—perhaps the situation is sufficiently alarming so that hysteria is the appropriate response. Furthermore, an obvious self-interest is not always a reason to distrust an opinion. Perhaps the president of Zoink Computers has done a great deal of research, knows a lot about computers, and wants to produce the best computer on the market. In this case, despite the fact that he stands to profit from the sale of Zoinks, his ideas could be worth believing.

TAKING CHARGE OF YOUR READING

When people are inexperienced in working with published works, whether in the form of articles, books, or online materials, they often approach them passively—that is, they note that the title seems related to their topic and then they simply begin reading, trying to understand the meaning of the text. The problem with this approach is that it adheres to a submissive, rather than to a "take-charge," model of the reading process. Reading submissively implies that the work exists as a separate, valid, believable entity, rather than part of a conversation, and that it is worthy of serious consideration simply because it has been published. Moreover, the submissive approach does not include the reader-initiated activities of reflecting on the subject and context of the work; questioning the motives, agendas, and qualifications of its author; or evaluating the quality of the argument.

If you recall the party discussion scenario outlined previously, the submissive approach to reading puts you, as the reader, at a great disadvantage because you will not be able to evaluate the validity of what you are reading. Such an approach is as if you had entered the party, had been immediately cornered by the man in the blue T-shirt who was screaming about the rash he had contracted from his Zoink laptop, and had listened only to his point of view without reflecting on your own perspective, understanding the context of the discussion, or questioning the reliability of the speaker.

To avoid being a passive reader, you should keep the following principle in mind:

> *Very few, if any, articles or books are written simply to present information in a completely objective way.*

Even what seems to be the most coldly and objectively written scientific piece of writing has, at its foundation, a complex set of beliefs about how the world is or ought to be, and if you are aware of what those might be, you will be in a better position to evaluate the text and decide whether or not to believe what it says. Competent readers engage actively in the reading process. They approach a published work by trying to learn as much information about it as possible before beginning to read it. Then, once they decide that the text is worth reading, they interact with it energetically, almost as if they were having a conversation with the author.

THE THREE-PASS APPROACH: AN OVERVIEW

The Three-Pass Approach will enable you to evaluate the credibility of articles, books, and online sources so that you will be able to decide whether or not to use them in your essays. At first, the method will seem as if it involves a lot of work, and maybe you will think initially that it is not worth your time. Keep in mind, though, that with practice, the first two steps quickly become collapsed into one, and that any new method may seem cumbersome at first but eventually becomes easy to use. Here then, is an overview of The Three-Pass Approach:

1. **The First Pass—Reflection and Quick Overview**
   During the first pass, the reader reflects on the subject and context of the topic, issue, or problem being addressed, evaluates the qualifications and motives of the author, and examines the reading for additional clues, such as the title, publication information, and easily discernible strategies of organization.

---

2.   The Second Pass—Reading for Meaning and Structure

During the second pass, the reader reads the text for meaning to determine what it is saying. To aid understanding, the reader uses structural clues within the text and facilitates his or her understanding by summarizing main points.

---

3.   The Third Pass—Interacting with the Text

During the third pass, the reader interacts with the text, actively engaging in a critical dialogue with it in order to determine how much of it to accept. Such interaction involves distinguishing between fact and opinion, evaluating the type of evidence cited, deciding whether the writer is aware of the complexity of the topic, and paying close attention to how language is being used to shape the reader's perspective.

A DETAILED LOOK AT THE THREE-PASS APPROACH
THE FIRST PASS—REFLECTION AND QUICK OVERVIEW

The first pass over a published work involves assessing what you already know about the subject matter, the context, and the author and then examining the easily detectable surface clues that the work provides. Before you begin reading a published work, ask yourself the following questions:

1.   What do I know about the subject matter of this work? Have I been brought up to have an opinion on this topic? Have I heard discussions on this topic or read anything about it? Is there a controversy associated with this topic?

2.   What is important to understand about this topic or issue? Is there some action or policy associated with it? Was it written in response to another piece of writing? For whom is it being written? Do I know anything about any particular groups associated with this issue?

3.   What do I know about the author? Does the author have a title or position that would indicate his or her qualifications or a particular agenda? Can I speculate on what the motive of the author might be?

Clues About the Text

Once you have reflected on the subject and context of the controversy and on the potential agenda of the author, you should then peruse the work for surface clues that can provide you with additional information. These clues include publication information, such as the title, the type of publication, and the copyright date, and organizational clues, such as section headings and bolded subtitles (for an article both in print and online) or chapter headings and the table of contents (for a book). If you know something about the topic, you can get a sense of where the author is situated in the conversation by looking at the bibliography, if there is one, and noting which sources the author has cited and whether or not you can recognize any names or publications. Then, in a brief glance, you should try to determine the type of evidence cited, such as the use of charts or graphs or the inclusion of statistics.

Begin by examining the title and thinking about what the title might suggest about the author's attitude toward the subject or purpose in writing. See if you can figure out what the article or book might be about simply on the basis of the title. Then, if the work is an article in a magazine or journal, both print and online, try to grasp the overall approach or agenda of that publication. Some journals are known to endorse a particular political approach, so you might be able to predict what the overall thrust of an article might be by thumbing or scrolling through it to see what other articles appear along with the one you are thinking of reading. If biographical information about other authors appears, read through it and see what other authors are included and the kind of backgrounds they have. Finally, check the copyright date. For some topics, the fact that a particular article was written fifteen or twenty years ago might not matter at all. For other topics, it might matter a great deal. Reflect on whether or not the date of publication will affect the believability or validity of the work.

Sometimes you can get a sense of an article by reading an abstract or by skimming over section headings or words that appear in bold. Think about how these subheadings relate to the title, or, if the work you are about to read is a book or a chapter from a book, see if there is a chapter summary at the beginning or end of each chapter or group of chapters that will provide you with additional clues. Frequently, if you skim over the first few and last few paragraphs of an article or chapter, you can quickly understand its main point.

Of course, not every article or book you come upon will be easily accessible to immediate scrutiny. Nevertheless, even those that are not written by readily identifiable authors with easily predicted agendas or those that do not state their main points explicitly usually yield at least *some* useful information during the first pass. Even if you find out very little information about the text, looking for clues in this way will at least help you begin looking at the work with a critical eye.

THE SECOND PASS—READING FOR MEANING AND STRUCTURE

During the second pass, you should read the material through reasonably quickly and write a summary of it so that you can easily refer back to it without having to reread it. Use the summary to encapsulate its overall point, as well as to record component supporting points and make the summary sufficiently complete so that even a reader who has not read the article will be able to understand what it is about. Also be sure to write or input all information you would need in order to be able to locate the article again if you wish to use it—that is, for an article, include the title, the author, the title of the journal, issue number, pages, and date; for a book, include the author, title, and publication information, such as publisher, place of publication, and date.

In reading a text for meaning, it is a good idea to focus attention on its purpose and structure—that is,

> Is it a response to another point of view? Can you situate it in a conversation? Is there a controversy associated with it?
>
> Does the article or book compare and contrast two or more ideas or recommendations?
> Does it make a point about cause and effect?
> Does it pose a question and then answer it?
> Does it trace the history of something, structuring its information chronologically?
> Is it developed through the use of many examples?

During the second pass, you will understand the text more easily if you think about how it has been organized, noting how different facets of the topic relate to the author's main point. Look also for signals in the text that indicate a shift of some sort is about to occur, noting how new content is introduced—subheadings are good indicators of this, but sometimes the author uses transitional sentences.

One point to note about the second pass is that after a quick read, you may decide that the work is not worth reading after all. Remember that there has been a lot written that may not be worth your time. Understanding the meaning of a text through a relatively quick appraisal can thus prevent you from expending unnecessary effort.

THE THIRD PASS—INTERACTING WITH THE TEXT

Once you understand the meaning and structure of the text, now is the time to take charge of your reading, which means reading critically with a questioning attitude toward your material and interacting with it as much as possible. Now is the time for you to enter the conversation, not accepting what you read unless the evidence is convincing. If you have printed out an article, you might wish to summarize main points in the margins or pose questions that the article raises in your mind. Keep in mind what you have learned about the author's agenda or qualifications for writing this particular article or book (or publishing it online), and use that information to formulate critical questions as you read. Following is a detailed discussion of the third pass:

1. Is the argument or ideas consistent with what you believe is true or possible about the world and about human behavior?

Your View of the World and Your Belief About Human Nature

In order for an argument to convince a reader, it must be consistent with what the reader believes is true and possible in the world and with his or her concept of human nature. Our view of the world and our beliefs and ideas about humanity serve as a kind of filter through which we can assess the quality of the information we receive, and the more we experience and read, the more we adjust our world view to accommodate new information. We believe, for example, that it is possible to fly from California to New York in about five hours, so that if a friend left my home in L.A. at 2:00 p.m. and then called me at 8:00 p.m., claiming that he was in New York, I would probably believe him (unless I suspected that he was playing some sort of joke or had a reputation for lying, etc.). But if my friend left my home in L.A. at 2:00 p.m. and then called me at 2:30 p.m., claiming to be in New York, I would be unlikely to believe him, even if he claimed that he had been whisked there in a new form of airplane.

Similarly, our concept of human nature—that is, what we believe human beings are likely to do or are capable of doing—is another source by which we evaluate what we read. To cite an obvious example of how one's world view and concept of human nature contribute to the credibility of an idea, imagine the difficulty you would have in convincing a local school board that a night watchman is needed to prevent aliens from landing on the school football field at night, since most people do not believe that aliens constitute much of a problem on a nightly basis (in fact, only some people think that aliens exist at all). On the other hand, it would be less difficult to convince the school board that a night watchman is necessary to prevent thieves from stealing expensive computer equipment from the science lab. Our world view tells us that there are, indeed, such things as thieves, and our concept of human nature tells us that, unfortunately, some human beings will avail themselves of the opportunity to steal, unless reasonable precautions are taken.

On an issue such as whether or not to have a night watchman at the local high school, most people would probably have little difficulty reaching agreement (assuming that the money was available and wasn't needed for something regarded as more important). However, on controversial, complex topics, people will often disagree, because they have differing concepts of human nature. Moreover, people sometimes make statements about human behavior on the basis of what they *wish* were true, rather than what the evidence suggests is really the case. Because we often wish that everyone was motivated by only the most noble of impulses and that deep down everyone wants to do the "right" thing, we often have difficulty believing stories that suggest otherwise, particularly about those we have set up as heroes or role models. Thus, when a president of a country, a film star, or sports celebrity behaves poorly or even illegally, many people refuse to believe even what seems evidently true. Many people seem to want to be deceived, easily believing reports that to others seem completely preposterous—belief in paranormal events or a chance at winning the lottery, for example.

In the third pass, then, you should question the extent to which a particular argument is consistent with your world view and concept of human nature. You can ask yourself whether the main point makes sense to you according to your own experience and what you believe is likely to be true. If it is not, you would then attempt to view the issue from the author's point of view, trying to understand why the author espouses these beliefs.

2.   Is the argument or thesis supported with appropriate and believable sub-points, examples, and facts?

Distinguishing Fact from Opinion

Reading a text interactively means being on the alert for statements that may appear to be facts but are actually opinions presented as if they were facts. An effective way to detect the difference, though, is to notice whether or not the main points are supported with specific, appropriate details and sub-points or consist simply of observations that the author *thinks* are true. Keep in mind that unless a writer is an acknowledged authority, you really have no reason to accept his or her point of view, and that even an expert is obliged to provide supporting evidence. For example, examine Jenny's paragraph that follows, which is concerned with the question of whether homework should be assigned to children in elementary school:

1) *Although many teachers and parents believe that homework is an important part of a child's elementary school education, homework in the elementary grades does little or nothing to help children learn. 2) Moreover, it detracts from a child's physical development and family life. 3) Young children need time after school to play in the fresh air and get physical exercise, and homework requires them to stay indoors, working on their schoolwork. 4) Moreover, most homework assignments are nothing more than busy work assigned by the teacher because they have always done so. 5) Homework also contributes to children's anxiety about school because the responsibility of getting homework done weighs on their minds, interfering with their ability to enjoy learning. 6) Finally, the need to supervise a child's homework puts too much stress on parents, who are already too busy trying to work and maintain family life.*

In this paragraph, Jenny has written a number of statements that are stated as if they are facts, but are actually Jenny's own opinion of what she believes to be facts. To determine the extent to which you should be convinced by Jenny's paragraph, read each statement carefully with a questioning attitude, reflecting on the nature of the support Jenny has provided.

1) *Although many teachers and parents believe that homework is an important part of a child's elementary school education, homework in the elementary grades does little or nothing to help children learn.*

This is Jenny's topic sentence. It expresses the idea that her paragraph is going to develop, and Jenny states it definitively. The implication of the statement is that homework should *never* be assigned in elementary school, and you might begin by reflecting on your own experience with homework, or that assigned to your own children, and the extent to which you agree with this idea.

2) *Moreover, it detracts from a child's physical development and family life.*

This is an extension of Jenny's thesis, and you might reflect on whether you think that this statement is a fact or only Jenny's opinion. You might ask, "How does homework detract from a child's physical development and family life?" Another point to consider is, "How much homework would have this effect?" You also might ask, "How does Jenny know this?"

3) *Young children need time after school to play in the fresh air and get physical exercise, and homework requires them to stay indoors, working on their schoolwork.*

You will probably agree that children need fresh air and physical exercise. But you might feel that Jenny's statement is an exaggeration. Unless children are assigned hours and hours of homework, it is unlikely to interfere completely with their play and exercise time.

4) *Moreover, most homework assignments are nothing more than busy work assigned by the teacher because they have always done so.*

This is Jenny's opinion, presented as if it were a fact. You might ask, "How does Jenny know that most homework assignments are nothing more than busy work?" or "What is the difference between homework that is worthwhile and homework that is 'just busywork?'"

5) *Homework also contributes to children's anxiety about school because the responsibility of getting homework done weighs on their minds, interfering with their ability to enjoy learning.*

Once again, you might question how Jenny knows this. Can she cite the statements of people whose children have suffered anxiety due to homework? Moreover, Jenny does not refer to the possibility that assuming responsibility for homework might be beneficial for children in that it could help them develop a sense of responsibility. The role of homework in fostering responsibility and aiding learning is an issue that people continually debate, so there is likely to be considerable discussion about this topic that Jenny could read that might help her develop her ideas. However, in this paragraph, Jenny has not indicated that she has "joined the conversation." She is simply voicing her own opinion.

6) *Finally, the need to supervise a child's homework puts too much stress on parents who are already too busy trying to work and maintain family life.*

This is once again an assertion, not a statement of fact, although it is presented as if it were. How does Jenny know that homework puts stress on family life? Is she simply basing her statements on what may have been the case in her own family?

Evaluating the Assumptions Behind the Thesis

During the third pass, it is important to try to understand the assumptions that lie behind the author's position; that is, the underlying values or statements about the world that provide the foundation for the main idea. The assumptions behind the text provide the basis for the author's point and are used to justify what the author is saying. For example, Jenny's paragraph is based on a number of assumptions that derive from her view of homework. Some of these assumptions are as follows:

- that anything that detracts from free time is not good for children;
- that giving a child responsibility for homework is harmful because it causes anxiety;
- that learning takes place only in the classroom under the supervision of a teacher;
- that parents should not be involved in schoolwork.

Once you are aware of the assumptions behind a work, you are in a better position to evaluate the quality of the argument and the extent to which you accept it. In the example of Jenny's paragraph, you may decide that you do, indeed, agree with it. But, on the other hand, you may also feel that homework can be beneficial.

3.   *Is the evidence reliable?*

The Quality of the Reasoning

Some arguments appear to be well thought out, but are really based on fallacious reasoning that cannot withstand careful scrutiny. To evaluate the quality of the reasoning, question whether or not the author's reasons seem logical to you, and be on the alert for arguments based on fallacies, which are discussed in Chapter 8.

An active reader also looks closely at the kind of evidence used to support an argument before deciding to accept it. Evidence in an argumentative essay can take many forms, such as examples, statements from authorities, and statistics, and it is important for a careful reader to examine that evidence with a questioning attitude.

Appeals to Authority in a Published Work

Since no one is qualified to make judgments about every topic, writers often use the statements of experts to provide support. However, as an active reader, you should check that a statement from an authority does indeed substantiate what the author is saying and that the authority can really be trusted. Try to find out who these experts are before accepting what they say as absolute truth, and evaluate their statements carefully. Sometimes a statement by an authority is quoted out of context, or authorities in one field are quoted as experts on topics that they really know little about (the use of athletes or movie stars to endorse certain products is an example of this). Keep in mind that you do not have to accept everything that you read, just because an alleged "expert" says that something is so. Maintain a skeptical attitude, and look for other perspectives on the topic before completely accepting a particular point of view, particularly if it does not seem sensible to you.

Statistics

Statistics constitute another means of supporting an argument, and they can be very convincing. In fact, many students are under the impression that when an article includes statistics, it is then automatically more reliable. A critical reader is aware, however, that although statistics can often provide valid support, they can also be used to distort rather than to clarify an argument. As an active reader, then, be wary of statistics—they may not mean what is initially suggested that they mean and can be used to suit an author's purpose.

Moreover, statistics can be reported inconsistently. During the Persian Gulf War, *Time Magazine* reported the number of Iraqi troops attacking Kuwait as 430,000 (November 12, 1990), 360,000 (October 1, 1990), 50,000 (September 1, 1990), and 100,000 (August 1, 1990). If you wanted an accurate reporting of how many troops Iraq sent to Kuwait during this period, you would need to consult additional sources.

4.   Is the text stylistically trustworthy?

Detecting Vagueness and Distortion in Language

Trying to figure out what a text is really saying is sometimes like trying to read through a rain swept window. Particularly when writers attempt to manipulate, rather than convince, their readers, they may use language to disguise meaning so that readers have difficulty knowing whether to trust what they read. An important characteristic of a stylistically trustworthy text is that it uses language to communicate with readers, not to confuse them; therefore, you, as an astute reader, should be on the alert for the following stylistic techniques that can sometimes muffle the meaning of a text:

- interpretive words
- words used for emotional effect
- excessive use of abstract rather than concrete language
- ambiguity and distortion

Interpretive Words

Reading with a questioning, critical attitude involves becoming alert to words that *interpret* as opposed to those that simply state the facts. For example, examine the following two statements:

1. A beautiful woman was sitting in the cafe, her elegant hand lightly holding a coffee cup.
2. A woman in her mid-thirties with long black hair was sitting in the cafe, her slender fingers lightly holding a coffee cup.

If you read the statements carefully, you will perceive that in statement #1, the reference to the woman as beautiful is only an opinion, the opinion of the author (the author thinks the woman is beautiful and the author wants the reader to think that the woman is beautiful), whereas the second statement presents particular facts (the woman's age, the color and style of her hair, the slenderness of her fingers, which also suggest that the woman is probably slender, since it is unlikely that the author would mention the slenderness of the woman's fingers if she was overweight). One method of distinguishing between facts and opinion, then, is to become sensitive to the many words that interpret; words such as *ugly, dangerous, elegant, bad, best,* etc.

Of course, it is not necessarily "bad" to use interpretive language, and, indeed, no text is entirely interpretation-free. However, in interacting with a text, it is a good idea to be sensitive to interpretive language and of the extent to which that interpretation either enhances or clouds the argument.

Words Used for Emotional Effect

Many words have positive and negative overtones and tend to trigger emotional responses in their readers or hearers. Because they stimulate an immediate response, writers may use them as a shortcut to providing adequate support. Saying that someone is a "bleeding heart," for example, suggests that such a person is inclined to spend money recklessly in a misguided impulse to help the human race. A writer may thus use this term without indicating what sort of spending or what type of misguided humanitarian impulse he or she may mean. Other examples of emotionally loaded language are *nerd, loser,* or *hippie.* Moreover, not all emotionally charged words are negative. Words such as *democracy, freedom,* and *family* are examples of words that stimulate an immediate positive response among readers. Whether such words are positive or negative, be on the alert for extreme statements and exaggerated expressions—they can generate a disproportionately emotional response that can affect your judgment.

For example, reacting against the political correctness (PC) movement on college campuses during the 1990s, Dinesh D'Souza writes that the "college classroom" has been transformed from:

> a place of learning to a laboratory of indoctrination for social change. Not long ago most colleges required that students learn the basics . . . . [Now] this coherence has disappeared . . . [and] most universities are . . . graduating students who are scientifically and culturally impoverished, if not illiterate.
> **D'Souza, Dinesh. "The Visogoths in Tweed."** *Forbes Magazine* **April 1, 1991.**

In this passage, D'Souza has used several terms that are likely to trigger a strong reaction in his reader, such as "laboratory of indoctrination,"—suggesting a dictatorial "1984"-like atmosphere—and the reference to students as "scientifically and culturally impoverished, if not illiterate." In essence, D'Souza is implying here that the PC movement is responsible for lack of freedom, cultural impoverishment, and illiteracy on college campuses.

Excessive Use of Abstract Rather than Concrete Language

In his famous and often anthologized essay, "Politics and the English Language," George Orwell argues that politicians often use abstract language to desensitize the reader to what a writer may actually be saying:

> . . . political language has consisted largely of euphemism, question begging, and sheer cloudy vagueness. Defenseless villages are bombarded from the air, the inhabitants driven out into the countryside, the cattle machine gunned, the huts set on fire with incendiary bullets: This is called pacification. Millions of peasants are robbed of their farms and sent trudging along the roads with no more than they can carry. This is called transfer of population or rectification of frontiers . . .
> **(Orwell)**

Orwell's point pertains to a writing style that still exists today. Bureaucratic language, in particular, is often characterized by a high degree of abstraction, the idea being that the reader becomes numb or bored, and hence more willing to accept what may be outrageous or preposterous statements.

Another form of ambiguity occurs when words are not adequately defined, a technique that is particularly common in advertising. A facial soap ad claims that the product will "enhance the beauty you were born with," but does not specify what "enhance" means in this context or define what it means by "the beauty you were born with." In examining a text with a critical eye, be especially suspicious of words that are not adequately defined; words such as "family values" or "work ethic" are used frequently to put down a particular ethnic or racial group, yet the terms are left undefined.

THE THREE-PASS APPROACH: USING THE METHOD

To illustrate how The Three-Pass Approach can help you gain insight into a source, access the article "Needed: A License to Drink" online (http://www.newsweek.com/needed-license-drink-186210

Following is the way in which The Three-Pass Approach could work with this article:

The First Pass

On first encountering the article, you might begin by asking the following questions:

1. How can your own experience help you understand the article?

Have you had any experiences, either personally or through the experiences of others, that suggest that it would be valuable to issue licenses for drinking? Do you think that people tend to drink irresponsibly? Do you think that legal restrictions lead to greater obedience?

2. What do you already know or believe about the topic that is suggested by the title and the subtitle?

The title, which includes a subtitle, suggests that drinking licenses are "needed" in order to prevent unnecessary deaths from excessive alcohol and those resulting from drinking while driving. The title and subtitle of this article, then, indicate clearly the position that the author is advocating.

3. Where and when was this article published? Will that indicate something about the perspective being emphasized?

The note at the top of the page indicates that this article was published in *Newsweek* on March 14, 1994, and that it was written by someone who writes for the communication department at the Oklahoma State Department of Education. Does the fact that this article was published in 1994 make it dated?

4. Who is the intended audience for this article?

Who reads *Newsweek*? Is the journal read mostly by people who are in a position to implement a law requiring licenses for drinking? Are students likely to read this magazine?

5. What can you learn from the first and final paragraphs of the article?

The first paragraph presents a personal example of several people the writer knew who died through excessive drinking. The last paragraph restates the main idea of the essay, that there should be licenses for drinking because it is a public health issue.

The Limits of The First Pass

Answering these questions during the first pass can be helpful. But unless you were very familiar with a journal, you would not necessarily know the answer to questions about its intended audience. Also, even if you can identify the writer's agenda, the article may still be worth reading or that the author may be worthy of trust. In fact, someone who has suffered personal loss due to alcohol may be in an excellent position to write about alcoholism as a social problem. However, awareness of a potential agenda can alert you to possible bias, which might be reflected in a one-sided or unintentionally distorted presentation of information or facts.

The Second Pass

During the second pass, the reader does a quick appraisal of the article, reading it for meaning and trying to get a sense of how it develops its main point. A quick perusal of "Needed: A License to Drink" would enable you to see that the early section of the essay discusses the author's personal connection to the topic both through personal loss and his work as a counselor in the chemical dependency treatment center. He cites statistics that indicate how dangerous excessive drinking can be. Then he presents his main idea, that there should a license to drink.

The Third Pass

During the third pass over "Needed: A License to Drink," the reader could evaluate the text by responding to the following questions:

1. Is the argument consistent with what you believe is true or possible about the world and with your concept of human nature?

In asking yourself this question, you might reflect on your own view of whether a law requiring a drinking license would discourage excessive drinking. To what extent do you think that people, especially young people, would obey or break this law? Do you believe that excessive drinking is due to people's lack of understanding of how dangerous this habit can be, both to oneself and to others?

2. Is the argument supported with appropriate and believable sub-points, examples, and facts?

In evaluating the support provided in this article, you might note that the author cites his own experience both through people he knows and through working as a counselor in a chemical dependency center. He also cites statistics and compares a drinking license to other types of licenses, such as fishing or hunting licenses.

3. Is the evidence reliable?

Although it is sometimes impossible to evaluate the reliability of statistics unless you are very familiar with the subject and the method of sampling, this article cites figures that can be checked, and in fact you should check them to see how the numbers have changed since the article was written. However, the author uses a judicious tone and doesn't seem to be making outrageous claims.

4. Does the argument acknowledge the complexity of the topic?

You might note that the author does not delve too deeply into the issue of alcoholism. He does not mention that some people are more prone to alcohol addiction than others or that alcoholism may be due to social and psychological factors. Moreover, he doesn't address the issue of whether people are likely to obey a law that requires a license for buying or ordering alcoholic beverages. The comparison of a drinking license to a hunting or fishing license might also be questioned.

5. Is the text stylistically credible?

The author uses a measured tone, devoid of language that is inflammatory or hysterical. Consequently, the article overall seems believable.

A FORM FOR CRITICAL READING

In this chapter, we have discussed a three-pass approach to reading an outside source, a method that will enable you to "join the ongoing conversation" about issues for your argumentative essays. Some of you may be thinking, though, that analyzing a text in this way will take more time than you are in the habit of devoting to your reading and that you prefer to complete your reading as quickly and efficiently as possible. Critical reading to evaluate the credibility of a published work does require analytical thinking, a process that usually takes more time than a quick skim will allow. Ultimately, though, you will be able to use The Three-Pass Approach quickly and efficiently. Like any new procedure, once you have practiced it, the more efficiently you will be able to do it—and the gain in insight will more than compensate for the additional time you spent initially.

MATERIALS TO HELP YOU READ MORE EFFECTIVELY

Following are several forms that will help you read published works with greater insight:

BEFORE YOU READ . . .

By Emmanuel Sabaiz-Birdsill

We always seem to jump into our readings and never really stop to think about what we know and need to know before we start reading. Before you read anything, use this brief outline and fill in the blanks to get a bit of an understanding of what you are going to read before you read it.

Name of the author/s:	What do you know about this author/s?
Name of the publication:	What do you know about this publication?
Source of the publication:	What do you know about this source? Is it reliable?
Year of the publication:	Does the year this was published change the information? Why/why not?
Title of the piece:	What does the title tell you about what you are about to read?
Headings and Subheadings:	What do the headings and subheadings tell you about what you are about to read?
References:	Do the references help with the ethos of the writer? Can you trust all of the references? Why/why not?

SUMMARY AND PARAPHRASE

Developed by Sean Curran

You will be asked in your writing assignments to provide your opinion on particular issues and in reaction to your assigned readings. *However,* writing is not solely comprised of sharing your opinion. Often you also need to demonstrate your understanding and knowledge of what a reading *says.* Using quotations from the reading is one means of doing this, but two related and possibly more important means are **paraphrase** and **summary.**

> **Paraphrase** means to use your own words and phrasing to relay someone else's ideas.
> **Summary** is to take a reading of some size and to *more briefly* and *in your own words* convey the *main idea(s)* of that reading.

How Can You Find the Main Idea(s)?

- Typically in a multiple-paragraph reading, the main ideas that whole reading conveys are stated in the first and/or last paragraphs.
- The main idea of a single paragraph is usually its first sentence.
- Look through the reading to see if any significant words (don't bother with "the" or "thing") are repeated. Which words are repeated most?

If there is a story told in the reading, look for sentences that *explain* the story rather than *tell* the story.

SUMMARIZING AN ARGUMENT

Developed by Andrea Hernandez

When writing essays in the genre of argument, it is important to acknowledge what others have said about the issue or controversy that you are discussing. You can show that you are acknowledging what others have said by **summarizing** their arguments. Summarizing arguments is slightly different than summarizing texts in other genres. For instance, you may have previously been told that a summary should include the author's "main points." But how do you find the "main points" of an argument? Instead of searching for main points, your summary of an argument should include the following:

1. The author's **thesis statement,** or primary claim.

In arguments, the author's thesis statement is often his or her opinion or stance on a particular issue. Some authors will have a clear, explicitly stated thesis statement; others will have one that is implied or implicitly stated. If the author's thesis statement is easily identifiable, highlight or underline it. If the thesis statement is not readily apparent, write in one sentence what you think the author's primary claim is.

2. The **reasons** that the author gives in support of their thesis statement.

Find the specific reasons that the author gives for making their primary claim. Some authors may give only a couple of reasons while others will give several. Make sure that you identify all the reasons that the author gives in support of their thesis statement.

Things to keep in mind:

- Include the author's name and the title of their text. This can be included in the opening statement of your summary.
  - **EXAMPLE:** "In the article, *TITLE, AUTHOR NAME* discusses *TOPIC/ CONTROVERSY.*"

- Restate the author's thesis and reasons for support clearly and concisely. Remember to phrase these elements of their argument in your own words.

  - **EXAMPLE:** "*AUTHOR NAME's* argues that *THESIS STATEMENT.* The first reason that *AUTHOR NAME* gives for this is *REASON #1.*"

- Remain **objective.** You are not critiquing or analyzing their argument; you are simply restating what they have claimed.

EVALUATING OUTSIDE SOURCES

Bibliographic Information:

Author: _____

Title: _____

Publication Information (Publisher, Place, Date of Publication):

_____

_____

Main Point: _____

Short Summary: _____

_____

_____

_____

THE WRITER

Describe the expertise and motives of the writer.

Describe how the writer acknowledges the complexity of the topic.

THE QUALITY OF THE ARGUMENT OR MAIN POINT

Characterize the beliefs about the world implied in this argument.

Characterize the view of human nature that underlies this argument.

Summarize the evidence used to support this argument.

Analyze the use of language. Does it contribute to the credibility of the text?

READING/WRITING CONNECTIONS: LOOKING AT RHETORICAL MOVES

A very useful approach to reading is to learn to read rhetorically—that is, to read not only to understand what a published work is saying, but also to figure out how it works—how the author has used thought patterns, techniques, and strategies to achieve his or her persuasive goals. Focusing on these thought patterns, techniques, and strategies will not only help you read more effectively; it will also help you become aware of various strategies you can use in your own writing.

Looking at various texts in terms of their rhetorical moves has become an important research direction for scholars who analyze various genres, and in his book, *Genre Analysis,* the scholar, John Swales, discusses the use of rhetorical moves in the introductions commonly used in social science articles. Swales studied many introductions, eventually developing a three move scheme that he called "Create a Research Space" (CARS) model. That model consists of the following components:

Move 1   Establishing a territory
Move 2   Establishing a niche
Move 3   Occupying the niche

In the first move, the writer presents a topic or "territory" about which the article or essay is concerned. That territory may have been addressed by other writers and scholars.

In the second move, the writer shows that there is a **gap** within that topic or area that hasn't been adequately explored. Essentially, this gap provides the exigence which the author's claim or thesis will address.

In the third move, the writer explains how he or she will address that particular gap. The thesis, argument, or main point arises from the author's wish to fill that gap. Here is an example:

Video Games: Good, Bad, or Other?

(Move 1) The relations between media consumption, especially TV viewing, and school performance have been extensively examined. **(Move 2)** However, even though video game playing may have replaced TV viewing as the most frequent form of media usage, relatively little research has examined its relations to school performance, especially in older students. **(Move 3)** We surveyed 671 college students concerning their history of video game usage and school performance. **(Thesis)** In general, video game players reported a greater likelihood of playing video games to avoid doing homework. There were consistent native associations between liking to play violent video games and school performance.

Burgess, Stephen R, Stermer, Paul, and Melinda C.R. Burgess. "Video Game Playing and Academic Performance in College Students." *College Student Journal* 46.2 2012. 376–87. Print.

Analyzing a text by looking at rhetorical moves will enable you to understand how an article "works"—how the form, structure, and style have been used to support a main claim. You can then consider how you might wish to imitate these moves in your own writing.

The rhetorical moves in "Needed: A License to Drink."

Mike Brake's article "Needed: A License to Drink, " which argues for the use of "license" for the purchase of alcohol, uses the following rhetorical moves in support of his proposal:

Paragraph 1 Use of an Emotional Appeal. Brake begins by referring to his cousin who killed himself at age thirty-two to introduce his proposal, which appears at the end of the paragraph.

Paragraph 2 Citing of statistics to support the claim that alcohol is a big problem.

Paragraph 3 The author indicates that he has had experience in working with the effects of alcoholism on young people.

Paragraph 4 The author reiterates his proposal that a national system of licensing for the purchase of alcohol be instituted.

Paragraphs 5–6 The author compares the licensing of alcohol to other types of licenses.

Paragraphs 7–9 The author explains how the system would work.

Paragraphs 10–11 The author argues against potential objections.

Paragraph 12 Concluding Paragraph—The author reiterates the thesis and affirms the value of his proposal.

FOR THINKING, DISCUSSION, AND WRITING

Mike Brake's article may be considered a "proposal" in that it proposes a solution to a problem. Find another article with a similar purpose and analyze it rhetorically. Does it use similar "moves" as those in "Needed: A License to Drink?" Do you find these moves effective? Does this article utilize moves that you think are more effective? Are there rhetorical moves you would like to use in your own writing?

EVALUATING WEB SOURCES

Developed by Emmanuel Sabaiz-Birdsill

Today, a great deal of information is obtained through Websites, which also have to be read critically, if they are used as sources. When people look at a Website, they need to be very careful about how they use the information that they find. Since not all Websites go through a review or editing process, it is important to gather as much information as possible, in order to decide if the information is reliable. Below is a worksheet to help evaluate information on a Website.

1. What is the name of the Website?

2. What is the URL of the Website?

3. Who wrote the content? What type of credentials do they have?

4. Is the information provided in text form, audio, or images?

5. What year was the content created or updated?

6. Is it associated with a particular organization or group?

7. What references are used in the site? Are they in-text references, or are they links to other Websites?

8. Can you reach the creators of the site in case you have a question? If so, how?

9. Is this a blog or a personal Website?

10. Is this an informative site or an opinion site?

By gathering as much information as possible in the early stages, you will be able to determine if the site is appropriate to use, and you will also have all the information you need for in-text citations and Works Cited page.

3

CHAPTER

Audience Awareness

One of the first questions many students have when they begin writing an essay has to do with their readers or audience. "For whom am I writing this?" they might wonder. "Who is the audience supposed to be?" or "Am I writing this for my professor or someone who does not know the subject?" It is clear that the idea of audience, or audience awareness, is a topic that students have on their minds. If the purpose of any essay is to have an impact on its readers, it is important to think about who those readers, or intended *audience,* might be and consider how they might react to your ideas. Sometimes figuring this out can be challenging and thus we need to look at how we can keep working with this concept as part of the writing process. This chapter discusses several strategies for thinking about your audience and explains *Rogerian Argument,* a form of argumentation that is based almost entirely on understanding the feelings of an intended audience.

THE MANY DIFFERENT AUDIENCES

Although all college arguments, whatever type they might be, are written to be read by an audience, it is sometimes difficult to define exactly who that audience actually is. If you think of "audience" as referring only to those who will actually read your essay, you may believe that your audience consists only of your teacher or maybe your fellow students who may help you peer review it. This is a reasonable assumption. After all, college essays are usually written for specific classes, and the teachers in those classes are usually those who read and evaluate them. However, a college essay, as a genre, is not written for just one person, not even your teacher. Rather it is intended for an "academic" audience, of which your teacher is a representative. To help our students understand the concept of an academic audience, we sometimes refer to it as *anyone with sufficient background in, and concern for the subject who might choose to read the essay.* If you left your essay on a table in the library, students and teachers should be able to understand its purpose and decide whether its ideas are worth considering. Notice that YOU are the first in the line of people who make up the academic audience. We often hear students say that they need a hook, or something to capture the audience's attention, but keep in mind that YOU are the first audience. So if you think your essay is boring and needs a hook, you most likely need to work on how you approach your intended audience. If you cannot convince yourself that your arguments are valid, then you are not going to convince anyone else. Knowing that you are the first audience is a powerful approach that will help you with your ownership of your work. It is the first step to understanding the complexity of audience awareness.

Teachers may sometimes add to the confusion about audience by saying, "consider your audience," without specifying what sort of audience should be considered. As a result, students may write without thinking about audience at all, or if they do, they think only of the teacher. But it is not a good idea to think of audience only in terms of those who already know the requirements of the assignment. If you write only to your teacher, you may omit a lot of important information—explanations, definitions, or support—because you will assume that the teacher is already familiar with the topic and will therefore not need very much background. Think of your teacher as a *representative* of a group of teachers. Other members of the group will have similar expectations and standards, but they will not know as much about the assignment or contexts as your teacher does, so it is important to include that information in your essay.

Another problem that results from confusion over the concept of audience is that students may inadvertently use an inappropriate tone or present only one side of an issue. On occasion, a few of our students have written blatantly one-sided, aggressive, or poorly reasoned harangues on a topic, rather than the thoughtful, reasoned response appropriate to the genre of academic argument because they have not thought about the reaction of an audience. Remember that statements such as "Anyone who thinks this is just a racist," or "These ideas are hopelessly old fashioned," are more likely to offend than to convince an audience and will therefore not contribute to the persuasiveness of your essay. Most students may not be aware that they are already experts in tone, and thus they already know how to use tone to convince their audience. Let us do a little exercise to see how well you know tone and audience.

EXERCISE

Same Genre, Two Audiences

Pretend that you work for a company and rumor has it that the boss is going to hand out some great promotions soon. Your boss walks into your office and tells you that he would like you to attend a BBQ at his house that weekend. You accept, knowing that this may be the time you may get a promotion. As soon as your boss walks out, your best friend calls you and tells you that she was able to get front row tickets for a concert of your favorite band. Not only do you get front row tickets, you also get back stage passes to meet the band and get to hang out with them at the after party. The problem is that the concert will take place the same day as your boss' BBQ!

> **Part 1**—Write a note to your boss letting him know you are not going to make it to the BBQ anymore.

Now pretend that it was not your boss, but rather your parents who invited you to have dinner with them. Again, pretend that you do not live with them and this is a time you already set up to spend time with them. Yet the same thing happens, your friend has called and has these great tickets.

> **Part 2**—Write a note to your parents letting them know you are not going to make it to dinner.

Now let us compare the notes. Did you use the same diction? Are there certain phrases or types of sentences found in one of the notes but not the other? Are they even the same size? Most likely you were more formal with your boss than with your parents. Maybe with your boss, you used words like "Dear Mr./Miss." or "Thank you for your understanding" and with your parents, you may have addressed them as "Hi Mom and Dad," and end with "Love you and miss you!" Maybe you gave more reasons to your boss, and decided to be more brief with your parents. Notice that you wrote the same genre, an excuse, and that it was based on the same ideas. The main difference was the audience, and by being aware of who the audience was, you changed your writing style. In this book, we discuss the idea of tone a bit further but for now be aware that tone comes into play when writing for your audience.

Being aware of audience and focusing on audience as a way of exploring the topic thus has the following advantages:

1. It helps you keep in mind that the teacher is not the only audience for an argumentative essay;

2. It serves as a means of generating ideas and of figuring out what additional information is needed;
3. It focuses attention on the purpose of argumentative writing—to address a reader—not simply to express your own ideas;
4. It enables you to distinguish when it is appropriate to confront an opposing viewpoint directly and when it is more appropriate to strive for change through mutual acceptance and understanding;
5. It helps you decide what to emphasize.

CREATING YOUR AUDIENCE—LOCAL, NATIONAL, OR TRANSNATIONAL

Even though college essays are usually intended for an audience of more than one particular person, it can be helpful to think about a *representative* toward whom the writing will be addressed. You should not think of this audience as someone in particular, such as one particular person with a certain level of education or from a specific place. More and more students are being asked to write to broader audiences, so that their work can show a level of sophisticated writing that can be shared by many. This idea comes into place when we are dealing with complex issues that may reflect ideas from members of different communities and cultures. For example, let us pretend you are writing an essay in which you need to convince your audience that the local government should spend more money on education and less on prisons. Who would be your audience? It could be the local politicians, school board supervisors, the teachers and the parents, along with those in the judicial system and victims of crime. Now let's say that you are calling for a national shift of funds so that the country would spend more on education and less in military defense. Who will your audience be in this instance? Now you will need to take into consideration more politicians, such as governors whose states are awarded military contracts. You will need to think about military personnel and how shift in funding would affect their jobs. You will even have to think about our foreign partners who rely on our military for their defense. So as you can see, audience can range from local, to state, to national to even international audiences you need to think about as you develop your essay.

Now think about issues in which not only the community needs to be taking into consideration, but the culture as well. For example, let's say that you are writing an essay in which you have to discuss the use of natural resources in rural areas of the US. Part of your audience would be those who live in those areas. Those communities may react differently to your arguments if their culture has different values than yours. You will have to show that you understand the culture of this community and create your argument by doing research and showing that you know the values of those cultures. This can also be applied to an international audience as well. Imagine you are writing an essay where now you are arguing that we need to look for these natural resources around the world. How would you approach audiences that are from different cultures, with different languages and different values? It may seem impossible but the key is to focus on one audience at a time. International business writers do it all the time, since the way they would approach a business in Japan, would not be the same way they would approach a business in South America. They understand that they need to be culturally sensitive to the specific audience in order to close the deal.

Always ask yourself who will have a say on the subject you are arguing about as a strategy to help you create a more specific audience.

CONVINCING AN AUDIENCE THAT YOU ARE KNOWLEDGEABLE

Although you are probably not an expert on the subject you are writing about, you can demonstrate that you have researched your topic adequately and provide a lot of pertinent and appropriate information in support of your position. In writing, we call that your Ethos, and we will discuss Ethos, Pathos, and Logos further in the book, but for now remember that Ethos is your character. This means that as a writer you need to convince members of your audience that they can trust you because you know and understand what you are arguing about. Convincing writers support their statements with examples, statistics, and references to reliable authority. They are people who have "done their homework," and their work indicates that they have thought carefully about the topic and have located sufficient and appropriate information to strengthen their position. Do not confuse the idea of adequate support simply with having random quotes, or many quotes throughout your essay. A convincing argument contains carefully selected sources that enable the reader to develop understanding. Too many or random quotes confuse the reader and instead of contributing to your credibility, they may suggest that you really do not fully understand what you are talking about.

Adequate information on a researchable topic will enable you to have an impact on your audience. The following paragraph lacks sufficient supporting material.

Philip's Paragraph

> To my understanding, exams, in many cases, do not promote learning. They exert pressure on students and result only in cramming, not in real education. Many students stay up all night studying and then find that their minds have blacked out before the test because of lack of sleep and too much input of information all at once. Often, the effort put into studying throughout the year is not reflected on how well a person does on an exam. Sometimes, all the information learned before an exam is forgotten in one week.
>
> **(Phillip)**

The claim in Phillip's paragraph is that exams do not promote learning, but instead, result in all-night cramming that neither guarantees a high performance on a test nor reflects how much the student has actually learned. Phillip's claim is clearly stated, but his argument is not convincing because his topic is so broad that he could not research it adequately and because he does not use supporting material that would strengthen his position. In his reference to college exams, Phillip did not specify what sort of exams or college courses he means. Does he believe that all exams are useless and that there is no exam that can measure student learning? Would he advocate the elimination of licensing exams for doctors and lawyers? How about exams for licensing drivers? Most people would not feel comfortable consulting an unlicensed doctor or lawyer or hiring an unlicensed driver, so it is important that Phillip define more specifically what he means by useless exams.

Discerning readers know that one cannot be an "expert" on a topic that is too broad, nor can one research a broad topic adequately. Therefore, Phillip cannot write a convincing argument about the effectiveness of all exams in all college courses. In fact, because Phillip has not adequately narrowed his subject, his paragraph sounds more like a student complaining about all the studying he has to do than someone who has carefully researched the topic.

The other reason that Phillip does not appear credible is that his claim is based solely on his own experience. Although personal experience can often provide relevant support for many subjects, readers of academic argument usually expect additional support—having a strong view on a topic can be an advantage, but it is a disadvantage if you have nothing else. Phillip's paragraph would have been a great deal stronger if he had cited studies or reliable authorities concerning the relationship of particular exams to learning. In its current form, it does not indicate that Phillip has "done his homework," and his audience is unlikely to be convinced.

UNDERSTANDING AUDIENCE THROUGH DIALOGUE

Conceiving of argumentation in terms of a **dialogue** or exchange about a topic is another strategy that can help you focus your ideas. Jon, a college student who wants to transfer to a different college, might find it useful to imagine himself having a dialogue with his Aunt Maria in order to anticipate any points she might make about why he should remain where he is. Similarly, in writing argumentative essays for your college classes, you might find it useful to imagine a potential opponent, anticipate opposing points this opponent might make, and think about how you might refute them.

The idea that the genre of argument begins in dialogue is useful not only because it can help you develop ideas and strategies that can be used against a potential opposition, but also because it can highlight points of agreement between you and your reader. When writers acknowledge that they understand how their opponents might feel or believe, they present themselves as thoughtful and trustworthy because these points of agreement serve as a bridge or a link. If Jon can demonstrate that he understands Aunt Maria's point of view, Aunt Maria is more likely to trust Jon and pay attention to Jon's ideas. It is as if Jon is saying, "I understand how you feel and, in fact, there are many aspects of this topic about which the two of us agree. But here is where the two of us differ."

WRITING A DIALOGUE

To utilize dialogue in the exploration of a topic, create a character with an opinion on a controversial topic and another with a differing opinion. Script an exchange between them in a dialogue of one to two pages, remembering that both participants should be presented as polite and intelligent people. In this interchange, no one should make outrageous or insulting statements and no one should win. The aim is to generate an exchange of ideas, not to score points over an adversary. Here is a dialogue between Jon and Aunt Maria:

Jon's Dialogue

Jon: Aunt Maria, I've been spending a lot of time thinking about where I ought to go to college.

Aunt M: But you're already in college. Haven't you been enrolled at State since last September?

Jon: Yes, of course, and I've actually been pretty happy. I mean, State has a great Business School and fantastic sports teams. It's pretty well-known on a national level also. People are impressed when I say I go to State.

Aunt M: That's right. Even when I went to State, its reputation was terrific. It was known nationally—even in Europe, people knew about it. And those teams ... I really loved the games—getting to cheer on the State Walruses. I still go to the homecoming game. And I had a really excellent grounding in business, a really excellent grounding.

Jon: You know, Aunt Maria, I used to feel exactly the same way.

Aunt M: What do you mean "used to feel"?

Jon: Well, this year, I've done some serious investigation into job opportunities. And the jobs for people with straight business degrees just aren't there anymore.

Aunt M: Is that so?

Jon: Right. Today, with tight economic conditions, the jobs are for people in newer fields, people with specialties. People who get the jobs are those who have all of the training that used to be associated with business—lots of math and computer experience, for example—but they also know about some of the newer fields.

Aunt M: What fields are you talking about?

Jon: Well, like environmental studies, for example. I took a geography course last semester and I learned about all sorts of job opportunities in environmental policy; jobs involving field work, government jobs—lots of possibilities.

Aunt M: It sounds like that's what you plan to major in at State.

Jon: Well, not exactly. You see, State doesn't have a major in environmental policy. But there is a terrific program at Northern College.

Aunt M: Northern? That's a smaller school, isn't it? It certainly didn't have much of a reputation when I went to State. In fact, the kids who went to Northern were the ones who didn't get into State.

Jon: That's all changed now, Aunt Maria. Northern's reputation has really come up. It's still true that Northern is smaller than State, but that means the classes are smaller and that you get more attention from the teachers. For me, that's really important. I learned so much from just talking with my geography teacher after class—in a way, I learned more in those conversations than I did in class.

Aunt M: And you say that there are job opportunities in environmental studies?

Jon: Yes. I've even got a list of jobs that graduates in environmental policy have gotten right after graduation. It looks like they're doing okay.

Aunt M: Well, it looks as if you know what you're doing. At least you did your homework. So you want to transfer to Northern?

Jon: Oh yes, Aunt Maria. Environmental policy is such an interesting field. I can see all sorts of possibilities in it for me. I know this is the right choice.

This dialogue, of course, presumes that Aunt Maria is a reasonable person and will not simply shout, "I went to State. You're going to State. That's all there is to it." If Jon thought that Aunt Maria was someone like that, there would be no point in trying to convince her of anything. So one of the functions of writing dialogue is that it enables you to envision your audience as reasonable, an audience who will listen to convincing reasons supported by credible evidence.

EXERCISE

SCENARIO: THE RIGHT TO SEARCH TRASH

The scenario that follows is concerned with the rights stated in the Fourth Amendment of the Constitution of the United States for all Americans to be free of unreasonable searches. The amendment reads as follows:

> The right of the people to be secure in their houses, papers, and effects against unreasonable searches and seizures, shall not be violated and no warrants shall issue, but upon probable cause, supported by oath or affirmation, and particularly describing the place to be searched, and the persons to be seized at the time.

The Fourth Amendment is designed to protect an individual from unwanted government intrusion. However, for the Fourth Amendment to apply, a person must have a reasonable expectation of privacy, and anyone who searches must have "probable cause"—that is, a valid reason for conducting a search. Often, that reason is a concern for public safety or well-being, and it is this conflict between the right to privacy and public safety that is open for interpretation. If a search violated a person's Fourth Amendment rights, and if no probable cause was established, evidence obtained could be excluded.

Related to issues of public safety and privacy rights is the question of whether incriminating evidence found in a trash bag placed outside of a person's home can be used against that person. In a 2003 case in South Dakota, a drug agent had been informed that a couple was distributing and using illegal drugs. The agent searched a trash bag found outside the couple's home and found evidence of drugs. He then obtained a search warrant, searched the couple's home, and found more incriminating evidence. The couple was convicted and appealed the case, but the judge in the case ruled that the search was "reasonable," based on probable cause, and the conviction was upheld. The couple was sentenced to two years in jail.

A Scenario Concerned with Privacy

Read the following scenario, which is concerned with the issue of trash search at a university:

> Mrs. Glenwood-Jones is worried about her daughter, Cindy, who is a first-year college student living in a residence hall. She is concerned that the residence hall is not adequately supervised and that many of the students drink excessively, especially on the weekends. Concerned that Cindy will not do well in school if she parties too much on the weekend, Mrs. Glenwood-Jones learns that all students place their trash cans outside their rooms on Monday for garbage collection the next day. One Tuesday morning, when she knew that most of the students were

in class or still asleep, Mrs. Glenwood-Jones went to her daughter's residence hall and confiscated the contents of several trash cans that were left outside the rooms. Just as she had suspected, every can, including that of her daughter, was filled with liquor bottles and beer cans, as well as other evidence that the weekend had been spent in excessive partying. Furious, Mrs. Glenwood-Jones wants to take her evidence to the school authorities in order to require them to exercise more stringent restraints on students' behavior.

THINKING, DISCUSSION, AND WRITING

Discuss this situation in small groups, considering some of the following questions:

1. How similar is this situation to the one in the South Dakota case?
2. What do you think Mrs. Glenwood-Jones ought to do?
3. Was Mrs. Glenwood-Jones violating the students' rights to privacy?
4. Do you think it was right for her to steal the trash?
5. Do you think it was legal for her to steal the trash—that is, do you think she had probable cause?
6. Do you think she can use the trash as evidence?
7. What effect do you predict her action will have on the school authorities? On her daughter?

Write a dialogue between Mrs. Glenwood-Jones and the Vice President for Student Life at the University. Then write a short essay evaluating Mrs. Glenwood-Jones' action from both a social and legal point of view. Do you consider her action justified? Do you think her behavior was socially acceptable?

THE ROLE OF AUDIENCE IN ROGERIAN ARGUMENT

The concept of audience is especially important in a form of argumentation known as "Rogerian Argument," which takes its name from the psychologist, Carl Rogers. In working with his patients, Rogers noted that although reason is an important component of making a point or instituting change, many people are not convinced by reasons alone—often they need to feel understood before they can even contemplate changing their ideas. Rogers thus postulates a defensive fearful audience, resistant to any new position, an audience that does not easily tolerate differences in opinion but which can be swayed if it does not feel threatened. Rogerian argument is not used very much within the genre of argument, but it can focus a writer's attention on the psychological factors that influence the effect of an argument on an audience.

Writers who utilize Rogerian argument maintain that they will not impact their audience if they simply present their ideas and cite their reasons, because for some audiences, a direct statement of a new idea might generate hostility. Given this notion of a threatened, fearful audience, those who advocate Rogerian argument claim that it is preferable first to engender empathy from the audience by indicating that the writer understands its position, delaying the thesis statement until the audience is comfortable. It is as if the writer is saying: "I understand your view very well. Here is a restatement of it and here are all the aspects of it that I agree with." Then, once the writer has gained the audience's confidence, he or she can present a claim or position and perhaps move the audience to consider alternative viewpoints.

The Structure and Tone of Rogerian Argument

An argument based entirely on Rogers' model differs considerably from other models used in the genre of argument. Where the writer of traditional argument may state the thesis directly in the first or second paragraph, the writer of Rogerian argument begins by communicating understanding and empathy and often waits until further along in the essay to indicate points of disagreement. One may also see differences in the conclusion. In traditional argument, the writer aims for agreement or at least serious consideration, so the conclusion may reaffirm the writer's claim. In Rogerian argument, all the writer can hope for is that the audience will acknowledge that the writer's view is worth considering, or perhaps allow for the existence of alternative possibilities. The conclusion may, therefore, call for further discussion or exchange of ideas.

Whether or not you ever write a true Rogerian argument, Rogers' concept of empathy can be applied to all forms of argumentative writing because it defines an attitude that can influence the writer's tone. If you are aware of the importance of empathy and of assuming a sufficiently judicious and qualified tone, you will be more likely to win the trust of your audience, whatever form your actual text may assume.

WRITING ASSIGNMENTS

1. Write a brief Rogerian argument responding to one of the following scenarios. Use small groups to discuss your strategy.

    A. A mother is worried about sending her twelve-year-old son to summer camp. Write a Rogerian argument to help her understand that the child would benefit from the experience.

    B. Your roommate does (or doesn't) want to join a club, team, sorority, or fraternity. Write a Rogerian argument to help him or her understand the opposing position.

2. For the essay assigned in Chapter 6, which is concerned with the appropriateness of fairy tales in a nursery school, write a Rogerian argument to help a worried mother understand that fairy tales are not likely to traumatize her four-year-old daughter. Use the fairy tales with which you are most familiar.

Following is the essay that Teeanna wrote on this topic. Note how she indicates awareness of her audience's position and the placement of the thesis.

ARE FAIRY TALES STILL RELEVANT?

Every day, you read about it—violence in the streets, dysfunctional families, sexual harassment—and you see it everywhere in our society. What has been done to our children? How can we teach the next generation that certain behaviors are not acceptable? Can old-fashioned fairy tales, which are filled with vicious actions and harmful sexual stereotypes, possibly hold anything useful for today's child? Or will they simply make matters worse?

The most disturbing problem in society is that of violence, and unfortunately, most violent acts are committed by young people. We can blame TV and gangs, but the fact remains that somehow along the line, today's children are missing something in their education or upbringing that makes them unable to cope with everyday stresses that ultimately explode into violence. Can anything be done to make our young people less violent? Can education in early childhood have an impact on how young people learn to cope with anger and frustration?

The psychologist, Bruno Bettelheim, in *The Uses of Enchantment,* states that young children need to work through anger and hostility through the imagination, and that old-fashioned fairy tales, which contain many violent elements, are extremely helpful in enabling children to express these feelings vicariously. This doesn't mean that fairy tales are some kind of cure-all for juvenile delinquents, but maybe if some of our violent teenagers had read fairy tales when they were young, they could have learned to express anger or frustration using their imagination rather than a gun.

Sexism is another problem in society, which is difficult to solve because it involves bucking a system that has existed almost as long as we have history. We work hard to erase sexist terms and imagery in all areas of our lives, and especially in the lives of our children. We hope that if we teach our children these lessons early enough, they will be comfortable being loving fathers, involved in their children's lives, and confident women, capable of earning equal respect (and income) in the workplace. And yet, so little progress has been made and so many stereotypes still exist. Doesn't it seem likely that if we expose children to traditional fairy tales we will only make matters worse?

Of course, traditional fairy tales do contain unflattering portraits of both men and women. Some of the women are depicted as passive characters who wait for Prince Charming to show up on a white horse and rescue them. Others are evil, witch-like creatures, who perpetuate nasty deeds on one another out of jealousy. Moreover, a number of the fathers in fairy tales are not heroes either. Many are depicted as uninvolved or even absent from their families. It doesn't seem possible that fairy tales with all of these terrible stereotypes will help children avoid harmful views of both sexes. Isn't it more likely that if we teach our children that all people are equal and they carry that lesson with them as they read fairy tales, that the fairy tales themselves will destroy what we have taught?

In response to this concern, Bruno Bettelheim argues that fairy tales can help children understand the importance of struggling against great difficulties, even those caused by age-old sexist stereotypes. Bettelheim points out that fairy tales are stories about characters who are good overcoming characters who are evil and powerful, and he maintains that if children read fairy tales in that way, they will be encouraged to succeed, regardless of their sex. In deciding whether or not to include traditional fairy tales in early childhood education, then, the answer must be "yes." Although fairy tales contain elements we no longer find acceptable, they are still useful to children because fairy tales allow children to learn how to express themselves and to empower themselves.

HOW AUDIENCE DETERMINES OTHER COMPONENTS OF A TEXT

Following are citations for two essays concerned with the topic of underage drinking. Each is intended for a different audience. Find these articles and note how the audience for each determines other aspects of the text, such as the introduction, types of sentences, tone, and evidence cited.

"Surgeon General's Call to Action to Prevent and Reduce Underage Drinking" *http://www.surgeongeneral.gov/topics/underagedrinking/*

"Colleges Move Boldly On Student Drinking; Exploiting an Exception to Federal Privacy Laws, Schools Increasingly Notify Parents When Kids Are Caught With Alcohol" *http://online.wsj.com/article/SB119690910535115405.html* Originally published by Elizabeth Bernstein in the *Wall Street Journal* (Eastern edition) on Dec. 6, 2007, pg. D.1.

4

CHAPTER

Translating Your Assignment

Chapter 1 explained the terms "genre" and "argument" as they are used in this book, and Chapter 2 focused on rhetorical and critical reading, referring to several concepts associated with genre and argument that are important to understand when you write and read for your college classes: Rhetoric, exigence, rhetorical situation, problem, thesis, audience, and purpose. These are important concepts that we will continue to refer to throughout the book, and we suggest that you review them to make sure you understand their meaning and their connection to college writing assignments.

In this chapter, we discuss a process we call "Translating Your Assignment," and you might wonder why a student should have to "translate" a writing assignment. After all, assignments are usually written in a language that students can read and understand, and teachers distribute them in order to help students figure out what sort of essay they are supposed to write—they are intended to be like a set of directions, a guide, or a road map. However, although writing assignments are *supposed* to be easy to follow and may *seem* clear-cut and straightforward, they sometimes contain hidden assumptions and cues that require special understanding and interpretation, especially when students are unfamiliar with college writing. Following are four suggestions for **translating your assignment,** a process that can help you to understand college writing assignments more clearly:

1. Translate unstated time requirements into a plan.
2. Translate the topic into something meaningful for *you.*
3. Translate key terms.
4. Translate the teacher's assumptions about the genre of essay you are expected to write.

1. TRANSLATE UNSTATED TIME REQUIREMENTS INTO A PLAN

Although assignment sheets will usually tell you when the assignment is due and may indicate how many drafts you are expected to write, they usually do not specify how long each part of the writing process is likely to take, and many students do not leave enough time to complete an assignment effectively. Upon receiving an assignment sheet, they may glance at it briefly, stuff it into a folder, and put it completely out of their minds—that is, until the night before it is due! Then they will panic, rush off to the library, grab whatever materials they happen to find that are pertinent to the assignment, and stay up all night writing a draft, drearily cranking out the necessary number of pages just to get the paper finished. Students who write like this cannot "engage" with the topic because they don't give themselves a chance to find something meaningful in it—that is, to locate an exigence and a purpose for writing it—and the essays they write usually reflect this lack of engagement. They are as painful to read as they were to write! Sometimes, students who write in this way will suffer from writer's block, unable to write anything at all beyond a few unsatisfactory beginnings.

Students who are aware of what it means to engage with a topic successfully understand that a good piece of writing requires personal investment, that writing requires intellectual and emotional involvement, and that if a writer thinks about it seriously, understands it thoroughly, wrestles with it mentally, finds a way to connect with it, and leaves enough time to work on it—unconscious processing can occur that can lead to a really good essay. Creativity is often erroneously viewed as occurring through an inspirational lightening bolt, striking without warning, a belief that implies that one has to wait passively for good ideas to come. Our experience as writers and writing teachers tells us that creativity is more likely to occur when we have been grappling with a topic for a while, both consciously and unconsciously. Then, after many rejected efforts, an idea will strike—and most likely it will be a good one. Go after the lightening bolt; don't wait for it to come to you! Also—if you think about an assignment in advance, you will be able to figure out what might be unclear to you. Then you will be able to ask questions of your teacher, other students, or tutors in a writing center.

With sufficient effort, **you can engage with a topic even if, at first, you didn't care about it at all.** If you wish your brain to percolate, to work on the assignment even when you are driving, cooking, working, even sleeping, and if you want to come up with something interesting and meaningful to say, you should start thinking about your assignment immediately. Don't dismiss it with too-commonly used phrases such as "this is boring," "who cares about this topic?" or "this is easy. I can write this essay the night before it is due." Use the time you have to find something about it that is interesting to you, and give your brain a chance to work on it.

Planning Your Time

Translating unstated requirements into a workable plan can be accomplished if you construct a list in which you write down everything you must do in order to finish your paper. You can construct the list as follows:

1. **List all the activities you will engage in when you write your paper.** These could include talking with someone about the topic, brainstorming, going to the library, searching the Internet, reading, taking notes, summarizing and comparing sources, writing early drafts, revising, printing the final draft—perhaps creating a blog or Website.
2. **Estimate the time you think you will need for each of these activities.** Decide when and where you will actually complete these activities so that you can leave enough time.
3. **Add up the total.** If possible, add at least an hour to each estimate. Most of the time, activities take more, not less, time than anticipated.

Of course, we understand that it is difficult to plan, and sometimes even more difficult to stick with a plan, no matter how well intentioned a person might be. Life sometimes interferes with the best of plans, and this is true for all of us. But it is a good idea to develop a plan anyway. The *Writing Time Management Form* below is offered as a possible way of organizing your time. But you should develop a plan that works particularly for you.

WRITING TIME MANAGEMENT FORM

Type of Activity	When?	Where?
Reading assignment		
Writing exploratory draft		
Reading sources		
Brainstorming		
Developing preliminary topic		
Creating an outline		
Writing first draft		
Getting feedback on first draft		
Writing second draft		
Revising second draft		
Editing second draft		
Checking documentation		
Printing and copying		
Creating a blog		
Creating a Website		

2. TRANSLATE THE ASSIGNMENT INTO SOMETHING MEANINGFUL FOR *YOU*

During the impeachment hearings of President Clinton in 1998, there was a humorous discussion about the meaning of the word *is*, a word whose meaning seems obvious. The same could be said for the word *you*, because when we encourage you to translate your assignment into something meaningful for "you," we mean that there are many "yous," and that the process of writing in college involves your becoming aware of them, and, in some instances, creating new ones. There is "you" the student, "you" the child," "you" the wage earner, "you" the friend," and many other "you's," depending on the different contexts of your life. Certainly you play a different role when you are with your parents or children than when you are with friends or at work, and each role involves a different "you." We will discuss the relationship of "you" to college writing in Chapter 5. But in the early phase of the translation process, you should focus on the everyday "you"—the "you" who wakes up in the morning, the "you" who is a member of a family, the "you" who hangs out with friends sometimes, the "you" who answers the phone, the "you" who texts with friends, and the "you" who recalls childhood experiences.

To translate your assignment into something meaningful for "you," then, you should think about your initial responses to the following questions concerning the topic you wish to write about. It is also useful to respond to these questions in writing.

ESTABLISHING CONNECTION WITH YOUR TOPIC

1. What is your immediate reaction to this topic?
2. Was this topic ever discussed in your home when you were a child? If so, how?
3. Was this topic ever discussed when you were in high school? If so, how?
4. If you are currently working, is this a topic that is discussed among co-workers? If so, how?
5. Can this topic be considered controversial in any way? If so, how?
6. Can you think of at least two people who might hold differing opinions on this topic? If so, describe them and summarize what you think they believe.
7. Do you think this topic is important for people to think about? Why or why not?
8. Can you find an exigence in this topic?

FOR THINKING, DISCUSSION, AND WRITING

Think about what sort of job you would like to have five years from now and write two letters describing that job—one to a close friend, the other to an authority figure, a parent, a teacher, or an employer. How do the "yous" in these two letters differ from one another? How are these different "yous" presented in each letter?

3.   TRANSLATE KEY TERMS

College writing assignments often require the writer to translate terms into workable definitions. These terms may seem self-evident but can have special meaning in the context of college writing. For example, if you were asked to write about a teacher who was particularly "effective," you might think about your high school history teacher, Mr. Casey, who told jokes in class and held lively debates. Mr. Casey made history come to life for you! But does that mean that Mr. Casey was effective? Is an effective teacher someone who brings a subject to life? Someone else might think that an effective history teacher is someone who requires students to memorize dates of historical events. If you were writing about this topic, then, you would need to define what you mean by an *effective* teacher. In the context of a film, if you were asked to write about whether the movie *Bowling for Columbine* was an "effective" piece of social commentary, you would have to think about what you mean by "effective" and incorporate that definition into your writing. Look for key terms in your assignment and think about which ones need definition.

FOR THINKING, DISCUSSION, AND WRITING

1. Write a short essay about an effective or ineffective teacher you have had. Be sure to include a definition of the term.
2. Write a short essay in which you discuss whether or not team sports are beneficial for children. Be sure to include a definition of what you mean by "beneficial."

Writing assignments may also include terms that require students to write in a particular genre. For example, a common assignment might ask you to "respond" to a published article. What does the word *respond* mean in this context? Usually it means that you begin by summarizing the main points of the article and then indicate whether or not you agree or disagree with those points. For example, a response to an article that focuses on the negative impact of television might point out that the article overlooks some important benefits that television has had on young children—teaching children the alphabet on *Sesame Street* and exposing children to other cultures in discovery or adventure programs. If you are asked to *respond* to an article, it is important to acknowledge its main points, not simply to use the article as a springboard for an essay that is concerned with the same subject. For example, if you were asked to respond to an article that argues against the policy of allowing companies to distribute credit cards to entering college students, it is important to indicate that you have read and understood the article. You might, in fact, agree completely with its main point, but your essay must refer to the article in some way, not simply argue a similar idea about the problems students often have with credit cards.

Other terms that students sometimes misunderstand are *compare* and *contrast*. An assignment may require students to write an essay in which they "compare and contrast" two articles on a given subject, and many students will follow those directions quite literally. They will discuss first one article and then they will discuss the other without really doing much comparing or contrasting. In fact, if students respond to the assignment in this way, they are not really writing an essay at all, because essays usually have a main point or thesis that provides unity and coherence. A college writing assignment that asks students to "compare and contrast" two articles usually expects students to write an essay with a main point that incorporates information from both articles. For instance, in a writing class, Maria was assigned to compare two articles, one a news article and the other an opinion piece, both of which are concerned with the impact of television on adolescent girls on the Pacific Island of Fiji. The study focused on how television has changed Fijian girls' ideas about body image and altered their eating practices. Here is how Maria began her essay:

Maria's Essay

Two Reports on the Becker Study

An article by Erica Goode entitled "Study Finds TV Alters Fiji Girls' View of Body" discusses the results of a study by Dr. Anne E. Becker, director of research at the Harvard Eating Disorders Center of Harvard Medical School. Dr. Becker studied Fiji Island girls' concept of body image over three years. The study showed that since the introduction of television to Fiji, adolescent girls are rejecting the traditional Fijian association of beauty with being big and now feel that beautiful women must be thin. The study found that girls who watched television for three or more nights a week "were 50 percent more likely to describe themselves as 'too big or fat' and 30 percent more likely to diet than girls who watched television less frequently" (399).

The article by Ellen Goodman entitled "The Culture of Thin Bites Fiji" also discusses the Becker study. Goodman cites statistics from the article to show that in "just 38 months, and with only one channel, a television-free culture that defined a fat person as robust has become a television culture that sees robust, as, well, repulsive" (401). Goodman notes that being thin in Fiji is no longer seen as a disease, but rather as a "requirement for getting a good job, nice clothes, and fancy cars" (402).

Sonia began her essay like this:

Sonia's Essay

Body Image Insecurity in Fijian Girls

Every woman I know seems to be on a diet or at least is worrying that she is too fat. Very few seem to be satisfied with their bodies. This situation pertains not only to women in the United States but also to those in far away Fiji, an island in the Pacific Ocean, as a result of their being exposed to American television. Recently, Dr. Anne E. Becker, director of research at the Harvard Eating Disorders Center of Harvard Medical School, conducted a three-year study of Fijian girls' concept of body image, and the results of the study have been reported in two news articles. The article by Erica Goode cites evidence from the study about how adolescent Fijian girls who watched a lot of American television have changed their notion of what is beautiful. The article by Ellen Goodman, however, uses information from the study to build an argument about how unrealistic body images portrayed on television can have a devastating impact on women, causing them to "hate and harm themselves" (402).

Both articles cite alarming statistics about what happened when adolescent Fijian girls were exposed to television for three years, but Goode presents the results objectively without expressing anger. She notes that girls who watched television three or more nights a week "were 50 percent more likely to describe themselves as 'too big or fat' and 30 percent more likely to diet than girls who watched television less frequently" (399), but she recounts this information simply as fact. Goodman, though, is angry about the results of the study. She uses a more strident tone to show her strong disapproval of the unrealistically thin body image promoted by Hollywood and to express her belief that Hollywood ought to take responsibility for the insecurity and self-loathing it foists on women, not only in Fiji, but everywhere. The Goode article is a report, but the Goodman article is an argument.

Note the differences between these two short essays, paying particular attention to the thesis statement in each essay. Can you restate the thesis of the second essay? How does the thesis statement reflect the idea of "compare and contrast" and influence what information is included for comparison and contrast?

Other terms used in writing assignments that might need definition and clarification are as follows:

Analyze—to break down an event, an idea, a process, or a text into its component parts. For example, you can analyze the components of a holiday celebration or a business letter.

Define—to state the essential feature of something. You can define the essential characteristics of a particular holiday or action.

Discuss—a word often used in exam questions but sometimes in essay assignments as well. It means to present information in the context of a main point, as in, discuss the factors that will influence your choice of major.

Describe—to tell about a person, a scene, or a process to give a vivid picture of it. You can describe a room that was meaningful to you or a scene you will always remember.

Evaluate—to assess the value of something. You can evaluate the impact of affirmative action on educational opportunity, the importance of team sports in a high school experience, or the advantages and disadvantages of laptop computers.

Explain—to make a topic as clear as possible. You can explain the significance of a cultural ritual or the meaning of a particular text.

4.   TRANSLATE THE TEACHER'S ASSUMPTIONS ABOUT THE WRITING GENRE YOU ARE EXPECTED TO WRITE

When teachers construct writing assignments, they sometimes do not clarify what genre of essay they are expecting students to write. Without that clarification, students tend to write the sort of essay they have written before, perhaps in high school—personal narratives based on their own experience, five paragraph essays, summaries, or information-based reports. Your prior knowledge is certainly important, and the genres you are most familiar with might be appropriate for a particular writing assignment. However, it may not be, so it is important to clarify for yourself what sort of genre you are expected to produce. As we discussed in Chapter 1 college writing is usually a thesis-driven argument—that is, it begins with an exigence, is written to address a rhetorical situation, and is focused around a central point or thesis that serves as a unifying principle that organizes the entire essay. Its purpose is to influence an audience to say, "That is a well-developed idea that is worth considering."

For example, if you are given an assignment that asks you to *analyze* a film, you should not simply summarize the plot and discuss how boring it is. Rather, you might discuss how components of the film, such as the setting or main characters, reinforce or raise questions about gender stereotypes. Similarly, an assignment that uses the word *describe* may require a simple description of something. But it may mean that description should be used to support a main point or thesis. For example, a memo to the Director of Student Services may describe the unsanitary conditions in the cafeteria and the poor quality of the food, but its central purpose is to institute necessary changes.

Applying A Conceptual or Theoretical Framework

Some college writing assignments may expect students to apply a concept or theory to a particular scene, situation, or literary work. Here are some examples:

- an essay concerned with Ibsen's play, *A Doll's House,* may use feminist theory to explain Nora's behavior and her departure from her home at the end of the play;
- an essay that focuses on analyzing advertisements may use theories of color and spacing to explain how a particular ad creates its effect;
- an essay concerned with literacy acquisition may use Deborah Brandt's idea of "literacy sponsors" as the basis for a personal narrative concerned with that theme.

Some students find this type of assignment difficult because they may not be familiar with this writing genre, and a particular problem we have noted is that the essay may focus more on summarizing the scene, situation or literary work, rather than showing how a concept of theory explains it in some way. Maintaining a balance between the theoretical concept and the details of what is being analyzed or explained is important for this type of essay. Also, it is important to recognize that not all readers will be familiar with the particular concept or theory being used, so it is important to set up definitions and explanations of that theory as a basis.

If you are unclear about the kind of essay you are being asked to write, be sure to ask questions until you understand the teacher's expectations. Ask about its purpose and the audience for which it is intended. Perhaps you can see an example or model. Another useful strategy is to write your draft early and confer with your teacher or someone in a writing center about whether or not it fulfills the expectations implied in the assignment. Do not assume that the essay you are expected to write will be exactly like those you have written before.

FOR THINKING, DISCUSSION, AND WRITING

Writing assignments, like many types of directions, omit some information on the assumption that the reader already knows it. They also contain words that need definition. Read the following sets of directions. Then, in small groups, discuss what information has been omitted and which words need further clarification.

1. Recipe for Exceptional Coffee
   - Use 1 tablespoon YUBAN and 3/4 measuring cup (6 fl oz) cold water for each serving. Use more or less coffee to suit your taste.
   - Refrigerate container to help preserve flavor.
   - Makes 80–90 suggested strength servings.
2. To disinfect non-porous surfaces: Sprinkle Comet on wet surface, rub gently to cleanse, let stand five minutes, and rinse. To disinfect toilet bowls, flush, sprinkle 4 oz of Comet onto bowl surfaces, scour thoroughly, let stand 10 minutes, and flush.
3. Use 1/3 cup marinade per 1/4 lb of steak or chicken. Pour marinade over steak or chicken. Cover and refrigerate for at least 30 minutes. Marinate longer for richer flavor. Remove from marinade, discard marinade (DO NOT REUSE). Grill or broil steak until done. Bake or grill chicken until done. Refrigerate any leftover steak or chicken.
4. 1) Bring 4–6 quarts of water to a rolling boil. Add salt to taste, if desired.
   2) Add contents of package to boiling water. Stir gently.
   3) Return to a boil. For authentic "Al Dente" pasta, boil uncovered, stirring occasionally for six minutes. For more tender pasta, boil an additional one minute.
   4) Remove from heat. Drain well.
   5) Serve immediately with your favorite sauce.

TRANSLATING YOUR ASSIGNMENT

WORKSHEET #1

This worksheet will help you translate your assignment before you begin writing so that you will be able to write your essay with greater understanding.

1. Read the assignment aloud to yourself. Note areas that need translation. Then read it again, slowly. This will help you to see things that you may not have seen on your first read.

2. Find the writing task and try to summarize it. What kind of writing does this assignment require? (Remember that most college writing assignments require a thesis or main point. You may not know what that main point will be, but you can begin to think about what it might be.)

3. Underline or circle key phrases. List any terms that need definition.

4. Ask yourself what sort of essay you are expected to write in terms of form and genre. How is this essay similar to and different from essays you have written before?

5. Think about how you can you make this topic meaningful to you.

6. Consider the audience for this essay. How can an understanding of audience influence what you plan to write?

7. Consider the resources you will need to begin and complete work. Do you need to review articles or books on this topic? Do you need to conduct a survey? How important are outside sources for this assignment?

Translating Your Assignment *Developed by Andrea Hernandez*		
Common Writing Tasks of College Essays	**Translation**	**Example**
"Agree or disagree" (with author's position)	State whether you agree or disagree with the author's position on a particular issue and explain why.	"State whether you agree or disagree that American high school students are given too much homework."
"State your position" (on a topic/practice/ controversy)	Give your opinion on the issue raised; often either pro or con, for or against.	"State your position on the practice of banks marketing credit cards to college students."
"To what extent. . ."	Determine the degree to which you support or oppose something; to which something is harmful or helpful, etc.	"To what extent does the Internet enable students to cheat?"

Common Genres of College Essays	Explanation
Personal Narrative	Personal narrative assignments will require you to write about a personal experience. Personal narratives can still be argumentative; what's important to keep in mind is that you do not merely summarize an experience, but create an exigence for writing about that experience.
Problem/Solution	Problem/solution essays will require you to first identify a type of problem and then offer a solution (or solutions) that will potentially solve that problem. For example, a student may claim that college textbooks are too pricey and then propose textbook rentals as a solution.
Response	Response essays require you to read an article and identify its main point. You then begin by briefly summarizing that point and then find a perspective or idea that you will develop in your essay. Some options to consider in responding to someone else's text are: to agree, to disagree, or extend the author's perspective in some way.
Rhetorical Analysis/ Critical Analysis	A rhetorical or critical analysis will require you to evaluate the effectiveness of someone else's argument. In other words, you will examine how different aspects of that argument function in order to fulfill the argument's purpose.
Applying a Conceptual or Theoretical Concept	A conceptual or theoretical application essay will require you to use a theory or concept to explain or shed light on a scene, situation, or literary work. You will not merely explain the concept or theory, or summarize the scene, situation, or literary work, but show how that concept or theory can be used to help a reader understand something more insightfully. For this type of essay, it is important to maintain a balance between the concept or theory and the scene, situation, or literary work being analyzed.

AN EXAMPLE OF A RESPONSE ESSAY

The assignment below requires students to write a response to the article "How Learning a Foreign Language reignited My Imagination: Pardon My French," using a personal example. Below is the assignment and an example of an introductory paragraph that responds to the assigned article.

Assignment

Read the article "How Learning a Foreign Language Reignited My Imagination: *Pardon my French*" by Ta-Nehisi Coates. You can find this article at

- http://www.theatlantic.com/magazine/archive/2013/06/pardon-my-french/309316/

Once you have finished reading it, write a response which agrees or disagrees with Coates' idea about how learning a new language can reignite the imagination. Use a personal example from your own journey to learn a new language.

Example opening paragraph:

In the article "How Learning a Foreign Language Reignited My Imagination: *Pardon my French*," Ta-Nehisi Coates recounts his experience of learning French in a small French town in the summer of 2011, when he was in his mid-thirties. Coates remembers that at first, he could barely understand anything—that the words he "overheard were only the music of the human voice," moving him into a state of silence and incomprehension that triggered his imagination, helping him to feel young again. This idea, that silence and being a linguistic outsider, can stimulate the imagination is an interesting one that obviously worked well for Coates. But my own experience of learning English, which began on the first day of the fifth grade, was nothing like that. On that day, I learned that instead of being in a classroom with the friends I had since kindergarten, I would be in a class for bilingual students. At that time, I did not know what this would mean for me. I was scared, intimidated and nervous to meet my new teacher. The incomprehension I experienced did not feel at all positive, and even though I can now speak the English language well (in fact,

I now have difficulty speaking Spanish), I can still recall how awkward it felt to be around people who speak a language really well that you are trying to learn.

Below is the same opening paragraph that explains the function of each sentence:

In the article "How Learning a Foreign Language Reignited My Imagination: *Pardon my French,*" Ta-Nehisi Coates recounts his experience of learning French in a small French town in the summer of 2011, when he was in his mid-thirties. Coates remembers that at first, he could barely understand anything—that the words he "overheard were only the music of the human voice," moving him into a state of silence and incomprehension that triggered his imagination, helping him to feel young again. **(The first three sentences summarize the main points in the article. They cite the author and title and the main points that the article develops.)** This idea, that silence and being a linguistic outsider, can stimulate the imagination is an interesting one that obviously worked well for Coates. **(This is a transition sentence that indicates the worth of the author's main point.)** But my own experience of learning English, which began on the first day of the fifth grade, was nothing like that. **(This sentence shows that the writer will disagree with the main point of the article.)** On that day, I learned that instead of being in a classroom with the friends I had since kindergarten, I would be in a class for bilingual students. At that time, I did not know what this would mean for me. I was scared, intimidated and nervous to meet my new teacher. **(These sentences provide the personal example that the assignment requires.)** The incomprehension I experienced did not feel at all positive, and even though I can now speak the English language well (in fact, I now have difficulty speaking Spanish), I can still recall how awkward it felt to be around people who speak a language really well that you are trying to learn. **(These sentences state the writer's main point—to disagree with the writer of the article.)**

5

CHAPTER

The Identity of the Writer

"Who are *you*?" said the Caterpillar.

This was not an encouraging opening for a conversation. Alice replied, rather shyly, "I–I hardly know, sir, just at present—at least I know who I *was* when I got up this morning, but I think I must have been changed several times since then."

"What do you mean by that?" said the Caterpillar sternly. "Explain yourself!"

"I can't explain *myself*, I'm afraid, sir," said Alice, "because I'm not myself, you see."

Lewis Carroll *Alice's Adventures in Wonderland*

In the children's classic, *Alice's Adventures in Wonderland,* the conversation between Alice and the Caterpillar suggests that the word *you* can have multiple meanings, an idea that also applies to the differences between the "you" of everyday and the "you" who writes college essays. Writing involves performing a role, at least to some extent, and when you write essays for your college classes (or for any other purpose), you should **choose** the role you wish to play—who you would like to be. To a certain extent, writing is a type of performance, and you, as the writer, can **choose** how you wish to perform—the tone you assume, the language you use, the ideas you want to discuss in your writing. All of these elements contribute to the "you" as it is manifested in your writing.

This chapter discusses some of the factors that can enable you to choose your role as a writer—to consider how you want to present yourself when you write college essays. At one time, students were taught that there was only one way to present oneself in a college essay— to write as if you were the teacher—formally, seriously, and correctly. Or, sometimes students were taught that they had a fixed identity, an authentic **real** self and that once that self was located, that was the self they should always use. More recently, however, although we believe it is important for everyone to write authentically and be engaged honestly in their writing, we also think that everyone has the capacity to assume multiple identities when they write and that competent writers have the capacity to choose an identity that is appropriate for an intended audience or reader.

To begin, let us listen to a dialogue between Clementine and her friend, Jason:

Clementine:	I can't believe what's going on at the airport. They're stopping anyone who looks even a little bit foreign—making them open their bags, take off their shoes, and who knows what else.
Jason:	Well, that's okay with me. Don't you want to be protected from another terrorist attack?
Clementine:	Of course I do. But stopping people who look foreign is racial profiling, and it's really insulting to a lot of people.
Jason:	Oh—so because we don't want to insult a few foreigners, we should just let the terrorists blow up our country? I hate to tell you, but your idealism is pretty naïve sometimes.
Clementine:	And I hate to tell YOU that your racist views are pretty stupid, sometimes.
Jason:	You don't know what you're talking about.
Clementine:	And you're just a racist jerk!

This is an interchange that concludes with both people feeling angry, and, unfortunately, many of us have had unpleasant conversations like this. In fact, when we feel strongly about a topic, we sometimes WANT to express our anger and outrage. People who are involved with what is going on around them and in the world care deeply about a number of issues and are often not interested in hearing what anyone else has to say. But if Clementine and Jason wanted the conversation to continue or to have an influence on one another's perspective, neither one assumed appropriate roles. Calling someone "stupid" or "racist" is unlikely to be convincing and will not accomplish an important goal of college writing, which is to convince your readers that your ideas are worth considering.

As was discussed in Chapter 1, Ben Franklin's autobiography makes a strong case for considering the feelings of a potential audience and for not being overly aggressive or dogmatic, and we can imagine Franklin shaking an admonishing finger at Clementine and Jason. College writing often addresses complex and sensitive topics, but if you want your readers to pay attention to what you have to say, it is a good idea to assume the identity of a reasonable and thoughtful person—not someone who immediately starts calling names.

Presenting yourself as reasonable and thoughtful is particularly important if you post your writing on a blog or Website. You may have strong feelings about a topic but your ideas will not be considered if you seem overwrought or hysterical. The "you" of college writing, whatever the genre or type of argument, is a thoughtful, involved person who is concerned about the topic, has taken the time to gather information about it, and presents his or her point of view honestly and reasonably. The "you" of college writing, above all, is *credible*—that is, concerned, informed, believable, and trustworthy, although, of course, who is considered credible varies according to the audience for whom the writing is intended.

The Role of Ethos in College Writing

The classical rhetorician, Aristotle, recognized the importance of *ethos,* or the credibility of the speaker, in influencing an audience. In his *Rhetoric,* Aristotle argued that credibility is most effectively established when the audience thinks of the speaker as a person of intelligence, moral integrity, and good intentions. These qualities are important in effective college writing as well.

Can a college student assume the role of someone who has intelligence, moral integrity, and good intentions? The answer to this question is a resounding "yes!" Although recent articles in newspapers and journals have claimed that today's students are apathetic, uninvolved in world events, interested only in themselves and their social lives, we have never found this to be the case. College students may be busy, but they are concerned about social and political issues. Even people who prefer to remain uninvolved have at least a few issues about which they care deeply. As a student, you may be troubled about fairness in grading standards or about the quality of teaching. If you are a parent, you may have strong feelings about available childcare or obtaining an excellent education for your children. Or as a concerned citizen you may be outraged by invasions of privacy or cruelty to animals.

FOR THINKING, DISCUSSION, AND WRITING

Writing a Manifesto

A manifesto is a strong and often impassioned declaration of one's beliefs and opinions, and writing in this genre can help you think about your identity as a writer. It will enable you to know yourself a bit better and become conscious of what matters to you, what you feel strongly or passionate about. A manifesto can also serve as an inspiration for further exploration and writing. So—to begin, write a list of topics about which you have strong feelings. These topics may be political, social, or personal, and they may be concerned with changes you would like to see or actions you would like to take. Then choose one of these topics and write as many ideas, principles, or beliefs about it as you can. If appropriate, share your manifesto with other students in a small group.

Below is an example of a manifesto written by an adult student. How does this manifesto differ from a traditional academic argument?

ERIC'S MANIFESTO

Everyone these days has access to all sorts of information—on phones, laptops, computers—everywhere—and young people are especially good at accessing various types of technology. But what is the use of that expertise if they have no sense of history, no political ideals—not even embarrassment about not knowing.

Last semester, I stood in front of my class of college freshman students and asked them if they knew what the Occupy Wall Street protests were about. None of them had an answer. After a brief discussion, I asked them why we were still at war in Iraq and Afghanistan. They had no answer. I was shocked to find that they had no understanding of the failed policies of the Bush Administration other than what they could glean from a Green Day song. This was a generation that quite possibly did not witness or process the 2001 attacks the same way older people did. How could they? They were only three or four years old at the time. When I asked them if any of them heard of the Vietnam War, very few raised their hands. And when I followed up with the question of why America fought the Vietnam War, there was a silence. A minute went by and someone blurted out an answer. He had recited a description from Wikipedia off of his phone. This immediate access to contextual information can be enough to make for a more progressive and politically informed generation, but only if they are compelled to take advantage of it.

It was very different for my generation. As a young boy attending middle school in Queens during the early 1990s, I had more appreciation for the New York Mets and the music of Kurt Cobain than politics, but I was still aware of the socio-political issues of the time. Even before everyone had access to vast amounts of information via the Internet, I had history class in school. There, we did more than make dioramas about ancient Egypt or dress up as the white privileged "patriots" of the American Revolution. We covered current events through respected news magazines and newspapers (remember newspapers?). But we also had a context for the news. The foreign conflicts and domestic socio-economic disputes were not just trending topics that faded behind the scandal of the latest celebrity. That type of thing was reserved for the tabloids. So when George Herbert Walker Bush led the country into the first war with Iraq in the Persian Gulf, I sensed there was something wrong. This was not the war my grandfather had helped fight against the Nazis. Saddam Hussein was a tyrant like Hitler but by no means on the same scale. I had also been acquainted with stories of Vietnam, the war my father escaped by dodging the draft. And though there was a clearer enemy in the Gulf War than in Vietnam, the 60s peace movement had been handed down to me in spirit. I became the first of my seventh grade cohorts to write "No Blood for Oil" on my trapper keeper.

A decade later, in my twenties I watched in horror as Al Qaeda terrorists flew commercial airplanes into the World Trade Center. Like every American in that moment, I wanted justice to be served. After watching those towers fall in real time, like some horrific Hollywood thriller film depicting the apocalypse, the entire world was on our side, our enemies included. A little less than a year later, the second Bush Administration had begun to squander all of the world's good will by promoting a false narrative that 9/11 was somehow connected to Iraq and the infamous dictator Saddam. America, still reeling from the shock of the attack on our homeland, allowed for the president, the vice president and his cronies to lead our young soldiers into a preemptive war. But I knew better because I had context. I knew all about the members of the first Bush Administration and the Project for a New American Century. Cheney, Wolfowitz, Powell, Rumsfeld. These were all the same players from the 1990s. This context provided me a focus to my protest. My efforts were concentrated on stopping the war and removing the Bush Administration from power. This was my twenties, the time I really became involved with politics. I joined anti-war rallies in different cities, handed out flyers, promoted awareness in public arenas. My friends and I organized fundraising events for John Kerry's campaign in 2004. None of this was enough to change the direction of the country but that did not stop me. I continued with a spirit and a specific cause to support.

When I look around at the younger people today, I see less of that spirit. Some say there's disenchantment with, or even a disdain for politics. Some say it's a growing culture of complacency, that "millennials" are lazy or unmotivated to do anything but at worst, post photos of themselves on social media sites and at best, create Apps that help them take better quality photos of themselves. Though a few of these general statements seem to be true and others just hyperbole, the one thing that stands as truth is that we are currently living in a culture deficient of historical and social context and the younger generations are suffering for it. If we look at the quagmire that ensued and the overall destabilization of a region that was never a peaceful place to begin with, it is not difficult to view George W. Bush's Iraq War as the biggest foreign policy failure in the history of this country. The seven years following the September 11th attacks were among some of the darkest this country had experienced politically but I am afraid they've been forgotten. In 2008 the decade had been erased with the election of Barack Obama, the nation's first African American president. I will admit I myself was swept up in the moment and the younger politicians soaring rhetoric and obvious superior intellect to his predecessor. But I was astounded how the country treated the previous administration like it was last week's news cycle. George W. left to take up painting and Dick Cheney to continue consulting for oil companies. The financial crisis they facilitated and the trillion dollars worth of debt they accumulated for war costs they never actually included in their federal budgets were forgotten. A few years later near the end of Obama's first term, the younger generation all chanted "U.S.A.! U.S.A.!" outside the White House gates when the president announced the killing of Osama bin Laden the mastermind behind the 9/11 attacks. There was little consideration of the fact that since 2001 more terrorists groups had begun to form in Iraq and neighboring countries. Again, very little context was given to this largely symbolic victory. It is my belief that this lack of perspective or ignorance of history that made any of the younger generations protest movements lack focus.

One does not have to look long and hard at the Occupy Wall Street movement of 2011 to find the fatal flaw that brought it to an unsuccessful end. Arguably it raised the awareness of society that youth of our countries had social, economic, and political grievances. But that was ultimately what made it ineffective. The movement was without a focused goal. Unlike the LGBT movement fighting for marriage equality or organizations like Green Peace and the ACLU who were committed to one issue or one range of issues, Occupy was the equivalent of a global blog post of a manifesto written by a discontent unemployed graduate student. If the engineers of the movement had looked at the context of successful social and political protest in this country they might have had enough sense to pick a clear spokesperson and narrowed their cause to a more specific immediate policy change that was attainable.

When I think of my parents at the ages of eighteen through twenty-five, I am reminded of the black and white news footage of the civil rights marches or the anti-war protests at Berkeley or Kent State in the 1960s. No matter if some of the hippie movement was just about drugs as an escape from reality than any real freedom of mind, there was an overall shift in consciousness throughout the nation about many issues at once. The African American minority fought the injustices that had plagued their communities through non-violent protests lead by leaders such as Martin Luther King as well as through violent acts of civil disruption lead by groups such as the Black Panther Party. Women's liberation sprang forth in the fight for gender equality as the decade spawned the widespread feminist movement. We can even trace the birth and organization of the LGBT movement to this time. All of the movements for social equality and justice coincided with the mass protest against the Vietnam War. In spite of the almost cartoonish nature of the hippie communes and "flower power," the outcry for world peace among the youth of America was palpable. The 1960s into the early 1970s were the time of a cultural and socio-political seismic shift. The youth of the 60s counter-culture was arguably a new enlightenment in a post-modern era. Popular music, film, and art reflected the undercurrent of feeling. But this only happened because of a conglomeration of specific movements. Though they differed in their specific causes, all of these young men and women of different race, creeds, and colors were unified in one idea, revolution. If this "revolution" was a vague idea to just fight authority, or a long list of complaints about the government and the economic system of the country, very little "revolutionary" changes in society would have occurred. And if the young people of that generation didn't know anything about history and didn't worry that they didn't know, then nothing at all would have happened.

Presenting Oneself as Credible

Writing a manifesto can enable you to become aware of what you care about, and caring about a topic will contribute to your credibility—to write with concern, commitment, and conviction. Of course, we all know that there are some people who can *pretend* to have an interest in a topic even if they don't. They have a natural charm and a compelling manner that make people believe them. Their manner of speaking, their expression and tone of voice, their body gestures—their entire being—create the impression that they are honest and informed. These people are naturally convincing, even when they know little about their subject. If they choose to misuse this talent, they make very successful swindlers. Credible writers, though, are not phonies; they care about what they have to say, assume an appropriate role and play it seriously.

On the other hand, there are people who are sincere and involved with a topic but are not credible because they express their feelings with anger but no information. Often they are poorly informed about their subject and simply assert their ideas without proof or evidence. These people attempt to dictate what people ought to think, without acknowledging that other people may have ideas, too. Both Clementine and Jason are examples of this sort of person.

That sort of writing may be tolerated in a manifesto. But college writing requires the writer to be informed about a topic. A credible "you" is neither falsely polite nor abrasively aggressive. The credible "you" of college essays aims for a tone that people will believe and trust. Your goal is to convince your readers that you have thought about the topic, have considered different facets of it, know what you are talking about, and are honest, informed, and reasonable. This is the "you" that develops when you engage with a topic, think about it seriously, and prepare for writing by gathering information.

ACHIEVING CREDIBILITY

How can you establish credibility in your writing? Here are two strategies:

1. Become knowledgeable about the topic.
2. Create believability and trustworthiness through tone and style.

BECOMING KNOWLEDGEABLE ABOUT THE TOPIC

We tend to associate credibility with authority, an idea that advertisers use when they use a famous person or an actor dressed to look like a doctor in their ads. Credible people are those who have attained high status in their fields. But how do you establish credibility if you are only a student writing about a topic that is relatively new to you?

Even if you are not an expert in your field, you can establish credibility by knowing your subject well. When you thoroughly understand your topic, you will be able to write about it with conviction, and it is therefore important that you examine the background of your topic, define your terms, and read several sources that can give you multiple points of view.

Personal Experience as Knowledge

As a student, you are probably not a recognized expert in any field, and so your name on an essay or a reference to yourself within the essay would not immediately signal credibility. However, for some topics, your personal experience may serve to establish you as knowledgeable. Your experience may be typical of a particular situation, or it may indicate why you think the topic is important. In the following opening paragraphs, Professor Stephen L. Carter, an African American professor at Yale University, uses his own experience with affirmative action to argue in favor of racial preferences for college admission:

> I got into law school because I am black.
>
> As many black professionals think they must, I have long suppressed this truth, insisting instead that I got where I am the same way everybody else did. Today I am a professor at the Yale Law School, I like to think that I am a good one, but I am hardly the most objective judge. What I am fairly sure of, and can now say without trepidation, is that were my skin not the color that it is, I would not have had the chance to try (3).
>
> **Carter, Stephen L. *Reflections of an Affirmative Action Baby.***
> **New York: Harper Collins, 1991.**

Carter goes on to argue that African Americans should not be insulted if they are questioned about how they gained admission to a prestigious college. Referring to his own case, Carter maintains that the most important way of evaluating a person's worth is not on how he got into a university, but on his performance once he was there and on his achievement once he graduated. Carter's personal investment in this topic thus lends credibility to his ideas.

ESTABLISHING CREDIBILITY THROUGH TONE AND STYLE

The word *tone* is difficult to define, although we all recognize tones that we like and dislike. In the context of establishing credibility in a college essay, a credible tone is characterized by the use of a *balanced* approach—forceful, but not strident, a tone that suggests the writer's awareness of the sensitivity and complexity of the topic. Clementine and Jason, of course, did not use a balanced approach in their conversation, and it is easy to understand why they didn't. The topic they were discussing, the use of searches at airports, is a complex and controversial one; it is a topic about which many people have difficulty in determining right and wrong. No one wishes to allow terrorists the freedom to plot destruction, but the idea of searching people who "look" like terrorists seems wrong as well.

Many social issues and policies are similarly complex and controversial; they are topics about which even concerned, intelligent, informed, and well-meaning people find it difficult to decide what is fair or just. In addressing complex topics, then, writers are more likely to be accepted by readers if they navigate between extreme positions and acknowledge the difficulty of making definitive predictions or absolute value judgments. Their goal is to have readers say, "That is a complex topic and it is difficult to know what to think. But this writer's idea is worth thinking about." Moreover, readers are more likely to be convinced if the writer acknowledges what is worthwhile in other people's views.

The Use of Qualifying Terms

As we have noted in the first two chapters, a great deal of academic writing in the humanities and social sciences uses words that "qualify"—that is, "soften" a statement. Words such as *seems, suggests, indicates, to some degree, or to a certain extent* are examples of qualifiers and have the effect of softening statements that a reader might find difficult to accept. The use of these words indicates a writer's recognition that making bold statements can sometimes antagonize a reader and that any statement about what is best for society must be tentative. In the following paragraph, Adam Bellow argues that nepotism (obtaining one's job through family connections) may not be such a bad thing in government, because it has long been the practice in other professions. Note the facts with which Bellow supports his main point:

The men who built the movie industry in the 1920s were nepotists on a grand scale, and some of Hollywood's greatest figures owed their breaks to family ties— though many of them denied it. In the 1960s and 1970s there were dozens of second-generation actors, including Jane and Peter Fonda, Tatum O'Neal, Michael Douglas, Sally Field, and Sissy Spacek (the cousin of Rip Torn). Today there are hundreds—far too many to list. Kate Hudson is the daughter of Goldie Hawn. Gwyneth Paltrow, the daughter of Blythe Danner and the late Bruce Paltrow, got her break when "uncle" Steven Spielberg cast her in *Hook*. Family ties also prevail among producers, directors, and writers and also film and sound editors, cinematographers, makeup artists, costume and set designers, stunt men, and musicians—among them the Newman family, which has included eight composers.

Bellow, Adam. "In Praise of Nepotism."
The Atlantic Monthly, July/August 2003: 98–105. Print.

In the following excerpt, the writer anticipates that his readers will be resistant to his ideas. He, therefore, uses the bolded qualifying words to soften his statements.

Here is another example from an article titled "When Parents Are Not in the Best Interests of the Child," an article which takes the controversial stance that sometimes living in an institutional setting is better for children from troubled homes than living in an intimate family environment. Since our culture is so strongly in favor of family living, even under troubled circumstances, the writer is careful to qualify her statements so as to acknowledge the opposing viewpoint.

Life without parents is a difficult sentence to pronounce upon a child, but it's happening more and more often. "**Sometimes** children have gone beyond the opportunity to go back and capture what needed to be done between the ages of three and eight," says Gene Baker, the chief psychologist at The Children's Village. "**Sometimes** the thrust of intimacy that comes with family living is more than they can handle. **Sometimes** the requirement of bonding is more than they have the emotional equipment to give. As long as we keep pushing them back into what is our idealized fantasy of family, they'll keep blowing it out of the water for us.

Weisman, Mary-Lou. *Atlantic Monthly*, July 1994.

In this paragraph, Mary-Lou Weisman has anticipated an audience that feels strongly about keeping children in a family environment as much as possible, an audience that distrusts institutionalization except under the most extreme circumstances. Therefore, Weisman acknowledges her audience's reaction at the beginning of the paragraph and repeatedly uses the word "sometimes" to qualify her statements.

From *The Atlantic Monthy*, July/August 2003: 98–105 by Adam Bellow. Copyright © 2003 by *The Atlantic Monthly*. Reprinted by permission.

The Accommodating "You"

Qualifying words indicate that the writer has respect for the reader and is aware of the complexity of the issue under consideration. No reader is going to be persuaded by your ideas if you simply proclaim, "You are absolutely wrong and I am absolutely right,"—that approach rarely works under any circumstances, as most of us know from our own lives. My guess is that if someone says, "Let me show you how wrong you are about this issue and then I'll tell you how you can improve your thinking," you are likely to resist and hold on even more tightly to your own position. For most people, a dogmatic approach is more likely to engender hostility than agreement. You will be more successful, then, if you approach your subject politely and judiciously, indicate that you are aware that some people have different ideas, and project a "you" that is accommodating and respectful. Your message to your reader should be:

> "I understand how you feel and here are the points on which both of us agree.
> But here is where I differ from you, based on the following reasons."

Usually, whether we are listening to a speech or reading an essay, we are more likely to pay attention to what someone has to say if we feel that he or she understands our own point of view.

Qualification and Commitment

Suppose you care very strongly about the topic you are writing about. Will qualifying words undermine the forcefulness of your position? Actually, the use of qualifying words in academic writing indicates that you are someone who is aware of alternate possibilities because you are knowledgeable. Qualifying words, therefore, *contribute* to your credibility. An effective piece of writing is both committed *and* qualified, and combines a thoughtful presentation with strong feelings, maximizing the chances that the essay will accomplish its purpose—to have an impact on your reader.

Qualifying Words and "Emphatics"

Following is a list of qualifying words you can use to soften some of the statements in your essay. These words can be helpful when you make statements with which a reader might disagree.

> usually, often, sometimes, almost, virtually, possible, perhaps, apparently, seemingly, in some ways, to a certain extent, sort of, for the most part, may, might, can, could, seem, tend, try, attempt, seek, hope

From *The Atlantic Monthy,* July 1994 by Mary-Low Weisman. Copyright © 1994 by The Atlantic Monthly. Reprinted by permission.

The opposite of qualifying words are those that underscore the writer's point. These are called "emphatics." Emphatics are words that tell the reader that the writer believes strongly in his or her ideas. Here are some common emphatics:

> as everyone knows, it is generally agreed that, it is quite true that, it's clear that, it is obvious that, the fact is, as we can plainly see, literally, clearly, obviously, undoubtedly, invariably, certainly, always, of course, indeed

FOR THINKING, DISCUSSION, AND WRITING

A. Write a letter to a friend to convince him or her to do something or change an opinion about something. You can choose from an everyday topic (to get a dog, to buy a new car, to take or drop a course, to change his or her appearance in some way, to take a trip with you, or anything else you can think of). You can also write about less personal social issues.

Write one version without the use of qualifying words and one that uses them.

B. In small groups discuss the effect that the following statements are likely to have on a reader. Then rephrase the following statements so that they reflect a qualified view of the topic.

1. Watching television news gives a completely distorted picture of what is going on in the world.
2. Homeless people are alcoholics who beg for money in order to drink. They don't want to work.
3. Searching everyone at the airport is a complete waste of time and money.
4. The use of hidden video cameras in department stores is necessary to prevent shoplifting.
5. Terrorist acts are caused by religious fanatics.
6. The only humane way to alleviate the suffering of animals is to become a vegetarian.

C. Discuss the "you" that is projected in the following excerpts. What features in the text contribute to the creation of that "you"?

1. A writing center tutor who is concerned with helping students find both focus and fluency should aim not only to engage them in activities that will help them with a specific assignment, but also to demonstrate a strategy for generating ideas in future writing tasks. In the following section, I present several activities that have been useful both to me and to my students.

2. No one had ever warned me about the pitfalls of "Pre-Wedding Syndrome." . . . Now I know the truth. Anyone who survives planning a wedding with a sense of humor intact and new spouse in tow could take a respectable crack at negotiating peace in the Middle East.

   Whitney, Jane. "Pre Wedding Syndrome" *New York Times* 3 June 1990.

3. In recent years, an increase of violence in America, both individual and political, has prompted a backlash of public opinion on capital punishment. But, however much we abhor violence, legally sanctioned executions are not a deterrent and are, in fact, immoral and unconstitutional. Although I have suffered the loss of two family members by assassination, I remain firmly and unequivocally opposed to the death penalty for those convicted of capital offenses.

   **King, Coretta Scott. *The Death Penalty Is a Step Back.*
   Cleveland Publishing Company, 1981.**

4. I'm a 21-year-old black born to a family that would probably be considered lower-middle class—which . . . is a polite way of describing a condition only slightly better than poverty. [But when] I talk, some of my black peers ask, "Why do you talk like you're white?"

   **Jones, Rachel L. "What's Wrong with Black English?"
   Newsweek, 17 Dec. 1983 Print.**

TONE—YOU KNOW IT

By Emmanuel Sabaiz-Birdsill

When writing, we are constantly being asked to watch our tone. Professors may write statements next to your sentences such as:

Watch your tone
Inappropriate use of tone
Do not use exclamation points!!
Do not use slang
This is not an academic tone

All of these comments are referring to the type of tone that you are using. Tone is directly associated with diction and the type of vocabulary that you are using; therefore, sometimes you will get comments that say:

Improve your diction to bring up the tone of your argument
Diction and tone problem
Change diction to improve tone

All of these comments are telling you that the vocabulary you are using is creating a tone that may not be appropriate for academic argument, or it may sound judgmental or out of line. Many students think that tone and diction are two elements that they do not know how to handle because they seem so foreign. Yet every year they are surprised to find that they not only know tone and diction, they are masters at it. An exercise in Chapter 3, which is concerned with different audiences, is also useful for helping you become aware of tone and diction. Here is the scenario once again:

Let's pretend you were invited to a dinner at your boss' house this coming Saturday. You have agreed to attend, sent your RSVP, and confirmed via e-mail that you are coming. It is Friday and your best friend calls you telling you he has a free ticket, front row, to a concert this Saturday. It is sold out and your favorite band is playing. You say "yes" to your friend and now need to write a note to your boss excusing yourself from the dinner. Write the note that you would send to your boss.

Now let's pretend that the same thing happened, but the dinner you were invited to is not at your boss' house, but rather your parents' house. The situation is the same: you said "yes," you told them over the phone you are coming, and now you have been offered this free ticket. Now you have to write a note excusing yourself to your parents. Now write this note.

Compare the two notes. Did you use the same tone and diction in both notes? Most likely you did not. The way you approach your boss will be very different than the way you approach your parents. You probably used more serious or sophisticated language when you wrote the note to your boss, maybe addressing him/her by using the last name, using a very important excuse, and using a formal thank you statement. With your parents you did not use their last name, you did not call them Sir or Madam, and most likely ended with an "I love you and miss you" note rather than a formal thank you note. Notice how the diction you used affected the tone that the notes had. The goal was the same, to excuse you from dinner, and yet you have two very different notes due to the diction and tone you used. You are an expert in using the proper tone and diction. You just didn't know it.

FOR DISCUSSION

In small groups, read each of the following paragraphs aloud, noting how the writer establishes credibility. Which writer is more credible? What features of the text contribute to the writer's credibility?

DEBBIE'S PARAGRAPH

Many of today's problems are blamed on the disintegration of the family. Yet what often remains unacknowledged is the fact that the well-being of the family is strongly influenced by economic factors. During the post World War II period, a time of economic prosperity, there were many jobs available and it was possible for a father's single income to support the entire family. Now times have changed dramatically. One income is usually not enough for the family to sustain itself on, so both fathers and mothers have to work. Moreover, a large percentage of families consist of only one parent, with the increase in single mothers, teenage mothers, or divorced families. As David Eggebeen points out in an issue of *Generations,* "the ability of families to survive economically has been further exacerbated by the fact that an increasingly larger percentage of them are single-parent families—by definition dependent on one income" (45). Thus in both one-parent and two-parent households, parents are busy trying to support their children and are unable to spend as much time with them as might be desirable. The U.S. Bureau of child development reports that fewer than forty percent of children are cared for by a parent after school. Moreover, "a recent Children's Defense Fund Report notes that 31 states and the District of Columbia had waiting lists for child care with up to 30,000 names and projected waiting periods of over a year" (Kagan 5).

JASON'S PARAGRAPH

Today we are living in a very violent society in which even children and teenagers are committing crimes. Every night on the news we hear of gang-related incidents in which very young children commit murders and don't even seem to feel guilty about it. What seems pretty obvious, though, is that this increase in violence in society is strongly influenced by television and that television is having a severely negative effect on the morals and values of our society. Elementary school children watch over forty hours of television a week and a lot of what is on television is extremely violent and immoral. Even if children don't actually imitate what they see on television, watching violence continuously on their favorite shows desensitizes children to violence and confuses them about what is morally right. If educators and lawmakers are looking for the cause of our increasingly violent society, they should examine the impact of television.

QUALIFICATION ENHANCES CREDIBILITY

Qualification contributes your credibility because it indicates that you are a thoughtful person who is aware of the complexity of the issue. It indicates that you are someone who has done research and is aware of alternate possibilities, someone that the reader can respect and trust. It does not, however, mean that you are uncommitted to your topic or that you do not feel strongly about it. An effective piece of writing is both committed and qualified. It combines a thoughtful presentation with intensity of feeling, maximizing the chances that the essay will accomplish its purpose.

CHOOSING A PROPER TONE (YOUR LIFE MAY DEPEND ON IT)

Developed by Cesar Soto

After many years of ruthless pursuit, your mortal enemy, agent 008, has finally tracked you down to the edge of the Grand Canyon. You hang over a cliff, clutching a rope desperately, about to fall to your death. Agent 008 looks down at you with a cruel grin, ready to cut the rope with a Swiss army knife. It's almost over for you. But—aha!—you see a flicker of doubt in his/her eyes, and you take that moment to persuade them that you should live. How would you persuade them?

Use at least *two or more* of the following elements in your response:

- Tone: Do you use a (1) loud, aggressive voice, (2) a calm voice, or (3) a soft-spoken voice? Why? Explain.
- Identification: How can you make him/her relate to you and get them to step into your shoes? Why is this important? Explain.
- Authority figure(s): Mr. Oz is your (anonymous) boss and a very important man in spy world. Can you convince 008 that Mr. Oz is important enough to get him anything he wants? What are Mr. Oz's credentials?
- Reasoning: What are some good reasons why you should live and not die? For example, what do you have left to accomplish and how would 008 benefit from letting you live? Convince 008.

Please respond by writing two to three paragraphs. Your goal is not to be funny but to answer truthfully and to think logically about all this.

IDENTITY, LANGUAGE, DIALECT

At one time, the only form of English considered appropriate for college writing was Standard Written English, the formal English that is associated with scholarly academic writing and the language of the business world. This is a type of English that is still used in many places, and we think it is important for students to be able to use it. However, recently, language scholars have recognized that college students speak many different dialects and languages and that perhaps the restrictions about what is considered academically "appropriate" should be loosened to include a variety of "world Englishes." These scholars suggest that students should be allowed to combine local and vernacular forms of English with Standard Written English (SWE) in their college essays as a move toward pluralizing academic writing and recognizing the great variety of world Englishes (See Canagarajah, A. Suresh. "The Place of World Englishes in Composition: Pluralization Continued." *College Composition and Communication*. 57.4 (Jun. 2006): 586-619).

You may be one of the many students who speak several languages or dialects—perhaps Spanish, Korean, Farci, or Chinese at home, English in school. Some of you may speak African American Vernacular dialect with your friends. In thinking about the idea of identity, perhaps you would feel more like "you," more authentic, if you could include at least some elements of your everyday language or dialect in your writing. This is an idea that is only recently being discussed, and we suggest it as a topic for further exploration in your writing class. However, what is most important to keep in mind as you explore this topic is that no language or dialect is intrinsically better than another. Some people have the impression that one language is "correct" and other types of Englishes are inferior or "wrong." But that idea is now recognized as untrue. Although we do think that it is important to be able to write in Standard English, we also think that the idea of including other forms of English is an idea worth exploring.

FOR THINKING, DISCUSSION, AND WRITING

To begin thinking about the possibility of code meshing in your college writing, it is important to think about how language is associated with your identity and the preconceptions you may already have about Standard versus non-Standard Englishes. To gain this awareness, please write briefly in response to the following questions. Then share your responses with other students:

1. What language or dialect do you speak at home or with friends? Is it different from the language that you use in school?
2. When you hear the way a person speaks, do you gain a particular impression of that person? Do you judge a person as intelligent or not intelligent on the basis of his or her speech? Can you give an example?

3. Do you think that there are genres and situations when certain types of speech and writing should be used and others avoided? Can you give an example?
4. Would you be comfortable writing or reading college essays that include other Englishes besides Standard English?

AN EXAMPLE OF AN ESSAY THAT INCLUDES WORDS AND SENTENCES FROM ANOTHER LANGUAGE

Cuidando Los Chivos

"No quieres estudiar, vete a Mexico a cuidar los chivitos." This was something my father would always say to me when I was a child, meaning if I didn't want to study, I should go to his hometown and take care of goats. My father and his childhood stories about Mexico would reach my ears whenever I put homework aside or when I complained about homework being too hard. To this day, he tells my younger sister the same, teaching her about a good future *"Como tener un buen future,"* and how important education is. On certain occasions, he'll even say to her, *"So no quieres estudiar vas a trabajar vendiendo elotes."* Because where I grew up, there were corn and raspado vendors trying to earn extra money on the streets of East Los Angeles.

Lizeth Avalos. "Cuidando Los Chivas." *New Voices: A Collection of Student Essays* 24th Edition. Hayden McNeil, 2015. 36.

(Title Translation: "Caring for Goats")

This essay includes several Spanish words that you may not know. How do these words function in this essay? Do you think they should be included? Why or why not?

Access the following readings: "Brother, Don't Spare a Dime" (online at http://www.newsweek.com/brother-dont-spare-dime-203574 and "The Culture of Cruelty" (included in this chapter). Both address the issue of providing help to the poor. How is the "you" in the first essay different from the "you" in the second? Which essay do you find most compelling?

The Culture of Cruelty

By Ruth Conniff

Not long ago I was on a morning radio show talking about welfare, when an irate caller from Milwaukee got on the line and introduced himself as "that most hated and reviled creature, the American taxpayer." He went on to vent his spleen, complaining about freeloading welfare mothers living high on the hog while he goes to work each day. "A whiff of starvation is what they need," he said.

I was chilled by the hatred in his voice, thinking about the mothers I know on welfare, imagining what it would be like for them to hear this.

One young woman I've met, Karentha Mims, recently moved to Wisconsin, fleeing the projects in Chicago after her little boy saw a seven-year-old playmate shot in the head. Mims is doing her best to make a better life for her son, a shy third-grader named Jermain. She volunteers at his elementary school, and worries about how he will fit in. The Mimses have received a cold welcome in Wisconsin, where the governor warns citizens that welfare families spilling across the border from Illinois will erode the tax base and ruin the "quality of life."

Of course, even in Wisconsin, life on welfare is no free ride. The average family of three receives about $500 a month in Aid to Families with Dependent Children—barely enough to pay the rent. Such figures are widely known. So is the fact that each state spends a small amount—about 3.4 per cent of our taxes, or a national total of $22.9 billion annually—on welfare. In contrast, we have now spent $87 billion—about $1,000 per taxpaying family—to bail out bank presidents at failed savings-and-loans.

But neither the enraged taxpayer nor my host on the radio program wanted to hear these dry facts. "What ever happened to the work ethic in this country?" the host demanded. "What about the immigrants who came over and worked their way up?"

I had the feeling I was losing my grasp on the conversation. I could see my host getting impatient, and the more I said the more I failed to answer her central question. *What's wrong with those people on welfare*?

The people on welfare whom I know have nothing wrong with them. They live in bad neighborhoods; they can't find safe, affordable child care; often, they are caught in an endless cycle of unemployment and low-wage work— quitting their jobs when a child gets sick, losing medical insurance when they go back to their minimum-wage jobs. They don't have enough money to cover such emergencies as dental work or car repairs. In short, they are poor. They are struggling hard just to make it, in the face of extreme hardship and in an increasingly hostile environment.

Reprinted by permission from *The Progressive*, 409 E Main St, Madison, WI 53703. www.progressive.org.

Meanwhile, rhetoric about lazy welfare bums is taking the country by storm. Policy experts keep coming up with new theories on the "culture of poverty" and its nameless perpetrators, members of a socially and morally deformed "underclass." "Street hustlers, welfare families, drug addicts, and former mental patients," political scientist Lawrence Mead calls them.

"It's simply stupid to pretend the underclass is not mainly black," adds Mickey Kaus in his much-acclaimed new book *The End of Equality*. Kaus and fellow pundit Christopher Jencks, who wrote his own book this year—*Rethinking Social Policy: Race, Poverty, and the Underclass*—are two of the most recent riders on the underclass bandwagon. But the essence of their work is uncomfortably familiar. Both writers start by asking the question: *What's wrong with the underclass?*, and both proceed to talk about the depravity of poor black people, devoting large though inconclusive sections to such ideas as genetic inferiority and "Heredity, Inequality, and Crime."

Kaus paints a lurid picture of young black men who sneer at the idea of working for the minimum wage, which he says they deride as "chump change." (It's not clear where Kaus gets this information, since he doesn't cite any interviews with actual poor blacks.)

Why don't poor black people just get jobs and join the mainstream of society? Kaus asks rhetorically. While many African-Americans have moved up to the middle class, he writes, the important question is "what enabled some of them, a lower-class remnant, to stay behind in the ghetto? And what then allowed them to survive in the absence of legitimate sources of income?"

The answer, of course, is welfare. Kaus compares black people's attachment to poverty with a junkie's addiction to a drug. Welfare is the "enabling" force that indulges ghetto residents' propensity for living in squalor. When they stopped working hard and learned they could collect welfare while living in the ghetto, Kaus theorizes, poor black people's values eroded and they became a blight on society.

Kaus's solution to the "underclass problem," then, relies largely on such motivational initiatives as instilling a work ethic in lazy black youth through hard labor and "military-style discipline." Likewise, he proposes cutting benefits to mothers who have more than one child, creating an example for their neighbors, who, he says, would "think twice" before becoming pregnant.

To his credit, J. Anthony Lukas, the writer who reviewed *The End of Equality* for *The New York Times*, noted near the end of his essay that Kaus had forgotten to talk to anyone on welfare in the course of writing his book. But Lukas detected no prejudice in Kaus's prescriptions for an overhaul of the underclass, and he found a touching note of "compassion" in Kaus's assurance that under his plan, "no one would starve."

What I want to know is how Kaus came to be considered even remotely qualified to analyze the psychology and motivations of poor black mothers and their sons. Kaus's whole program rests on a faith in his own ability to do exactly that: to surmise what ghetto residents are thinking and why they behave the way they do.

Kaus and Jencks show little interest in learning about the real lives or day-to-day difficulties of people who are poor. Rather, in the grand tradition of underclass theory, they invent hypothetical characters with demeaning little names.

"Phyllis may not be very smart," writes Jencks, in a revised version of underclass theorist Charles Murray's famous "Harold and Phyllis" scenario. "But if she chooses AFDC over Harold, surely that is because she expects the choice to improve the quality of her family life . . ." Furthermore, says Jencks, "If Phyllis does not work, many—including Sharon—will feel that Phyllis should be substantially worse off, so that there will be no ambiguity about Sharon's virtue being rewarded."

On the strength of the projected feelings of the fictitious Sharon, Jencks goes on to recommend a welfare system in which single mothers don't get too much money.

Incredibly, this sort of work then gets translated into concrete public policy.

Under the Family Support Act, states are now running a number of experiments designed to tinker with the motivations and attitudes of poor people—despite data that demonstrate such tinkering will have no positive effect. There is no evidence, or example, to back up one of the popular notions Kaus subscribes to—that "most" poor women would stop having babies if benefits were cut. Women who live in states with higher benefits do not have more babies. They do not have fewer babies in Alabama or Mississippi (or Bangladesh, for that matter), where benefits are shockingly low. Yet Wisconsin, California, and New Jersey are now cutting AFDC payments to women who have more than one child. Likewise, theories about the underclass have inspired initiatives to teach poor people job skills and "self-esteem"—despite the fact that in many of the areas where the training is done, no jobs are available.

The results of these policies are often disastrous for the poor. As more and more states treat poverty as an attitude problem, legislatures justify slashing the safety net and cutting back social programs that help poor people survive. The situation is particularly dire for the "extra" children of women on welfare, who are punished just for being born.

But in Kaus's estimation, the suffering of children is nothing next to the social benefits he thinks will accrue from causing pain to their mothers. "If we want to end the underclass, remember, the issue is not so much whether working or getting two years of cash will best help Betsy Smith" teenage high-school dropout, acquire the skills to get a good private sector job after she's become a single mother. It is whether the prospect of having to work will deter Betsy Smith from having an out-of-wedlock child in the first place . . . The way to make the true costs of bearing a child out of wedlock clear is to let them be felt when they are incurred—namely, at the child's birth."

The callousness and immorality of such thinking, I believe, are part of a pathology that is spreading throughout our society. We might call it a "culture of cruelty."

Such theorists as Kaus and Jencks build the rational foundation beneath our national contempt for the poor. They lend legitimacy to the racist and misogynist stereotypes so popular with conservative politicians and disgruntled taxpayers who feel an economic crunch and are looking for someone to blame. Understanding the roots of the culture of cruelty, and trying to determine how, through the adoption of decent social values, we might overcome it, would be far more useful than any number of volumes of speculation by upper-class white experts on the attitudes and pathologies of the "underclass."

Underclass theory as promoted by Kaus and Jencks has four main characteristics:

It is extremely punitive, appealing to a desire to put poor black people, especially women, in their place.

It is based on prejudice rather than fact, full of stereotypical characters and flippant, unsupported assertions about their motivations and psychology.

It is inconsistent in its treatment of rich and poor. While poor people need sternness and "military-style discipline," to use Kaus's words, the rich are coddled and protected. This third characteristic is particularly important, since treating the "underclass" as alien and inhuman permits the prescription of draconian belt-tightening that one would never impose on one's own family or friends.

Finally, there is the persistent, faulty logic involved in claims that we can "end the cycle of poverty" by refusing aid to an entire generation of children. These children are thus punished for their mothers' sins in producing them, and, if such programs persist, they will soon have no hope of getting out from under the weight of belonging to a despised lower caste.

In his book *Savage Inequalities,* Jonathan Kozol describes visiting a wealthy public school, where he talks to some students who argue that giving equal funding to the schools in poorer districts wouldn't make a difference. Poor children "still would lack the motivation," they say, and "would probably fail in any case because of other problems." Racial integration would cause too many problems in their own school, they say. "How could it be of benefit to us?"

"There is a degree of unreality about the whole exchange," Kozol writes. "The children are lucid and their language is well chosen and their arguments well made, but there is a sense that they are dealing with an issue that does not feel very vivid, and that nothing that we say about it to each other really matters since it's 'just a theoretical discussion.' To a certain degree, the skillfulness and cleverness that they display seem to derive precisely from this sense of unreality.

Questions of unfairness feel more like a geometric problem than a matter of humanity or conscience. A few of the students do break through the note of unreality, but, when they do, they cease to be so agile in their use of words and speak more awkwardly. Ethical challenges seem to threaten their effectiveness. There is the sense that they were skating over ice and that the issues we addressed were safely frozen underneath. When they stop to look beneath the ice they start to stumble."

Kaus and Jencks remind me of nothing so much as precocious sophomores, dominating the class discussion, eager to sound off about the lives and motivations of people they have never met.

This is particularly true of Kaus, since he is even less interested in empirical data than Jencks. Kaus postulates a problem: the loss of a work ethic among lower-class blacks. Then he deftly applies a solution: "military-style discipline." *Voilá*, the problem is solved. This virtuoso performance might earn an A in academia. But when it becomes the basis for real-world public policy, we are, indeed, on thin ice.

Kaus's ideas are not all unpleasant. In the first half of *The End of Equality*, he conjures up images of a new civic America with public squares, clean libraries, parades, and a wonderful, pervading sense of fraternity and equal citizenship. But loose reasoning and a wishful premise—that economic inequality is not the real problem in our society; the real problem is that people aren't trying hard enough to be nice to each other and get along—lead to some remarkably loony claims. For instance, Kaus proposes that being poor doesn't bother people so much in Los Angeles, because the roads are good, and everyone can equally enjoy driving on them. (There must have been a little forehead-slapping among the editors and publishers at Basic Books when *The End of Equality* came out in the wake of the L.A. riots.)

The real trouble starts when Kaus gets down to specifics. When it comes to social programs for the poor, Kaus poisons the well, deriding "Money Liberals" for their tiresome whining about economic justice. Money-based solutions are too simplistic for a creative thinker like Kaus.

Kaus wants to create a massive "neo-WPA" program, with guaranteed jobs for everyone. But the jobs, he says, should be "authoritarian, even a little militaristic," and they should pay less than the minimum wage. The program would not raise anyone out of poverty, since there would be no opportunity for advancement within it. We can't have a class of workers dependent on the state for permanent employment, Kaus reasons. Instead, once people have gained work "skills" through his jobs program, Kaus says, the transition to a job in the private sector will "take care of itself." Never mind the recession, the thousands of former middle-class workers who are now out of work, or the fact that even in the best of times we do not have a full-employment economy.

Anyway, Kaus never explains why the poor black men he talks about would abandon employment in the illegal economy to work in labor gangs, for even less than "chump change." Nor does he note that there is already an extensive discipline-dispensing institution for black men: our ever-expanding prison system.

(Jencks, for his part, declares that we don't have enough prisons. "We claim that crime will be punished, but this turns out to be mostly talk. Building prisons is too expensive. . . ." It is hard to know what Jencks is talking about, since America's prison population doubled in the last decade. Prisons were the second fastest-growing item in state budgets last year, behind Medicaid. And the United States far surpasses the country with the next largest rate of incarceration, South Africa.)

It seems that Americans are insatiable gluttons for punishment when it comes to punishing the "underclass." But locking people up has not stemmed the tide of crime, and Jencks is right that it is extremely expensive. Nonetheless, our policy experts, along with our politicians, keep calling for more punishment and incarceration.

Perhaps because Kaus senses, on some level, that he cannot compete in getting hold of black men and disciplining them, he focuses most of his wrath on women, who are more vulnerable anyway since they get pregnant and have young children who depend on them.

When Kaus turns to his plans for poor women and children, he reaches the absolute shallow end of his thinking. Mothers should be forced out of the home to do a job—any job—rather than be allowed to stay home with their children, Kaus says. The state should be prepared to invest a great deal of money in creating such jobs. "Even a leaf-raking job rakes leaves," he reasons. "If that's all someone's capable of doing, does that mean she shouldn't be paid for doing it? The alternative, remember, is to pay her to stay home and raise children."

Kaus takes his contempt for child-rearing to its logical extreme. First, the state must deny benefits to women who have more than one child, and insist that mothers go to work. Then, we must be on the lookout for signs of neglect when poor parents fail to provide a proper home for their children. "The long answer, then, is that society will also have to construct new institutions, such as orphanages . . ."

So much for family values.

While Kaus deplores the "female-headed household" and the breakdown of the family as a central problem of the "underclass," his grand solution is to warehouse the children of the poor in vast institutions, away from love and nurturing care. Perhaps the state could also hire appropriate role models to come in and deliver speeches to the kids on the value of work. Kaus seems to think that's all they need.

Work, in Kaus's book, is supposed to become the value that binds society together. Work—at menial tasks for poverty-level wages—is supposed to give poor people a sense of citizenship and social equality. Work is even supposed to bring the family back together, since, without AFDC, "soon enough ghetto women will be demanding and expecting that the men in their lives offer them stable economic support." And children will want to work "because they will have grown up in a home where the rhythms and discipline of obligation pervade daily life."

You would think Kaus was talking about a group of people who had it too easy. He fails to consider the fact that AFDC already does not pay enough to live on. And he ignores the fact—a fact even Jencks points out—that most people on welfare *already* work. Because AFDC payments are not enough to support a family, almost everyone who receives AFDC does some sort of labor. Many do not report it, since the Government docks a dollar of benefits for every dollar a welfare recipient earns.

A front-page story in *The New York Times,* part of a series entitled "Rethinking Welfare," recently highlighted the irony of saying there is something wrong with people who stay on AFDC. The subject of the article was Linda Baldwin, a young woman who gave up welfare for minimum-wage work and is now making $169 less each month.

"While no one knows how many women on welfare would work if the financial rewards were greater," the article states, "most analysts agree it takes an especially motivated woman like Ms. Baldwin when there are no financial rewards at all." *Motivated* hardly seems the appropriate term here. Motivation usually implies some potential for upward motion, rather than submissiveness in life below the poverty level and a future of dead-end work.

Furthermore, while Kaus sees only moral turpitude in welfare mothers' efforts to care for their children by staying home, the more "moral" option—stashing the kids and taking a low-wage job, often means abandoning a sick child. Even free medical care and Kaus's offhand promise to provide day care for everyone (something the Family Support Act also promised, and failed to produce) are unlikely to lead to safe, nurturing environments for kids. This may not be a primary concern for Kaus, but it is for mothers who love their children.

Interestingly, Jencks points out all of these problems in his last chapter, when he finally comes into contact with some real-life welfare recipients. Through interviews conducted by his colleague, Kathryn Edin, Jencks discovers that concrete obstacles connected with poverty—as opposed to vague problems of immorality—account for the troubles these women face. He ends the chapter by making a series of fairly benign policy recommendations—better access to health care, tax credits for low-income housing—ideas that have nothing to do with race, the "underclass," or the rest of his book.

Kaus, on the other hand, holds firmly to the principle that the uppity attitude of the "underclass," not poverty, is our most salient social problem.

The solutions he comes up with, although he says they will be good for the poor, are really mostly good for the readers he addresses. Many wealthy suburbanites will undoubtedly agree that "foul-smelling" people in the library and the post office, a general lack of "civility," and poor black people who are not eager to labor and to serve present major difficulties to whites who want to lead lives of comfortable privilege in clean and pleasant communities.

But Kaus certainly doesn't intend to make his own children, or the children of affluent suburbanites, clean up the streets and subway stops or work at raking leaves.

Privilege and economic hierarchy are carefully preserved in Kaus's "civic liberal" dream. The rich must be bribed and coddled and persuaded to permit a nodicum of integration (which would not extend to full integration of the public schools), Kaus says.

As an incentive toward integration, he offers tax advantages to the rich. Income and property taxes could be cut, he says, and regressive taxes which disproportionately affect the poor—the sales tax, for example—could be raised to pay for the schools. In addition, tracking within the school system might soften the blow of integration for wealthy people who do not want their children tainted by coming into contact with the poor. (Kaus says he would not want his own child to go to school with the children of welfare recipients, because they might absorb some damaging "underclass culture.")

In any case, Kaus says, integration of the schools must be a very gradual process—nothing to get alarmed about. You can almost hear his suburban readers letting out a collective sigh of relief.

Kaus feel so sympathetic toward the rich that, in another bit of virtuoso reasoning, he discovers a noble motive in the suburbanite's flight from the city (a trend he himself blames for much of the decline of civic life). "We don't like to act superior to people we actually come into contact with in daily life, so we set things up so we don't have to come into contact with people who might provoke such feelings," Kaus deduces. "One reason Americans must stratify themselves is that they aren't such natural snobs at all."

Segregated neighborhoods and schools, for Kaus, prove a secret yearning for social egalitarianism.

Among the poor, in contrast, Kaus roots out the most vile and despicable motives behind such activities as being poor and being a mother.

Kaus just can't fathom the idea that not having money could seriously affect people's lives. He places arch quotation marks around the word "homeless," as if it strains credulity to imagine that someone in America might not have a place to live. Perhaps all those cardboard shanties, those families sleeping in bus stations and subway cars, are part of an elaborate put-on sponsored by the Money Liberals, who, it seems, will go to almost any length to drain the tax dollars and try the patience of the professional class.

The End of Equality is a particularly scary piece of work because it drags bigotry into the daylight and presents it as egalitarianism, making disdain for the poor safe for liberals. In a way, Kaus brings the hidden agenda of underclass theory to fruition. He shifts the blame for a range of social ills—from crime to poverty and unemployment to segregation—onto the disenfranchised. This is the very heart of the culture of cruelty; blame and punishment replace compassion and justice. Unburdened of the archaic principles of civil rights, Kaus says it proudly: The underclass means black people, and what blacks need is to be brought to heel.

Rather than addressing the inequities in our society—segregated schools, unjust wages, inadequate health care, things that social policy could actually fix—Kaus throws away the whole idea of economic injustice. He replaces it with a new villain—the "underclass," whom he blames not only for the problems of poor people on welfare, but for the problems of our society as a whole. Suddenly, the middle-class taxpayer, the politician, and the wealthy upper class are all victims. United in having been wounded by the "underclass," they are all innocent of any responsibility in society. Ominously, Kaus declares that it is only by gathering together and dealing with the "underclass problem" that we can make America a good place to live.

While Kaus bills his book as a manual for reform of the Democratic Party, a new platform that will give the liberal reputation a boost, the Democrats have already discovered much of Kaus's prescription—though few are quite so bald-faced about emphasizing its more punitive aspects. "Personal responsibility," not Government aid for the poor, has become the rallying cry of Democratic politicians from Senator Daniel Patrick Moynihan to candidate Bill Clinton.

There is a lively market these days for political theories that defend the rich and disparage the poor. The poor are a perfect scapegoat. After all, as Kaus points out, it is the suburbanites who vote. "Throwing money at the problem won't solve anything," is the old conservative mantra, chanted in exclusive clubs and suburban living rooms all over America.

Meanwhile, the cities seethe.

6

CHAPTER

Exploring a Topic/Finding a Thesis

When you are assigned to write an essay in a college class, when do you usually begin? Do you start thinking about it right away? Do you think about it while you are completing other activities (like driving, exercising, showering, etc.)? Or do you put the assignment out of your mind until the night before it is due? Do you have a process for generating ideas that works well for you? Some students are under the impression that they need to wait for inspiration to strike. Others have found that if they keep thinking about a topic even while completing other tasks, possible ideas emerge.

Although some people claim to work best under pressure, we think that you are more likely to write effectively when you leave enough time for ideas to percolate. The process you use, of course, depends on the type of assignment you have been given, and some assignments may require you to access materials online or in the library. But whatever the assignment, we feel that it is beneficial to develop a set of strategies that will enable you to **engage** with a writing topic and **develop an idea or thesis** worth supporting. This chapter focuses on several possibilities for exploring a topic actively, beginning with your own experience and then moving beyond yourself to locate information elsewhere. The chapter also discusses several forms that a thesis can take within the various argument-based genres used in college writing.

EXPLORING A TOPIC ACTIVELY

In some of your college classes, you may have the option of selecting your own topic; in others, your teacher may assign one. In either case, you should begin working on your paper by doing **something active**—it is not a good idea to just sit staring at a computer screen or chewing your fingernails, hoping that ideas come to you through some mysterious process. Perhaps some writers are inspired in this way—these are the writers depicted in film and story who pace the floor and think until a brilliant notion emerges, springing like Athena from the head of Zeus. For most writers, though, ideas do not arrive without effort. Most writers discover ideas when they engage in preliminary writing activities that enable them to assess what they already know and believe about the topic. Being *active* in the process is an important idea to keep in mind.

Engaging in preliminary writing activities, of course, is no guarantee that you will discover wonderful, exciting ideas right away. In fact, you may find that you reject a lot of what you have written initially. Yet even if this happens (and it happens to everyone), you will find that doing some form of preliminary writing will stimulate the discovery of at least something that is useful. If nothing else, it will highlight what additional information you might need.

BEGINNING WITH WHAT YOU KNOW

Exploration Questions

A good place to begin the writing process is to start with what you know—that is, to reflect on experiences, facts, opinions, and values you already have about the topic. Understanding your own views on a topic will also help you figure out what you *don't* know about it, determine what you need to find out, and enable you to evaluate the material you find. One strategy for initiating work on any topic is by responding in writing to the following **"exploration questions"**:

1. Why is this topic important? Is it currently being discussed?
2. Is there a controversy associated with this topic?
3. Were you brought up to have an opinion on this controversy? What opinion did your family and community have on this topic?
4. How did your school experiences influence your conception of the topic? Did your teachers and classmates have similar opinions about it as your family? Were there any points of disagreement?
5. Can you think of at least two people who hold differing views about this topic? If so, describe these people and summarize what you believe were their points of view.
6. Has your opinion changed about this topic in any way? Why or why not?

To illustrate how "Exploration Questions" can enable a writer to gain an understanding of a topic, let us imagine the following scenario, which was addressed briefly in chapter 3:

A college student named Jon is currently in his first year at State College. State College is a large, well-known university that offers many opportunities, and Jon had entered State in the fall semester with the idea of majoring in business. However, after a semester at State, Jon is thinking about transferring to Northern

College, a smaller school that is not as well-known. Northern offers a major in Environmental Studies, which Jon would now prefer as his major.

Both schools are public institutions, and tuition fees are about the same in each one. But Jon cannot just "switch" schools without the approval of his Aunt Maria. Aunt Maria has been helping Jon with his college tuition and Aunt Maria is, herself, a graduate of State. Jon's writing task is to convince Aunt Maria that Northern College would be a better choice.

To gain a better understanding of his "topic," Jon responded to the exploration questions listed above, an exercise that enabled him to become aware of other facets of the topic that he needed to clarify and investigate.

Jon's Responses

1. Why is this topic important? Is it currently being discussed?

Choosing a school sometimes means choosing a profession, which is one of the most important decisions a person can make, and that is why the topic is important. But I don't think that a person should choose a profession just for the money. On the other hand, you have to make enough to live. People do think that choosing the "right" college is important, especially people who are concerned about making contacts and going to a school that has the right reputation when someone is looking for a job. The media does discuss the importance of a college education, and certainly my family has discussed it a lot.

2. Is there a controversy associated with this topic?

The choice of which college to attend can be a controversial topic for some people. Aunt Maria, for instance, thinks that choosing the "right" college is an extremely important decision for being successful in life and that the "right" college means one that has a great Business school where you can make lots of contacts and ultimately be financially successful. Other people think that the "right" college is one that has programs that are interesting to students. These people think that going to college to study business is not the only possibility and is not at all the right choice for someone who doesn't find business interesting.

3. Were you brought up to have an opinion on this controversy? What opinion did your family and community have on this topic?

I was brought up with the idea that being financially successful was important. Yet my mother always encouraged me to explore topics that interested me and that I felt were worthwhile. Actually, my mother is an elementary school teacher and she didn't choose that field because she would be able to make a lot of money. On the other hand, a lot of my friends think that making money is everything and that studying business is a great way to do it.

4. How did your school experiences influence your conception of the topic? Did your teachers and classmates feel the same way about it as did your family? Were there any points of disagreement?

In school we were taught that doing something worthwhile was more important than just going for the money. My community service class in high school really opened my eyes to the possibilities for working to help the environment. My geography teacher last semester showed me that there was important work to be done in environmental policy. That class really sparked my interest and showed me that I could study something interesting and worthwhile and still make a decent living.

5. Can you think of at least two people who hold differing views about this topic? If so, describe these people and summarize what you believe were their points of view.

Aunt Maria thinks that going to a big, well-known school and majoring in business is the only way to go. She thinks that making a lot of money is the most important thing in life.

My geography teacher thinks I should go to a school that has a program that interests me. He thinks that making enough money is important but that doing something interesting and worthwhile is just as important.

6. Has your opinion changed about this topic in any way? Why or why not?

I used to agree with Aunt Maria. When I first began high school and saw the other kids with fancy cars and terrific clothes, I used to think that all I wanted to do was make a bundle of money so I could buy all that stuff. Now I think that doing something interesting and worthwhile is more important for me. I don't want to be poor, but I think I can make a living doing environmental studies because there are lots of jobs in that area.

EXPLORING YOUR EXPLORATION

After you have written responses to exploration questions, you should reread them, looking for ideas and directions you can use in your essay or which you will need to explore further. In looking over his responses, Jon noted several ideas to use, as well as a few about which it would be a good idea to find out some additional information:

1. Why is this topic important? Is it currently being discussed?

In his response, Jon wrote about the connection between choosing a school and choosing a profession and perhaps this is a theme he could explore in writing to his Aunt Maria. Perhaps this idea is not as established as many people think. Perhaps there are other opinions about this topic.

2. Is there a controversy associated with this topic?

In his response, Jon had written that "other people" think that "business is not the only possibility" for having a successful professional life. In rereading this statement, he realized that aside from his geography teacher, he didn't really know the names of any other people who felt this way. He decided that it might help convince Aunt Maria if he could find some specific names.

3. Were you brought up to have an opinion on this controversy? What opinion did your family and community have on this topic?

In answering this question, Jon noted that he had referred to his mother's profession as an elementary school teacher, one that doesn't earn an extremely high salary. He then thought that maybe he should ask his mother about why she had chosen her career and find out if she was satisfied with her choice.

4. How did your school experiences influence your conception of the topic? Did your teachers and classmates feel the same way about it as did your family? Were there any points of disagreement?

In answering this question, Jon had written that "there was important work to be done in environmental policy." Yet, he really didn't have specific information to support that statement. What sort of job could he expect to get with a major in environmental policy? He decided that he would talk with his geography teacher about this and maybe do some research in the library to find out more specific information.

5. Can you think of at least two people who hold differing views about this topic? If so, describe these people and summarize what you believe were their points of view.

In answering this question, Jon had written that Aunt Maria "thinks that making a lot of money is the most important thing in life" and that majoring in business was the only way to do this. As he thought about this, he realized that maybe some of the courses needed for the environmental studies major would be just as likely to earn him a good job after graduation. More information about this would be useful, Jon decided.

6. Has your opinion changed about this topic in any way? Why or why not?

Because Jon's opinion had changed on this topic, he can use his previous opinion as a point of contact with Aunt Maria. Shared ideas, even when those ideas have changed, can be used as a bridge between you and your reader. Also, as in his response to question 4, Jon referred to "lots of jobs" in the area of environmental studies, a subject about which he will need additional information.

SCENARIOS FOR WRITING

Scenarios or situations that incorporate particular problems or controversies are useful formats for writing assignments. Following are several you might consider:

WRITING ASSIGNMENT

The head mistress of the local nursery school has decided to include a unit on classic fairy tales for all the children. Some of the parents, however, feel that fairy tales are unsuitable for young children. Based on the readings in this chapter, others you can locate on the Internet, and on the fairy tales you are familiar with from your own culture, write an essay in which you address the following question:

Is it valuable for children to hear fairy tales? Why or why not?

In responding to this assignment, you should complete the following activities:

1. In small groups, discuss the fairy tales you liked best when you were a child. Why do you think you liked them? Would you tell these tales to your own children? Can you perceive anything harmful about these tales?
2. Write responses to exploration questions.
3. Write a short, informal essay discussing the good and bad points of the fairy tales you liked best when you were a child.
4. Read Teeanna's (on the following page) responses and compare them with your own.
5. Read the essays at the end of this chapter.
   A. Bruno Bettelheim excerpt from *The Uses of Enchantment*
   B. "The Value of Fairy Tales in Education"
   C. Lisa Belkin. "Are Fairytales Too Scary for Children?"

Your essay should have the characteristics of the genre of argument and should include at least some information from the readings.

EXPLORATION QUESTIONS ON THE TOPIC OF FAIRY TALES

1. Is the topic of fairy tales important? Is it currently being discussed?
2. Is there a controversy associated with the topic of fairy tales?
3. Were you brought up to have an opinion on the topic of fairy tales? What opinion do you think your family and community have on this topic?

4. How did your school experiences influence your conception of the topic? Do you think your teachers and classmates feel the same way about this topic as does your family?
5. Can you think of at least two people who hold differing views about this topic? If so, describe these people and summarize what you believe are their points of view.
6. Has your opinion changed about the topic of fairy tales in any way? If it has, how has it changed?

Teeanna's Responses
EXPLORATION QUESTIONS ON THE TOPIC OF FAIRY TALES:

1. Is the topic of fairy tales important? Is it currently being discussed?

The topic of fairy tales has become pretty popular because they are often associated with promoting cultural values. There are also psychological issues that some people discuss— also gender and racial stereotypes that some people feel are being promoted through fairy tales.

2. Is there a controversy associated with the topic of fairy tales?

The question of fairy tales is hotly debated. Some, like Bruno Bettelheim, feel that fairy tales teach young children how to deal with frightening emotions. Others are afraid that fairy tales teach children harmful attitudes about male and female roles in society. Then there are people who consider the cultural ideas that fairy tales promote. The question that arises from these arguments is: do fairy tales help or harm children?

3. Were you brought up to have an opinion on the topic of fairy tales? What opinion do you think your family and community have on this topic?

I was encouraged to read everything I could get my hands on and my parents never disapproved of anything I chose to read. As far as fairy tales were concerned, my mother gave me copies of the original Grimm's brothers and Hans Christian Anderson stories when I was very young. She felt that they would be good for my imagination and would teach me moral principles. My father's family comes from a different culture, a culture that does not value imagination like Americans do. While he encouraged me to read as much as I could, he also thought that anything fictional was useless and that I would be better prepared for life if I chose more "sensible" topics: Science, math, or history, for example.

4. How did your school experiences influence your conception of the topic? Do you think your teachers and classmates feel the same way about this topic as does your family?

When I started school, I hadn't yet read any Mother Goose stories. My mother thought they were silly, unlike the moral messages in the Grimm's and Anderson. My teachers and classmates were surprised that I didn't know stories like "Jack Sprat" and "Little Miss Muffet," and the children teased me. I got the feeling that I had missed out on something important, so I read all the Mother Goose tales. I thought they were silly. I've never understood why my teachers thought they were important for me to know.

5. Can you think of at least two people who hold differing views about this topic? If so, describe these people and summarize what you believe are their points of view.

Ms. X is a college graduate working in a feminist bookstore and is pregnant with her first child. She is concerned about what she should allow her child to read because she wants to avoid dangerous sexual stereotypes. She wants her child to respect him/herself, no matter what sex he/she turns out to be. Ms. X is afraid that fairy tales give children harmful ideas about male and female roles.

Ms. Q went to college with Ms. X and works for a counseling service. She is excited about Ms. X's baby because Ms. Q is going to be its godmother. She is not as concerned about sexual stereotypes in fairy tales. In fact, she thinks Ms. X should allow her child to read fairy tales because they teach children about how to feel good about themselves, even when they have "bad" thoughts.

6. Has your opinion changed about the topic of fairy tales in any way? If it has, how has it changed?

My opinion about fairy tales is different from my parents' view. I feel that fairy tales expand a child's mind by giving him or her new and unusual things to think about, and that they provide insight into how our culture has developed its value system. Bettelheim's essay shows how fairy tales allow children to think about things that are frightening to them, and Lisa Belkin is afraid that they are too scary for children. I am not sure, however, that I feel that fairy tales are as potentially damaging as Belkin and the other reading say they are.

Following is Teeanna's essay, which incorporates readings she had found in the library.

Teeanna's Essay

The Role of Fairy Tales

Children have been reading fairy tales for generations, and until recently, people tended to accept that they were an important part of a child's education. Today, however, some people are concerned about how fairy tales affect children. They say that they are too violent and instill harmful sexual stereotypes. However, although there may be violent elements in fairy tales, and although many of them do present stereotypical concepts of both men and women, fairy tales should still be part of a child's upbringing because they can teach children how to deal with complicated and difficult emotional stereotypes.

One of the most compelling arguments against fairy tales is that they expose children to gender-based stereotypes that perpetuate an old fashioned and unflattering view of women. Many fairy tales such as "Cinderella" or "Sleeping Beauty" depict women as passive, waiting for a Prince Charming to show up on a white horse and rescue them. Those who are concerned with the impact of fairy tales on children point out that this view of women presents an outmoded model of male-female relationships that is inappropriate to today's society.

In addition to depicting women as passive, many fairy tales characterize women as evil, witch-like beings who are consumed with jealousy and anger. Marina Warner points out that in many tales, women are extremely nasty to one another or to other women's children and that "fairy tales told by women contain vivid examples of female evil: wicked step-mothers, ogresses, bad fairies abound, while virtuous figures like Cinderella's mother, are dead from the start" (25). Warner traces these evil figures to the necessity in the past for women to guard their children's and their own positions in a male-dominated society, claiming that "if you accept Mother Goose tales as the testimony of women, as old wives tales, you can hear vibrating in them the tensions, the insecurity, jealousy and rage of both mother-in-law and vice versa, as well as the vulnerability of children from different marriages" (28). Moreover, as Armin Brott points out, fairy tales are frequently unflattering to fathers as well, often depicting them as uninvolved or even absent from their families. Brott states that children's literature often ignores "men who share equally in raising their children" and contributes to "yet another generation of men who have been told . . . that mothers are the truer parent" (14).

In addition to their perpetuation of harmful gender stereotypes, fairy tales also contain considerable violence. In "Hansel and Gretel," the children face a witch who wants to eat them and finally defeat her by pushing her into her own oven. In the Grimm's version of

Cinderella, the evil step-sisters try to fool the Prince by cutting off parts of their feet so they will fit into Cinderella's tiny shoe. Later at Cinderella's wedding, birds peck out their eyes. Certainly it would seem as if these would be alarming things for a child to read.

Nevertheless, although one must acknowledge both the gender stereotypes and the violence, fairy tales should be retained in early childhood education because, as the psychologist, Bruno Bettelheim, asserts, they "teach children about the inner problems of human beings." Bettelheim points out that many of the elements present in fairy tales are those that children already think about. According to Bettelheim, children do not always think only good thoughts and sometimes have trouble feeling good about themselves because of this tendency. He tells us:

. . . children know that they are not always good; and often, even when they are, they would prefer not to be. This contradicts what they are told by their parents, and therefore makes the child a monster in his own eyes. (7)

A new brother or sister may anger a child because he/she is not getting enough attention from the parent, and the child may then think that pushing baby into an oven might be a good idea. The child understands that this is a horrible thing to do or even to think of doing, and therefore thinks that he/she is a horrible person as well. But if children can read about deeds such as this in a fairy tale, they can then pretend they are doing something awful, such as pushing the witch into an oven, and they will therefore feel less guilty about their own thoughts without acting on them.

Moreover, in many fairy tales, the hero or heroine must struggle against great difficulties—a hostile step-mother as in "Cinderella," fierce jealousy, as in "Snow White," or threats from fearsome beings, such as wolves, giants, or ogres, as in "Jack-in-the-Beanstalk." Identifying with the protagonist, children learn "that a struggle against severe difficulties in life is unavoidable, is an intrinsic part of human existence—but that if one does not shy away, but steadfastly meets unexpected and often unjust hardships, one masters all obstacles and at the end emerges victorious" (Bettelheim 8). This is an important message for children to learn.

Finally, fairy tales are an important transmitter of culture, providing children with links to previous generations. Whatever gender stereotypes they might embody, other influences within the culture can counteract their potentially harmful effect. But the magic and imagination found in fairy tales cannot be replaced by the perhaps more politically correct but certainly less vital modern tales that do not force children to confront the dark side of human existence. Fairy tales should continue to be part of children's early years, because they are psychologically and culturally beneficial, enabling them to grapple with the "inner problems of human beings" (Bettelheim 6).

Works Cited

Bettelheim, Bruno. Introduction. *The Uses of Enchantment.* New York: Alfred A. Knopf, 1976.

3–11. Print.

Brott, Armin. "Not All Men Are Sly Foxes." *Newsweek* 1 June 1992: 14. Print.

Warner, Marina. "The Absent Mother: Women Against Women in Old Wives Tales." *History*

Today 41. April 1991: 22–28. Print.

OTHER STRATEGIES FOR ASSESSING WHAT YOU KNOW ABOUT A TOPIC

Free Writing and Brainstorming

Exploration questions structure the direction of your thinking, but some writers prefer a less-structured form of becoming conscious of personal knowledge, either by writing freely about a topic or by simply jotting down ideas. When you use these methods, the images and possibilities that come to mind often suggest others, leading you in new directions and enabling you to discover information that you didn't know you had.

Clustering

Clustering, like free writing and brainstorming, can also be a useful means of beginning to explore a topic. It enables you to group ideas graphically and to perceive possible connections between them. To cluster on a topic, write the central idea or topic in the center of a piece of paper and draw a circle around it. Around this centered word, write other words that are connected with it in some way, and draw circles around them, too. Connect these circles to your main circle. Now, around each of the words surrounding your main topic, write other ideas that come to mind and use lines to connect these ideas to others on the page. Here is an example of a cluster on the topic of fairy tales.

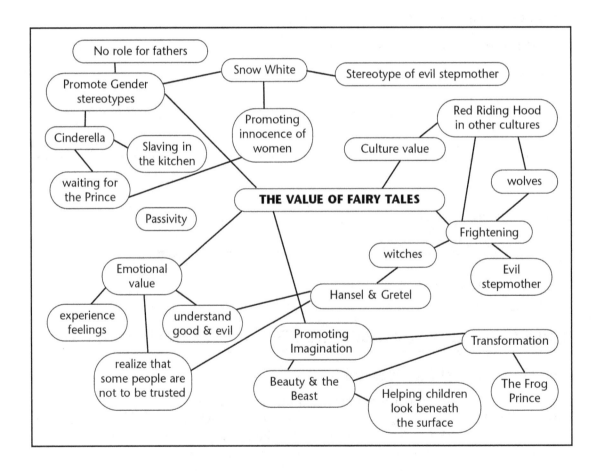

MOVING BEYOND YOURSELF IN DISCOVERING INFORMATION

Becoming conscious of your own ideas and beliefs is an important first step in exploring a topic. But personal topics may be assigned in college writing classes, other genres, including argument are assigned as well, so it is important to move beyond your own immediate background and discover additional information. That information may include the following:

- relevant background material
- key terms associated with the topic
- the main viewpoints on the topic
- the main reasons usually cited in support of these viewpoints

LOCATING RELEVANT BACKGROUND MATERIAL

Most, if not all, of the topics you will be writing about for your college courses have their roots in the past, and in order for you to formulate an opinion about what is happening in the present, you will find it useful to understand what happened in the past. Even in the most everyday occurrences, such as deciding on where to live, the past can play an important role. Suppose you were hunting for an apartment and discovered that one was available in a building in a section of town that was close to a large river. Before you formed an opinion on whether or not this was a good place to live, you would surely want to know if the river had ever overflowed its banks in the past, if any sort of damage had been done, and what sort of compensation was available were it to happen again.

Writing assignments concerned with social issues usually have their roots in past conditions. For example, in a political science or sociology class, you may be discussing policies concerned with immigration or admission to universities. However, in order to decide on whether a policy is "fair" or necessary for promoting equal opportunity to formerly oppressed groups, one must look to the past to find out why such policies were recommended in the first place and the extent to which they have been deemed effective. Thus, an important question to ask about most topics for argumentative writing is the following:

> What do I need to know about the past in order to develop an informed opinion
> on this topic?

LOCATING KEY TERMS ASSOCIATED WITH THE TOPIC

In addition to finding out about the past, exploring the background of a topic also involves locating key terms that are associated with it; terms that are likely to arouse strong feelings in a prospective audience. For example, if you were researching the topic of affirmative action, it would be important for you to be aware of such key terms as *equal opportunity, quotas, reverse discrimination,* or *The Fourteenth Amendment.* For every topic, there are a set of key terms that appear most frequently; usually these are terms that are likely to elicit strong reactions. These terms are also useful for conducting searches in the library or online.

LOCATING THE MAIN VIEWPOINTS ON THE TOPIC AND THE REASONS USUALLY CITED IN SUPPORT OF THESE VIEWPOINTS

When you begin to read about your topic, it is helpful to become aware of the major viewpoints that people hold about it and to become familiar with the reasons usually cited in support of these viewpoints. Understanding the extreme views on a topic does not mean that you must choose one or the other or that the genre of argumentation involves a "winner" and a "loser" in a debate. On the contrary, writers of academic argument usually situate themselves somewhere in-between extreme viewpoints, acknowledging that there is merit on both sides and adopting a thesis or claim that represents a compromise. However, in exploring a topic, it is a good idea to understand the extremes so that you can address them in your writing when appropriate.

EXERCISE

The following situations have generated controversy:

1. A community wishes to pass a law forbidding anyone between the ages of sixteen and eighteen from driving after 11:00 p.m.
2. A community wishes to organize a Neighborhood Watch to notify the police when a suspicious-looking person is seen.
3. An urban school wishes to require its students to wear school uniforms.
4. Some people feel that private citizens should not be allowed to own guns.

In small groups, explore each of these situations by answering the following questions:

1. What information about the past would it be necessary to know in order to develop an informed opinion on this topic?
2. What key terms are usually associated with these situations?
3. What are the extreme viewpoints on this topic and the main reasons usually cited in support of these viewpoints?

THE ROLE OF THE THESIS

Exploring a topic both through your own experience and by finding additional information about the background, key terms, and opposing viewpoints will enable you to discover a main idea for your essay. This main idea, which is developed and supported throughout the essay, is called the *thesis,* although sometimes it is also called a *position* or *claim* or *main idea,* and we will use these terms interchangeably in this book. A thesis in many college essays usually appears in the form of a statement about a rhetorical situation or problematic issue, and it exerts control over other features of the essay, serving as a sort of glue that holds the essay together. In fact, readers who wish to gain an overview of the major focus of an essay will often skim for the thesis statement before reading the essay. But a personal narrative can also have a thesis, often one that the narrative illustrates.

THREE WAYS OF PHRASING A THESIS STATEMENT

Three useful ways to state a thesis are as a *simple thesis statement,* an *expanded thesis statement,* and as an *expanded thesis statement using the word* although.

A SIMPLE THESIS STATEMENT

A simple thesis statement, as its name suggests, is a presentation of a position or main idea stated as a simple sentence. When Jon writes his letter to Aunt Maria about why he wants to transfer from one university to another, he may state his thesis this way:

> Northern College is a better choice for me than State University.

For other topics, examples of simple thesis statements are as follows:

1. Speech codes are an acceptable feature of campus life.
2. Marijuana ought to be legalized.
3. Immigration laws in California should be more restrictive.

A simple thesis statement presents a main idea or position, but it gives no hint of a writer's reasons, nor does it give readers a sense of what the structure of the essay is going to be.

THE EXPANDED THESIS STATEMENT

A more elaborated type of thesis statement is the expanded thesis, which uses the word *because.* Writing an expanded thesis can be a useful way of clarifying an argument for oneself because it forecasts what you plan to say. Here are examples of how a simple thesis may be stated as an expanded thesis.

Jon's Expanded Thesis

Northern College is a better choice for me than State because it offers programs in environmental studies, which is the field I wish to enter.

Here are some examples of expanded theses concerned with other topics:

1. Speech codes are an acceptable feature of campus life because creating a harmonious climate is more important than free speech.
2. Marijuana ought to be legalized because it has many medical benefits and because enforcement of restrictive laws is too expensive.
3. Immigration laws in California should be more restrictive because the local economy cannot afford to support illegal immigrants.

In an expanded thesis statement, the use of the word *because* indicates a *relationship* between the two parts of the thesis—the main idea and the reasons that will be used to support it. This relationship can also be suggested in other ways. For example, Jon could have written an expanded thesis as follows:

Northern College offers programs in environmental studies, has smaller class sizes, and fosters close interaction between professors and students. Therefore, it is a better college for me.

or

Northern College offers programs in environmental studies, has smaller class sizes, and fosters close interaction between professors and students so it is a better college for me.

The use of the word *because* (either actually or implied) is a useful strategy for clarifying your thinking and helping you to develop supporting points, so I suggest that you write an expanded thesis for all of your assignments, even if you decide you don't actually state it that way in your essay.

THESIS STATEMENTS USING "ALTHOUGH"

Another useful word that helps you clarify the goals of your thesis is the word *although*. "Although" often appears in a thesis statement to indicate how the thesis will differ from what is generally believed about the subject or how it will differ from an *opposing viewpoint*. A reference to what is generally believed or to what an opponent may believe is characteristic of college argument because it focuses attention on the viewpoint being refuted. Here are some examples of how the word *although* can help to focus a thesis statement:

Jon's Expanded Thesis Using "Although"

Although State College has an excellent reputation, Northern College is a better choice for me because it offers programs in environmental studies, has smaller class sizes, and fosters close interaction between professors and students.

Expanded Theses for Argumentative Essays Using "Although"

1. Although speech codes may sometimes interfere with the First Amendment right to free speech, they are an acceptable feature of campus life because creating a harmonious climate is more important.
2. Although marijuana has been considered a dangerous drug, it ought to be legalized because it has many medical benefits and because enforcement of restrictive laws are too expensive.
3. Although the United States has always offered a haven to immigrants, immigration laws in California should be more restrictive because the local economy cannot afford to support illegal immigrants.

Like *because,* the word *although* can be implied in other ways. Here is an example of the college student's thesis that implies the word *although* without actually using the word:

> Despite the fact that State College has an excellent reputation, Northern College is a better choice for me because it offers programs in environmental studies, has smaller class sizes, and fosters close interaction between professors and students.

The use of the word *although* indicates to the reader that the writer is aware of the complexity of the topic and understands that others may have different points of view. It, therefore, renders the thesis statement more "polite" or more "judicious." Writers of college argument need to be aware that they are more likely to have an impact on their readers by acknowledging their viewpoint and indicating that they understand and respect it, than by telling the readers that they are completely wrong. Argumentative essays are usually concerned with complex and controversial subjects in which the "truth" concerning these topics is difficult to "know" with absolute certainty. Thus, a thesis for an argumentative essay is one with which at least some people are likely to disagree, and often a position that one person may view as absolutely right may be viewed by another person as absolutely wrong (after all, that is why they are considered controversial). Therefore, writers of academic argument will be more successful if they approach their subject politely and judiciously, indicate that they understand the complexity of the subject, and acknowledge that they are aware of other points of view. The word *although* helps writers to frame thesis statements that accomplish this purpose.

EXERCISE

Working in small groups, find the thesis or claim for each of the essays included at the end of this chapter. State each in three ways—as a simple thesis statement, as an expanded thesis statement, and as an expanded thesis statement using the word *although*.

Writing Assignments

1. Reflect on some of the fairy tales you heard or read as a child. Then write a paragraph in which you recount the plot of one of these fairy tales. Share your recollection with other students in a small group.

    Using some of the material concerned with fairy tales included in this chapter and, possibly, supplementing your reading with additional texts, write an essay that addresses the following question:

    Is it valuable for children to hear fairy tales? Why or why not?

2. In "Feminism and Fairy Tales," Karen E. Rowe claims that although traditional fairy tales have presented a picture of young girls as passive, dependent, and subordinate, modern reformulations have aimed at countering this negative impact. Read this article online (http://www.tusculum.edu/faculty/home/smorton/womenslit/feminism.pdf and supplement it with at least two other articles, either print or online. Then focusing on a particular modern reconceptualization of a fairy tale, write an essay that addresses the following question:

    How successfully has this modern reformulation of a fairy tale countered the portrayal of women that characterized the original version?

3. Writing a Literacy Narrative

    In many Composition classes, and in other classes too, students are sometimes assigned to write a "Literacy Narrative" or "Literacy Autobiography". This genre is a narrative about one's own experience with some form of literacy—perhaps the learning of a language, struggle with learning to read, a description of a person who has been instrumental in helping you become a reader or a writer, the discovery of a book or literacy direction that has been significant for you, events or situations that have shaped your attitude toward reading and writing. Literacy narratives are often characterized by a **story arc**—essentially, a three-part format, in which the writer undergoes a transformation. For example, a writer may recount a struggle to learn English, beginning with feelings of isolation, frustration, perhaps conflict, then describing an event or person that has motivated or enabled a change, and finally showing that a transformation has taken place. In a story arc, the writer narrates how some form of growth or perhaps a triumph over adversity has occurred.

Below are some exploration questions to consider when generating ideas for a literacy narrative:

- Why are you telling this story? To share a memory? To teach a lesson? To help readers in a similar situation to gain encouragement?
- Who will care about this story? Are you writing for readers who are likely to share your attitude toward literacy?
- Where did this story begin? Did it take place over a long period of time?
- Where did this narrative take place?
- Who was involved in this narrative?
- What details will make your narrative compelling for your reader?
- What tone do you want to project? Humorous? Serious? Critical?
- How do you want your readers to think of you?
- Why do you think this narrative is significant? Why does it matter?

Keep in mind that a Literacy Narrative is a type of **argument** in that it is focused around a central idea and is intended to move a reader to view it as significant in some way. An effective narrative is focused, purposeful, and oriented toward the needs of its audience. It is enhanced by well-placed, vivid details and images that aim to capture the reader's interest. The story is well-told, and its significance is clear and perhaps memorable to the reader.

For an example of a literacy narrative that uses a story arc, please see Lida's essay in Chapter 14.

READINGS

Introduction: The Struggle for Meaning

By Bruno Bettelheim

If we hope to live not just from moment to moment, but in true consciousness of our existence, then our greatest need and most difficult achievement is to find meaning in our lives. It is well known how many have lost the will to live, and have stopped trying, because such meaning has evaded them. An understanding of the meaning of one's life is not suddenly acquired at a particular age, not even when one has reached chronological maturity. On the contrary, gaining a secure understanding of what the meaning of one's life may or ought to be—that is what constitutes having attained psychological maturity. And this achievement is the end result of a long development: at each age we seek, and must be able to find, some modicum of meaning congruent with how our minds and understanding have already developed.

Contrary to the ancient myth, wisdom does not burst forth fully developed like Athena out of Zeus's head; it is built up, small step by small step, from most irrational beginnings. Only in adulthood can an intelligent understanding of the meaning of one's existence in this world be gained from one's experiences in it. Unfortunately, too many parents want their children's minds to function as their own do—as if mature understanding of ourselves and the world, and our ideas about the meaning of life, did not have to develop as slowly as our bodies and minds.

Today, as in times past, the most important and also the most difficult task in raising a child is helping him to find meaning in life. Many growth experiences are needed to achieve this. The child, as he develops, must learn step by step to understand himself better; with this he becomes more able to understand others, and eventually can relate to them in ways which are mutually satisfying and meaningful.

To find deeper meaning, one must become able to transcend the narrow confines of a self-centered existence and believe that one will make a significant contribution to life—if not right now, then at some future time. This feeling is necessary if a person is to be satisfied with himself and with what he is doing. In order not to be at the mercy of the vagaries of life, one must develop one's

From *The Uses of Enchantment: The Meaning of Importance of Fairy Tales* by Bruno Bettelheim. Copyright © 1975, 1976 by Bruno Bettelheim. Reprinted by permission.

inner resources, so that one's emotions, imagination, and intellect mutually support and enrich one another. Our positive feelings give us the strength to develop our rationality; only hope for the future can sustain us in the adversities we unavoidably encounter.

As an educator and therapist of severely disturbed children, my main task was to restore meaning to their lives. This work made it obvious to me that if children were reared so that life was meaningful to them, they would not need special help. I was confronted with the problem of deducing what experiences in a child's life are most suited to promote his ability to find meaning in his life; to endow life in general with more meaning. Regarding this task, nothing is more important than the impact of parents and others who take care of the child; second in importance is our cultural heritage, when transmitted to the child in the right manner. When children are young, it is literature that carries such information best.

Given this fact, I became deeply dissatisfied with much of the literature intended to develop the child's mind and personality, because it fails to stimulate and nurture those resources he needs in order to cope with his difficult inner problems. The preprimers and primers from which he is taught to read in school are designed to teach the necessary skills, irrespective of meaning. The overwhelming bulk of the rest of so-called "children's literature" attempts to entertain or to inform, or both. Most of these books are so shallow in substance that little of significance can be gained from them. The acquisition of skills, including the ability to read, becomes devalued when what one has learned to read adds nothing of importance to one's life.

We all tend to assess the future merits of an activity on the basis of what it offers now. But this is especially true for the child, who, much more than the adult, lives in the present and, although he has anxieties about his future, has only the vaguest notions of what it may require or be like. The idea that learning to read may enable one later to enrich one's life is experienced as an empty promise when the stories the child listens to, or is reading at the moment, are vacuous. The worst feature of these children's books is that they cheat the child of what he ought to gain from the experience of literature: access to deeper meaning, and that which is meaningful to him at his stage of development.

For a story to hold the child's attention, it must entertain him and arouse his curiosity. But to enrich his life, it must stimulate his imagination; help him to develop his intellect and to clarify his emotions; be attuned to his anxieties and aspirations; give full recognition to his difficulties, while at the same time suggesting solutions to the problems which perturb him. In short, it must at one and the same time relate to all aspects of his personality—and this without ever belittling but, on the contrary, giving full credence to the seriousness of the child's predicaments, while simultaneously promoting confidence in himself and in his future.

In all these and many other respects, of the entire "children's literature"—with rare exceptions nothing can be as enriching and satisfying to child and adult alike as the folk fairy tale. True, on an overt level fairy tales teach little about the specific conditions of life in modern mass society; these tales were created long before it came into being. But more can be learned from them about the inner problems of human beings, and of the right solutions to their predicaments in any society, than from any other type of story within a child's comprehension. Since the child at every moment of his life is exposed to the society in which he lives, he will certainly learn to cope with its conditions, provided his inner resources permit him to do so.

Just because his life is often bewildering to him, the child needs even more to be given the chance to understand himself in this complex world with which he must learn to cope. To be able to do so, the child must be helped to make some coherent sense out of the turmoil of his feelings. He needs ideas on how to bring his inner house into order, and on that basis be able to create order in his life. He needs—and this hardly requires emphasis at this moment in our history—a moral education which subtly, and by implication only, conveys to him the advantages of moral behavior, not through abstract ethical concepts but through that which seems tangibly right and therefore meaningful to him.

The child finds this kind of meaning through fairy tales. Like many other modern psychological insights, this was anticipated long ago by poets. The German poet Schiller wrote: "Deeper meaning resides in the fairy tales told to me in my childhood than in the truth that is taught by life." (*The Piccolomini*, III, 4.)

Through the centuries (if not millennia) during which, in their retelling, fairy tales became ever more refined, they came to convey at the same time overt and covert meanings—came to speak simultaneously to all levels of the human personality, communicating in a manner which reaches the uneducated mind of the child as well as that of the sophisticated adult. Applying the psychoanalytic model of the human personality, fairy tales carry important messages to the conscious, the preconscious, and the unconscious mind, on whatever level each is functioning at the time. By dealing with universal human problems, particularly those which preoccupy the child's mind, these stories speak to his budding ego and encourage its development, while at the same time relieving preconscious and unconscious pressures. As the stories unfold, they give conscious credence and body to id pressures and show ways to satisfy these that are in line with ego and superego requirements.

But my interest in fairy tales is not the result of such a technical analysis of their merits. It is, on the contrary, the consequence of asking myself why, in my experience, children—normal and abnormal alike, and at all levels of intelligence—find folk fairy tales more satisfying than all other children's stories.

The more I tried to understand why these stories are so successful at enriching the inner life of the child, the more I realized that these tales, in a much deeper sense than any other reading material, start where the child really is in his psychological and emotional being. They speak about his severe inner pressures in a way that the child unconsciously understands, and—without belittling the most serious inner struggles which growing up entails—offer examples of both temporary and permanent solutions to pressing difficulties.

When a grant from the Spencer Foundation provided the leisure to study what contributions psychoanalysis can make to the education of children—and since reading and being read to are essential means of education—it seemed appropriate to use this opportunity to explore in greater detail and depth why folk fairy tales are so valuable in the upbringing of children. My hope is that a proper understanding of the unique merits of fairy tales will induce parents and teachers to assign them once again to that central role in the life of the child they held for centuries.

Fairy Tales and the Existential Predicament

In order to master the psychological problems of growing up—overcoming narcissistic disappointments, oedipal dilemmas, sibling rivalries; becoming able to relinquish childhood dependencies; gaining a feeling of selfhood and of self-worth, and a sense of moral obligation—a child needs to understand what is going on within his conscious self so that he can also cope with that which goes on in his unconscious. He can achieve this understanding, and with it the ability to cope, not through rational comprehension of the nature and content of his unconscious, but by becoming familiar with it through spinning out daydreams—ruminating, rearranging, and fantasizing about suitable story elements in response to unconscious pressures. By doing this, the child fits unconscious content into conscious fantasies, which then enable him to deal with that content. It is here that fairy tales have unequaled value, because they offer new dimensions to the child's imagination which would be impossible for him to discover as truly on his own. Even more important, the form and structure of fairy tales suggest images to the child by which he can structure his daydreams and with them give better direction to his life.

In child or adult, the unconscious is a powerful determinant of behavior. When the unconscious is repressed and its content denied entrance into awareness, then eventually the person's conscious mind will be partially overwhelmed by derivatives of these unconscious elements, or else he is forced to keep such rigid, compulsive control over them that his personality may become severely crippled. But when unconscious material is to some degree permitted to come to awareness and worked through in imagination, its potential for causing harm—to ourselves or others—is much reduced, some of its forces can then be made to serve positive purposes. However, the prevalent parental belief is that a child must be diverted from what troubles him most: his formless, nameless anxieties, and his chaotic, angry, and even violent fantasies. Many parents believe that only conscious reality or pleasant and wish-fulfilling images should be presented to the child—that he should be exposed only to the sunny side of things. But such one-sided fare nourishes the mind only in a one-sided way, and real life is not all sunny.

There is a widespread refusal to let children know that the source of much that goes wrong in life is due to our very own natures—the propensity of all men for acting aggressively, asocial, selfishly, out of anger and anxiety. Instead, we want our children to believe that, inherently, all men are good. But children know that *they* are not always good; and often, even when they are, they would prefer not to be. This contradicts what they are told by their parents, and therefore makes the child a monster in his own eyes. The dominant culture wishes to pretend, particularly where children are concerned, that the dark side of man does not exist, and professes a belief in an optimistic meliorism.

Psychoanalysis itself is viewed as having the purpose of making life easy—but this is not what its founder intended. Psychoanalysis was created to enable man to accept the problematic nature of life without being defeated by it, or giving in to escapism. Freud's prescription is that only by struggling courageously against what seem like overwhelming odds can man succeed in wringing meaning out of his existence.

This is exactly the message that fairy tales get across to the child in manifold form: that a struggle against severe difficulties in life is unavoidable, is an intrinsic part of human existence—but that if one does not shy away, but steadfastly meets unexpected and often unjust hardships, one masters all obstacles and at the end emerges victorious.

Modern stories written for young children mainly avoid these existential problems, although they are crucial issues for all of us. The child needs most particularly to be given suggestions in symbolic form about how he may deal with these issues and grow safely into maturity. "Safe" stories mention neither death nor aging, the limits to our existence, nor the wish for eternal life. The fairy tale, by contrast, confronts the child squarely with the basic human predicaments.

For example, many fairy stories begin with the death of a mother or father; in these tales the death of the parent creates the most agonizing problems, as it (or the fear of it) does in real life. Other stories tell about an aging parent who decides that the time has come to let the new generation take over. But before this can happen, the successor has to prove himself capable and worthy. The Brothers Grimm's story "The Three Feathers" begins: "There was once upon a time a king who had three sons. . . . When the king had become old and weak, and was thinking of his end, he did not know which of his sons should inherit the kingdom after him." In order to decide, the king sets all his sons a difficult task; the son who meets it best "shall be king after my death."

It is characteristic of fairy tales to state an existential dilemma briefly and pointedly. This permits the child to come to grips with the problem in its most essential form, where a more complex plot would confuse matters for him. The fairy tale simplifies all situations. Its figures are clearly drawn; and details, unless very important, are eliminated. All characters are typical rather than unique.

Contrary to what takes place in many modern children's stories, in fairy tales evil is as omnipresent as virtue. In practically every fairy tale good and evil are given body in the form of some figures and their actions, as good and evil are omnipresent in life and the propensities for both are present in every man. It is this duality which poses the moral problem, and requires the struggle to solve it.

Evil is not without its attractions—symbolized by the mighty giant or dragon, the power of the witch, the cunning queen in "Snow White"—and often it is temporarily in the ascendancy. In many fairy tales a usurper succeeds for a time in seizing the place which rightfully belongs to the hero—as the wicked sisters do in "Cinderella." It is not that the evildoer is punished at the story's end which makes immersing oneself in fairy stories an experience in moral education, although this is part of it. In fairy tales, as in life, punishment or fear of it is only a limited deterrent to crime. The conviction that crime does not pay is a much more effective deterrent, and that is why in fairy tales the bad person always loses out. It is not the fact that virtue wins out at the end which promotes morality, but that the hero is most attractive to the child, who identifies with the hero in all his struggles. Because of this identification the child imagines that he suffers with the hero his trials and tribulations, and triumphs with him as virtue is victorious. The child makes such identifications all on his own, and the inner and outer struggles of the hero imprint morality on him.

The figures in fairy tales are not ambivalent—not good and bad at the same time, as we all are in reality. But since polarization dominates the child's mind, it also dominates fairy tales. A person is either good or bad, nothing in between. One brother is stupid, the other is clever. One sister is virtuous and industrious, the others are vile and lazy. One is beautiful, the others are ugly. One parent is all good, the other evil. The juxtaposition of opposite characters is not for the purpose of stressing right behavior, as would be true for cautionary tales. (There are some amoral fairy tales where goodness or badness, beauty or ugliness play no role at all.) Presenting the polarities of character permits the child to comprehend easily the difference between the two, which he could not do as readily were the figures drawn more true to life, with all the complexities that characterize real people. Ambiguities must wait until a relatively firm personality has been established on the basis of positive identifications. Then the child has a basis for understanding that there are great differences between people, and that therefore one has to make choices about who one wants to be. This basic decision, on which all later personality development will build, is facilitated by the polarizations of the fairy tale.

Furthermore, a child's choices are based, not so much on right versus wrong, as on who arouses his sympathy and who his antipathy. The more simple and straightforward a good character, the easier it is for a child to identify with it and to reject the bad other. The child identifies with the good hero not because of his goodness, but because the hero's condition makes a deep positive appeal to him. The question for the child is not, "Do I want to be good?" but "Who do I want to be like?" The child decides this on the basis of projecting himself wholeheartedly into one character. If this fairy-tale figure is a very good person, then the child decides that he wants to be good, too.

Amoral fairy tales show no polarization or juxtaposition of good and bad persons; that is because these amoral stories serve an entirely different purpose. Such tales or type figures as "Puss in Boots," who arranges for the hero's success through trickery, and Jack, who steals the giant's treasure, build character not by promoting choices between good and bad, but by giving the child the hope that even the meekest can succeed in life. After all, what's the use of choosing to become a good person when one feels so insignificant that he fears he will never amount to anything? Morality is not the issue in these tales, but rather, assurance that one can succeed. Whether one meets life with a belief in the possibility of mastering its difficulties or with the expectation of defeat is also a very important existential problem.

The deep inner conflicts originating in our primitive drives and our violent emotions are all denied in much of modern children's literature, and so the child is not helped in coping with them. But the child is subject to desperate feelings of loneliness and isolation, and he often experiences mortal anxiety. More often than not, he is unable to express these feelings in words, or he can do so only by indirection: fear of the dark, of some animal, anxiety about his body. Since it creates discomfort in a parent to recognize these emotions in his child, the parent tends to overlook them, or he belittles these spoken fears out of his own anxiety, believing this will cover over the child's fears.

The fairy tale, by contrast, takes these existential anxieties and dilemmas very seriously and addresses itself directly to them: the need to be loved and the fear that one is thought worthless; the love of life, and the fear of death. Further, the fairy tale offers solutions in ways that the child can grasp on his level of understanding. For example, fairy tales pose the dilemma of wishing to live eternally by occasionally concluding: "If they have not died, they are still alive." The other ending—"And they lived happily ever after"—does not for a moment fool the child that eternal life is possible. But it does indicate that which alone can take the sting out of the narrow limits of our time on this earth: forming a truly satisfying bond to another. The tales teach that when one has done this, one has reached the ultimate in emotional security of existence and permanence of relation available to man; and this alone can dissipate the fear of death. If one has found true adult love, the fairy story also tells, one doesn't need to wish for eternal life. This is suggested by another ending found in fairy tales: They lived for a long time afterward, happy and in pleasure."

An uninformed view of the fairy tale sees in this type of ending an unrealistic wish-fulfillment, missing completely the important message it conveys to the child. These tales tell him that by forming a true interpersonal relation, one escapes the separation anxiety which haunts him (and which sets the stage for many fairy tales, but is always resolved at the story's ending). Furthermore, the story tells, this ending is not made possible, as the child wishes and believes, by holding on to his mother eternally. If we try to escape separation anxiety and death anxiety by desperately keeping our grasp on our parents, we will only be cruelly forced out, like Hansel and Gretel.

Only by going out into the world can the fairy tale hero (child) find himself there; and as he does, he will also find the other with whom he will be able to live happily ever after; that is, without ever again having to experience separation anxiety. The fairy tale is future-oriented and guides the child—in terms he can understand in both his conscious and his unconscious mind—to relinquish his infantile dependency wishes and achieve a more satisfying independent existence.

Today children no longer grow up within the security of an extended family, or of a well-integrated city. Therefore, even more than at the times fairy tales were invented, it is important to provide the modern child with images of heroes who have to go out into the world all by themselves and who, although originally ignorant of the ultimate things, find secure places in the world by following their right way with deep inner confidence.

The fairy tale hero proceeds for a time in isolation, as the modern child often feels isolated. The hero is helped by being in touch with primitive things—a tree, an animal, nature—as the child feels more in touch with those things than most adults do. The fate of these heroes convinces the child that, like them, he may feel outcast and abandoned in the world, groping in the dark, but, like them, in the course of his life he will be guided step by step, and given help when it is needed. Today, even more than in past times, the child needs the reassurance offered by the image of the isolated man who nevertheless is capable of achieving meaningful and rewarding relations with the world around him.

. . . .

From *The New York Times*, © January 12, 2009 The New York Times. All rights reserved. Used by permission and protected by the Copyright Laws of the United States. The printing, copying, redistribution, or transmission of the Material without express written permission is prohibited. (www.nytimes.com)

Are Fairytales Too Scary for Children?

By Lisa Belkin

Bedtime Stories

First came word that British Mums were no longer singing traditional lullabies and nursery rhymes to their children.

Now it seems that old-fashioned fairytales have fallen out of favor, too.

Of the 3,000 British parents polled by the TheBabyWebsite.com, earlier this month, 50 percent said they would not read fairy tales to their children until they were at least five years old. Of those, 20 percent said they rejected the oldies as politically incorrect, while close to that number, 17 percent, said the stories would give their children nightmares.

One in four prefer The Very Hungry Caterpillar, by Eric Carle, or the Gruffalo, by Julia Donaldson, to Rapunzel, which parents described as too dark, what with Dad locking the poor girl up in that tower, and Cinderella, which some parents reject as outdated because Ella is forced into a gender stereotype with all that housework. One in ten say that Snow White and the Seven Dwarfs should be re-titled because the preferred term is now "little people." And, while we're on the subject, why is Red Riding Hood allowed to walk alone in the woods?

My own question about these tales—Brother Grimm, Hans Christian Andersen, Disney (original and adapted)—has always been: where are the mothers? Cinderella, Snow White, Red Riding Hood, Rapunzel, Hansel and Gretel, Sleeping Beauty are all missing at least their Mom, and some of them have also lost Dad. And even as an adult I can't watch certain scenes in Bambi and Dumbo.

If my reactions are those of a overly sensitive Mama, others have more academic objections. A 2003 study out of Purdue University, analyzed how gender was portrayed in 168 Brother's Grimm fairytales. The short answer: not well. Longer answer: these stories give the message that unattractive people are evil, women can get by on their beauty, and you never see Princess Charming swooping in to rescue the Prince. In fact "Shrek" is the only tale for children in any of the annals where the ugly girl gets the guy. And don't even get the study's authors started on depictions of race. (And yes, Hermione turns out to be a brain and a beauty.)

If it is any consolation, a lot of the versions of the tales that we tell our children today, are actually sanitized forms of the originals. According to The List Universe, a site filled with this kind of triva, the Brothers Grimm version of Cinderella is a whole lot bloodier than the one you probably know. As described by the site:

> the nasty step-sisters cut off parts of their own feet in order to fit them
> into the glass slipper—hoping to fool the prince. The prince is alerted

to the trickery by two pigeons who peck out the step sister's eyes. They end up spending the rest of their lives as blind beggars while Cinderella gets to lounge about in luxury at the prince's castle.

It's the same with The Little Mermaid. The way Hans Christian Andersen wrote it,

the mermaid sees the prince marry a princess and she despairs. She is offered a knife with which to stab the prince to death, but rather than do that she jumps into the sea and dies by turning to froth. Hans Christian Andersen modified the ending slightly to make it more pleasant. In his new ending, instead of dying when turned to froth, she becomes a "daughter of the air" waiting to go to heaven—so, frankly, she is still dead for all intents and purposes.

But back to the poll of parents asking what they read to their children. Here is The Baby Website's list of the "TOP BEDTIME STORIES OF 2008":

1. The Very Hungry Caterpillar, Eric Carle (1969)
2. Mr. Men, Roger Hargreaves (1971)
3. The Gruffalo, Julia Donaldson (1999)
4. Winnie the Pooh, A.A. Milne (1926)
5. Aliens Love Underpants, Claire Freedman & Ben Cort (2007)
6. Thomas and Friends from The Railway Series, Rev. W. Awdry (1945)
7. The Wind in the Willows, Kenneth Grahame (1908)
8. What a Noisy Pinky Ponk!, Andrew Davenport (2008)
9. Charlie and Lola, Lauren Child (2001)
10. Goldilocks and the Three Bears, Robert Southey (1837)

And here is their list of the "TOP 10 FAIRY TALES WE NO LONGER READ":

1. Snow White and the Seven Dwarfs
2. Hansel and Gretel
3. Cinderella
4. Little Red Riding Hood
5. The Gingerbread Man
6. Jack and the Beanstalk
7. Sleeping Beauty
8. Beauty and the Beast

9.   Goldilocks and the Three Bears
10.   The Emperor's New Clothes

What do you read to your children at bedtime?

The Value of Fairy Tales in Education

In considering fairy tales for the little child, the first question which presents itself is, "Why are fairy stories suited to the little child, and what is their value for him?"

Fairy tales bring joy into a child's life. The mission of joy has not been fully preached, but we know that joy works toward physical health, mental brightness, and moral virtue. In the education of the future, happiness together with freedom will be recognized as the largest beneficent powers that will permit the individual of four, from his pristine, inexperienced self-activity, to become that final, matured, self-expressed, self-sufficient, social development—the educated man. Joy is the mission of art and fairy tales are art products. As such Pater would say, "For Art comes to you, proposing to give nothing but the highest quality to your moments as they pass, and simply for those moments' sake. Not the fruit of experience, but experience, is the end." Such quality came from the art of the fairy tale into the walk of a little girl, for whom even the much-tabooed topic of the weather took on a new, fresh charm. In answer to a remark concerning the day she replied, "Yes, it's not too hot, and not too cold, but just right." All art, being a product of the creative imagination, has the power to stimulate the creative faculties. "For Art, like Genius," says Professor Woodberry, "is common to all men, it is the stamp of the soul in them." All are creatures of imitation and combination; and the little child, in handling an art product, puts his thought through the artist's mould and gains a touch of the artist's joy.

Fairy tales satisfy the play spirit of childhood. Folk-tales are the product of a people in a primitive stage when all the world is a wonder-sphere. Most of our popular tales date from days when the primitive Aryan took his evening meal of yava and fermented mead, and the dusky Sudra roamed the Punjab. "All these fancies are pervaded with that purity by which children seem to us so wonderful," said William Grimm. "They have the same blue-white, immaculate bright eyes." Little children are in this same wonder-stage. They believe that the world about throbs with life and is peopled with all manner of beautiful, powerful folk. All children are poets, and fairy tales are the poetic recording of the facts of life. In this day of commercial enterprise, if we would fit children for life we must see to it that we do not blight the poets in them. In this day of emphasis on vocational training we must remember there is a part of life unfed, unnurtured, and unexercised by industrial education. Moreover, whatever will be accomplished in life will be the achievement of a free and vigorous life of the imagination. Before it was realized, everything new had existed in some trained imagination, fertile with ideas. The tale feeds the imagination, for the soul of it is a bit of play. It suits the child because in it he is not bound by the law of cause and effect, nor by the necessary relations of actual life. He is entirely in sympathy with a world where events follow as one may choose. He likes the mastership of the universe. And fairyland—where there is no time; where troubles fade; where youth abides; where things come out all right—is a pleasant place.

Furthermore, fairy tales are play forms. "Play," Richter says, "is the first creative utterance of man." "It is the highest form in which the native activity of childhood expresses itself," says Miss Blow. Fairy tales offer to the little child an opportunity for the exercise of that self-active inner impulse which seeks expression in two kinds of play, the symbolic activity of free play and the concrete presentation of types. The play, *The Light Bird,* and the tale, *The Bremen Town Musicians,* both offer an opportunity for the child to express that pursuit of a light afar off, a theme which appeals to childhood. The fairy tale, because it presents an organized form of human experience, helps to organize the mind and gives to play the values of human life. By contributing so largely to the play spirit, fairy tales contribute to that joy of activity, of achievement, of cooperation, and of judgment, which is the joy of all work. This habit of kindergarten play, with its joy and freedom and initiative, is the highest goal to be attained in the method of university work.

Fairy tales give the child a power of accurate observation. The habit of re-experiencing, of visualization, which they exercise, increases the ability to see, and is the contribution literature offers to nature study. In childhood acquaintance with the natural objects of everyday life is the central interest; and in its turn it furnishes those elements of experience upon which imagination builds. For this reason it is rather remarkable that the story, which is omitted from the Montessori system of education, is perhaps the most valuable means of effecting that sense-training, freedom, self-initiated play, repose, poise, and power of reflection, which are foundation stones of its structure.

Fairy tales strengthen the power of emotion, develop the power of imagination, train the memory, and exercise the reason. As emotion and imagination are considered in Chapter 11, in the section, "The Fairy Tale as Literature," and the training of the memory and the exercise of the reason in connection with the treatment of various other topics later on, these subjects will be passed by for the present. Every day the formation of habits of mind during the process of education is being looked upon with a higher estimate. The formation of habits of mind through the use of fairy tales will become evident during following chapters.

Fairy tales extend and intensify the child's social relations. They appeal to the child by presenting aspects of family life. Through them he realizes his relations to his own parents: their care, their guardianship, and their love. Through this he realizes different situations and social relations, and gains clear, simple notions of right and wrong. His sympathies are active for kindness and fairness, especially for the defenseless, and he feels deeply the calamity of the poor or the suffering and hardship of the ill-treated. He is in sympathy with that poetic justice which desires immediate punishment of wrong, unfairness, injustice, cruelty, or deceit. Through fairy tales he gains a many-sided view of life. Through his dramas, with a power of sympathy which has seemed universal, Shakespeare has given the adult world many types of character and conduct that are noble. But fairy tales place in the hands of childhood all that the thousands and thousands of the universe for ages have found excellent in character and conduct. They hold up for imitation all those cardinal virtues of love and self-sacrifice,—which is the ultimate criterion of character,—of courage, loyalty, kindness, gentleness, fairness, pity, endurance, bravery, industry, perseverance, and thrift. Thus fairy tales build up concepts of family life and of ethical standards, broaden a child's social sense of duty, and teach him to reflect. Besides developing his feelings and judgments, they also enlarge his world of experience.

In the school, the fairy tale as one form of the story is one part of the largest means to unify the entire work or play of the child. In proportion as the work of art, nature-study, game, occupation, etc., is fine, it will deal with some part of the child's everyday life. The good tale parallels life. It is a record of a portion of the race reaction to its environment; and being a permanent record of literature, it records experience which is universal and presents situations most human. It is therefore material best suited to furnish the child with real problems. As little children have their thoughts and observations directed mainly toward people and centered about the home, the fairy tale rests secure as the intellectual counterpart to those thoughts. As self-expression and self-activity are the great natural instincts of the child, in giving opportunity to make a crown for a princess, mould a clay bowl, decorate a tree, play a game, paint the wood, cut paper animals, sing a lullaby, or trip a dance, the tale affords many problems exercising all the child's accomplishments in the variety of his work. This does not make the story the central interest, for actual contact with nature is the child's chief interest. But it makes the story, because it is an organized experience marked by the values of human life, the unity of the child's return or reaction to his environment. The tale thus may bring about that "living union of thought and expression which dispels the isolation of studies and makes the child live in varied, concrete, active relation to a common world."

In the home fairy tales employ leisure hours in a way that builds character. Critical moments of decision will come into the lives of all when no amount of reason will be a sufficient guide. Mothers who cannot follow their sons to college, and fathers who cannot choose for their daughters, can help their children best to fortify their spirits for such crises by feeding them with good literature. This, when they are yet little, will begin the rearing of a fortress of ideals which will support true feeling and lead constantly to noble action. Then, too, in the home, the illustration of his tale may give the child much pleasure. For this is the day of fairy-tale art; and the child's satisfaction in the illustration of the well-known tale is limitless. It will increase as he grows older, as he understands art better, and as he becomes familiar with the wealth of beautiful editions which are at his command.

And finally, though not of least moment, fairy tales afford a vital basis for language training and thereby take on a new importance in the child's English. Through the fairy tale he learns the names of things and the meanings of words. One English fairy tale, The Master of all Masters, is a ludicrous example of the tale built on this very theme of names and meanings. Especially in the case of foreign children, in a tale of repetition, such as The Cat and the Mouse, Teeny Tiny, or The Old Woman and Her Pig, will the repetitive passages be an aid to verbal expression. The child learns to follow the sequence of a story and gains a sense of order. He catches the note of definiteness from the tale, which thereby clarifies his thinking. He gains the habit of reasoning to consequences, which is one form of a perception of that universal law which rules the world, and which is one of the biggest things he will ever come upon in life. Never can he meet any critical situation where this habit of reasoning to consequences will not be his surest guide in a decision. Thus fairy tales, by their direct influence upon habits of thinking, effect language training.

Fairy tales contribute to language training also by another form of that basic content which is furnished for reading. In the future the child will spend more time in the kindergarten and early first grade in acquiring this content, so that having enjoyed the real literature, when he reads later on he will be eager to satisfy his own desires. Then reading will take purpose for him and be accomplished almost without drill and practically with no effort. The reading book will gradually disappear as a portion of his literary heritage. In the kindergarten the child will learn the play forms, and in the first grade the real beginnings, of phonics and of the form of words in the applied science of spelling. In music he will learn the beginnings of the use of the voice. This will leave him free, when he begins reading later, to give attention to the thought reality back of the symbols. When the elements combining to produce good oral reading are cared for in the kindergarten and in the first grade, in the subjects of which they properly form a part, the child, when beginning to read, no longer will be needlessly diverted, his literature will contribute to his reading without interference, and his growth in language will become an improved, steady accomplishment.

CHAPTER

The Function of Form

The word "form," as it pertains to college writing, sometimes makes writing teachers uncomfortable because they are concerned that an emphasis on form will give students the idea that there is only one "right" way to structure an essay and that essay forms are fixed and absolute. These teachers want students to understand that organizational patterns should emerge from a writer's purpose, and they worry that focusing on form will stifle a writer's creativity. However, although we share this concern, we also think that an understanding of form can help writers organize their ideas and enable readers to understand what the writer is intending to say. Moreover, "form" does not necessarily stifle creativity, because it can be altered when a writer decides that an alteration would enhance communicative effectiveness.

In accord with the rhetorical and genre-based focus of this book, this chapter will emphasize that "form" is based on a number of factors—the content being developed, your teacher's expectations, the conventions of a particular discipline, and of course, your own purpose and the knowledge you have of your audience. On an essay exam, you might want to have a clearly stated thesis and easily discernible supporting points. But in other writing contexts, you may decide that this structure doesn't fit well with your writing goals. Remember that form, like other aspects of writing, is rhetorical, and its appropriateness depends on how well it suits your purpose.

THE RELATIONSHIP OF FORM TO CONTENT

In thinking about the concept of form, it is important to understand that the value of any formal features in an essay depends on their function, which, for many genres of college writing, is to have an impact on a rational, thoughtful audience. The "form" of any essay does not consist simply of a set of slots into which content is poured, because mechanical adherence to any form stifles creative thought and results in a boring, ineffective essay. Rather, the structure of your essay should reflect careful thinking about the relationship between form and function. Although it is important to be comfortable with the text structures that characterize established organizational patterns, you should not think of form as an end in itself. Think about how you want your text to "work"—how you want your intended audience to read what you have to say and how you can work with a form to make your essay effective.

FOR THINKING, DISCUSSION, AND WRITING

Briefly write about how form was taught in previous classes you have taken, perhaps in high school. How much do you think about form before, during, and after you write? Have you ever varied a prescribed form deliberately? Then share your responses with other students.

THE CLASSICAL FORM OF ARGUMENTATION

Some of your teachers may expect a particular essay structure that has been in existence since the time of the ancient Greeks, and therefore it is useful for you to become familiar with it, understand how it contributes to the development of your ideas, and utilize that understanding in your writing. The classical argumentative structure consists of an **introduction,** which states the thesis or claim; a **body,** which supports that claim and often addresses the opposing viewpoint; and a **conclusion,** which sums up the main ideas, perhaps restates the thesis, or affirms the importance of the topic. The components of this form, which are probably familiar to you, are outlined here.

1.   Introduction

In this section, which may consist of only one or two paragraphs, you indicate your topic, explain the rhetorical situation and the reason it is important to address this situation, and present your thesis or claim. The introduction may also include relevant background material. In some instances, it might summarize a viewpoint to which the body of the essay will respond, perhaps disagreeing entirely or indicating that it is limited in some way.

2.   The Body

The body of the essay consists of at least some of the following components:

- Further elaboration of the rhetorical situation
- Explanation of the problem, issue, or controversy
- Discussion of various viewpoints as a way of indicating that you understand the ideas of others and have researched the topic thoroughly

- Explanation of important key terms
- Support for your thesis
  This is usually the longest and most substantive section of the essay. It supports the thesis with compelling reasons and evidence that might include facts, statistics, data, statements by authorities, and illustrative examples. It may also establish common ground between you and your intended readers.
- Anticipation and refutation of opposing viewpoints
  In this section, you indicate areas where others will probably agree with your thesis, and then demonstrate that you are aware of areas where they are likely to disagree or where your ideas may differ in matters of degree or scope. Once you have indicated that you understand your other points of view, you can show the advantages of your perspective on the topic.

3. Conclusion

This section summarizes your main argument and perhaps suggests what action, if any, the readers ought to take. It may provide a sense of closure by restating the main thesis, postulating potential implications or consequences, or affirming the importance of the issues being addressed.

THE THESIS-FIRST STRUCTURE

Most of you have probably had experience with essays that use the form we have just outlined. In fact, some of you may feel you *must* use that form for school writing assignments, no matter what sort of writing you are doing, although you may not have considered *why* this should be the case. Has this form lasted simply because it was used in the past? Has it simply become a formula? Or are there sound reasons for using it that go beyond the constraints of tradition?

One reason that the classical structure continues to be used is that its placement of the thesis toward the beginning of the essay offers significant advantages to both writer and reader. A thesis with "because" clauses enables the writer to think about the entire argument in miniature, enabling him or her to predict and create structure. Placing the thesis up front also enables the writer to establish credibility, explain the rhetorical situation, and establish his or her perspective right from the beginning, involving the reader immediately. For the reader too, the thesis-first model also has advantages because it facilitates the efficient processing of information. By getting a clear sense of the main point of the essay and an overview of its structure, the reader will be able to understand immediately what direction the essay is likely to take and engage the issues with relative ease.

Ironically, although the classical form has been around for a long time and is associated with classical writers, it is particularly well suited for modern life, when many readers cannot afford the time to "hunt" for the main point in a text. Many of today's readers, both at the university and in the business world, are overwhelmed by the amount of reading they have to do, and consequently welcome the convenience of being able to predict where the thesis and main points in an essay will be located. An essay that does not establish its position and purpose early is sometimes frustrating to read. "Get to the point," readers are tempted to say. Depending on the context and type of essay, of course, an essay may be more interesting if the main point is not so obviously stated. But if one is in a hurry, being able to locate that statement easily can be very helpful.

Thesis-first writing is especially effective in composition programs that require students to prepare a portfolio of their work for evaluation at the end of the semester. Portfolio grading has many advantages for both students and teachers, but the process of grading many portfolios often requires evaluators to do a great deal of reading in a short period of time, and to understand what an essay is about very quickly. If your essays are going to be evaluated in this way, it is usually a good idea to utilize a thesis-first structure because it facilitates efficient reading.

The other advantage of the traditional form is that it provides a well-defined structure for the presentation of the writer's reasons and the support provided for those reasons. It thus provides a sense of order and expectation for both writer and reader, helping both the writer and the reader know how to structure supporting information. The advantages of the thesis-first form are summed up here.

ADVANTAGES OF THE THESIS-FIRST PLACEMENT

1. It enables the reader to know right away what the essay is about, thus facilitating the efficient processing of information.
2. It enables the writer to present an overview of the essay as a whole.
3. It provides the writer with an opportunity to address the opposing viewpoint and thus to grapple with the complexity of the topic.

ALTERNATIVES TO THE PLACEMENT OF THE THESIS

The advantages cited make the classical structure of argumentation a useful model, but there are times when you might wish to delay the presentation of your thesis until later in the essay. In some disciplines, essays begin with the posing of a problem and proceed to suggest a solution, which may occur toward the end of the essay. Some teachers may wish you to present evidence first and then see where that evidence leads, rather than beginning with a statement that must be proven.

For some topics and some audiences, it may be preferable to capture the audience's attention before making your position known. For example, you may be writing to an audience that is likely to be resistant to your point of view; in which case, you may wish to establish your credibility about the topic and indicate your understanding of the audience's position before presenting your main point. For such an audience, you may wish to write a Rogerian argument in which you first sketch out your audience's position and indicate that you understand it before you state points of disagreement. You might then place your thesis toward the end of the essay rather than at the beginning.

Generally though, it is easier to write essays using the thesis-first classical structure than it is to use the Rogerian model. So if you are unsure of your writing abilities or what your teacher expects, we would suggest using that form unless you have clear reasons for choosing an alternative.

SOME SUGGESTIONS FOR INTRODUCTIONS AND CONCLUSIONS

The Introduction

Some students have difficulty writing introductions because they have not clarified for themselves what they want to say. If you are having trouble—that is, your waste basket is filled with crumpled up pieces of paper, or you find yourself rephrasing the same sentence over and over again on the computer without making any progress—we suggest that you leave the introduction for later on and begin working on the middle of your paper, the place where you develop your supporting points and cite your evidence. Usually, once you have involved yourself sufficiently in the topic by developing several main points about it, the introduction will not be difficult to write.

Following are several suggestions you might find useful for writing an introduction:

1. Establish that a "problem" or "exigence" or some reason exists that is worth addressing in writing. It may take the form of an ongoing situation or condition, a plan that has failed, a proposal that is inadequate, etc. Your thesis or claim will then present another perspective. For example:

    How to get a baby to sleep through the night, or even sleep for several hours, has long been a problem for new parents. The inclination is to soothe a crying baby, no matter how often he or she may wake. And certainly, listening to a baby cry for an extended period is hard on the nerves and heartbreaking. Nevertheless, research on babies' sleep patterns suggests that it is important to teach a baby strategies for self-soothing, and the tendency for new parents to rush in and pick the baby up each time he or she cries is likely to result in many sleepless nights for everyone.

2. Establish that a controversy exists. Your thesis or claim will then indicate your position in the controversy. For example:

> At the Parent-Teacher Association meeting last week, a dispute broke out over whether all the children in the school should be required to wear school uniforms. Several of the parents were adamantly opposed to the idea, claiming that uniforms stifle children's creativity and self-expression. Others, however, felt that uniforms actually promote creativity because they eliminate children's preoccupation with clothing, leaving their minds free to explore other subjects. However, although it is probably impossible to determine whether uniforms stifle or promote creativity, they have an important advantage that neither group addressed adequately: Uniforms protect children from being mistaken for gang members, thus contributing to their safety. For this reason, school uniforms should be required for all students at the local high school.

3. Attract your reader with a thought-provoking or attention-getting statement or anecdote.

4. Briefly summarize the viewpoint that you wish to refute. Your thesis then is based on the distinction between your point of view and the point of view you are refuting.
    The beginning of the essay "Stop Banning Things at the Drop of a Rat" illustrates strategies three and four.

> In 1959, the nation experienced its first food related cancer scare: An official said that a chemical used on cranberries caused cancer in rodents. Panic ensued. Cranberry products were destroyed.
> **Whelan, Elizabeth M. "Stop Banning Things at the Drop of a Rat."**
> ***USA Today*, 19 October 1990. Print.**

These strategies can be helpful if you are having trouble getting started on an introduction. Keep in mind, though, that an introduction can utilize more than one strategy (as in those given) and that information you have about your reader can also influence the type of introduction you decide to write.

The Introduction and the "Although" Statement

Beginning with the ideas of an author whose ideas you wish to refute enables you to introduce your position using an "although" statement. That statement functions as a transitional sentence that distinguishes the writer's main idea from ideas that have already been proposed or are generally believed. The although statement is used when the writer states an existing point of view or proposal and then raises an objection to it, using the word "although," which naturally leads up to the thesis statement. In its essence, the "although" statement says the following:

Although something (another idea or proposal) may appear to be true (or good or beneficial or inevitable), the truth is actually something else—the writer's point. The word, *although,* indicates to the reader that what the writer has to say is superior to what has been said before. Following is an example:

> Multiculturalism—the notion that ethnic and cultural groups in the United States should preserve their identities instead of fusing them in a melting pot—has become a byword in education in Los Angeles and other cities. But now, educators . . . [are] worrying that past efforts to teach multiculturalism may have widened the ethnic divisions they were meant to close.
>
> **Bernstein, Sharon. "Multiculturalism: Building Bridges or Burning Them?"**
> ***Los Angeles Times* 30 November 1992. Print.**

The use of an "although" statement helps you think about the conversation to which the writer is responding, or as Gerald Graff and Cathy Birkenstein phrase it—to use the idea of "They Say, I Say." (*They Say, I Say: The Moves that Matter in Academic Writing.* W.W. Norton, 2006). For example, in an essay about whether students should wear uniforms to school, you might begin with a claim (They Say) that uniforms stifle students' individualism. Your idea (I Say) then might be that uniforms provide equality and eliminate competition over clothing. Below are a few commonly used ways to structure an introduction:

> Many students think that ---- However, I think that ------
> It is generally believed that ---- However, I believe that ------
> The well-known economist, Joe Smith, asserts that ---- However, other economists think
> ------

This way of thinking will help you sharpen the focus of your ideas and consider how your perspective contributes to an ongoing conversation.

Thinking about the Word "Although": How Much Do You Disagree?

Thinking in terms of what the word "although" means in an introduction to an essay doesn't mean that you must completely disagree with what others are saying. In fact, you might agree to a significant extent, but argue that there are other facets of the topic that need to be addressed. For example, in the paragraph below, authors Gary Null and Barbara Seaman, acknowledge that physical fitness is important and concern for appearance are important goals. But the thesis of the paragraph is that this concern is particularly difficult for women. Below is an example of this introductory move:

> Obesity and overeating have joined sex as central issues in the lives of many women today. In the United States, 50 percent of women are estimated to be

overweight. Every women's magazine has a diet column. Diet doctors and clinics flourish. The names of diet foods are now part of our general vocabulary. Physical fitness and beauty are every woman's goals. While this preoccupation with fat and food has become so common that we tend to take it for granted, being fat, feeling fat, and the compulsion to overeat are, in fact, serious and painful experiences for the women involved.

Gary Null and Barbara Seaman. *For Women Only:*
***Your Guide to Health Empowerment*. New York, 1999. 1065.**

The Conclusion

Like introductions, conclusions can also be problematic, particularly since writers sometimes lose patience by the time they get to the conclusion and are tempted to say, "Okay, I'm finished. This is all I have to say." Don't give in to that temptation, though, because conclusions are important, too. In fact, aside from the introduction, the conclusion is often what readers remember best. The conclusion is the place where you can direct the reader's attention back to the central problem discussed at the beginning of the paper, sum up your main thesis, and tie things together. Strong conclusions are usually concise and sometimes can be memorable, particularly if you can think of a thought-provoking or dramatic last sentence. Drama, though, is not the main requirement of the conclusion, so don't be concerned if you can't think of punchy concluding lines. Here are some suggestions you might find useful in writing a conclusion:

1. Return to the problem you discussed earlier

Since your thesis is likely to be concerned with a particular issue, it is sometimes useful to return to that issue in the conclusion to refocus your reader's attention on it. Perhaps you began with a specific example or a personal reference—if so, mention it again in the conclusion as a way of tying the essay together. Returning to something mentioned in your introduction can provide unity to your essay. In an essay titled, "Owls Are Not Threatened, Jobs Are," Randy Fitzgerald begins his essay by referring to a man named Donald Walker Jr., who received a letter from an environmental group forbidding him to cut down a single tree on his 200 acres of Oregon timberland. He then concludes his essay by referring to that example:

Spotted owls and logging are not incompatible—and Congress must take this controversy away from the courts and carve out a compromise that serves the national interest. "The reign of terror against private landowners must end," says Donald Walker, Jr.

Fitzgerald, Randy. "Owls Are Not Threatened, Jobs Are."
***Reader's Digest*, November 1992. Print.**

2. *Summarize your main points*

Conclusions frequently contain a summary of your main points, connecting them to your thesis. This is the place where you can restate your ideas, without having to provide additional explanation, since the body of the essay has already done that. Readers often find it helpful to conclude with a summary of main points, since it helps them remember what the essay was about.

3. *Direct your reader's attention to the implications and potential consequences of your ideas*

You might conclude your essay by showing how the issue you have discussed will impact society as a whole, thus widening the context of your discussion. A paper arguing in favor of bilingual education, for example, might conclude with a statement showing that the United States cannot afford to reduce a whole segment of society to a life of poverty because they are unable to speak English.

4. *Use an illustrative anecdote*

The significance of your thesis might be reinforced for your reader if you conclude with an illustrative anecdote or description. In an essay titled, "The New Immigrants," which argues against the idea that bilingual education will prevent young people from adjusting to American culture, James Fallows concludes with a reference to a young man originally named "Ramon" who, after having participated in a bilingual education program, wished his name to be spelled "Raymond," showing that Americanization occurs in spite of bilingual education. Here is how Fallows concludes his essay:

> Most of the young people I met—the rank and file, not the intellectuals who espouse a bilingual society—seemed fully willing to give what in Fuchs's view the nation asks. I remember in particular one husky Puerto Rican athlete at Miami Senior High School who planned to join the Navy after he got his diploma. I talked to him in a bilingual classroom, heard his story, and asked his name. He told me, and I wrote "Ramon." He came around behind me and looked at my pad. "No, no!" he told me. "You should have put R-A-Y-M-O-N-D."
> **Fallows, James. "The New Immigrants."** *Atlantic Monthly***, November 1980**

IMITATING STRUCTURAL MOVES

Although imitation is not emphasized a great deal in writing classes today, it was once considered an important strategy for helping students learn to write. The idea was that when students copied the work of established writers—imitating how other writers have written—they would develop awareness how other writers achieved their purpose. The idea of developing awareness is an underlying idea of this book, and we therefore suggest that imitation can be very useful for a developing writer. By paying attention to how other authors have structured their essays and thinking about connections between rhetorical moves and essay structure, you will gain insight into how to structure your own writing. Although we don't believe in the value of blind imitation or in the absoluteness of any text structure, we do believe that conscious attention to what other authors have done is valuable.

For an example of how imitation can help you decide on a particular structure for an essay, read the paragraph below from a student essay titled "From a Cat to a Lion:"

> "The difference between a successful person and others is not a lack of strength, not a lack of knowledge, but rather a lack of will" (Vincent T. Lombardi). This quotation pertains to comparisons people often make between four year universities and community colleges, with the university being the lion and the community college being the cat. In fact, community colleges are often referred to as "reject schools" or schools intended for the lower classes. This comparison, however, hides an important truth—that many people can transform themselves from a timid cat to a roaring lion by beginning higher education at a community college and working hard to achieve their educational goals. In today's rapidly changing world, community colleges provide equal opportunity for both academic and professional success, especially if a student has the will to succeed.
> **Prianka Heredia *Wings: A Collection of Student Essays*, Haydn McNeill 2012**

FOR THINKING, DISCUSSION, AND WRITING

To practice using imitation using structural moves, choose a topic about which you might wish to write. Then reread the paragraph above to figure out the pattern of the sentences with the goal of imitating that pattern. Below is an explanation of how each sentence is used in this paragraph:

1. The first sentence uses a quotation to begin the essay. To experiment with this structure, find a quotation you might like to use. Below are a few possibilities, and you can find many others on the Internet:

"When people ask me to compare the 20th century to older civilizations, I always say the same thing: the situation is normal.'"

Will Durant

"A good teacher, like a good entertainer first must hold his audience's attention. Then he can teach his lesson."

John Henrik Clarke

"You can get help from teachers, but you are going to have to learn a lot by yourself, sitting alone in a room."

Dr. Seuss

"Food is a central activity of mankind and one of the single most significant trademarks of a culture."

Mark Kurfansky, "Choice Cuts" (2002)

"In the Middle Ages, they had guillotines, stretch racks, whips and chains. Nowadays, we have a much more effective torture device called the bathroom scale."

Stephen Phillips

2. The second sentence applies the quotation to an idea that many people think is true. You can imitate this pattern by filling in the blank in the sentence below:

   This quotation pertains to _____.

3. The third sentence illustrates that statement. You can imitate this pattern by filling in the blank in the sentence below:

   However, _____

4. The fourth sentence provides an illustrative example of the idea in the third sentence. You can imitate this pattern by filling in the blank below:

   In fact, _____

5. The fifth sentence refutes the ideas in sentences 2, 3, and 4. You can imitate this pattern by filling in the blank below:

   This idea, actually, hides/emphasizes an important truth that _____ _____.

6. The last sentence in the paragraph is the thesis statement. Write yours and compare the paragraph you have written with those of other students. It does not matter if you have not imitated the pattern exactly. But analyzing how it works will enable you to think about how you might apply and vary that pattern in your own writing.

An important qualification: Imitating how other writers have structured their ideas is a type of **pattern practice** that can help you understand possibilities for structure. However, in encouraging you to use imitation in this way, our goal is to raise your consciousness about how various patterns "work." We do not advocate slavish imitation, nor do we believe that there is only one way to structure an essay.

STRATEGIES FOR CREATING STRUCTURE USING AN OUTLINE

Some writers create structure by writing a formal outline before beginning to write, complete with multi-layered subheadings down to the smallest detail, and if that system works for you, by all means continue to use it. Other writers object to the idea of a preplanned outline, claiming that the imposition of a formal structure is unrealistic since writers often discover ideas as they write; moreover, they feel that too much planning inhibits the creative impulse. Such writers do little advance planning on paper—once they know what their preliminary thesis is, they simply begin to write and see what develops, creating a concept of structure as they go along.

Unless you have already developed a system that works for you, our recommendation is to take the middle ground—that is, once you have a fairly clear idea of what position you wish to develop, that you then write down your main points and jot down possible examples and supporting pieces of evidence, thus giving you something to refer to as you write. Creating an informal outline such as this will give you an opportunity to think through your main ideas before actually beginning to write and to gain a sense of the preliminary structure of your paper, enabling you to see what may be weak, missing, or disproportionately emphasized. Once you have created an outline, it can serve as a guideline for proceeding and indicate to you where your paper might need additional research, development, or balance. However, because it only involves noting ideas, it will not absorb as much time as creating a formal outline.

ORGANIZING YOUR MAIN POINTS

Most writers prefer to organize subsections of their essays so as to parallel the overall structure of the essay as a whole—that is, they use a deductive structure for each of their major points, stating a point, supporting that point, stating the next point, supporting that point, etc. On the other hand, for variation and for calling attention to a point you wish to emphasize, you may wish to use an inductive structure, presenting facts or observations and leading your readers to make discoveries for themselves.

When considering possibilities for arrangement, one possibility is to consider which of your points is most important or compelling and discuss that point first. Readers often pay most attention to points presented at the beginning of a text, and if you present your most significant point first, it is likely to have the most profound impact on your reader. You can then develop your major points in descending order of importance, ultimately reminding your reader of your most important point when you refute the opposition and perhaps in your conclusion as well.

In an essay entitled "Living Under a Veil of Denial" (*Los Angeles Times* 1992) Alfee Enciso argues a position about racism through the following main points:

1. Racism is promoted through magazines, television, shoes, and billboards.
2. Racism is implicit in the ideal of beauty that young men and women adopt as a standard.
3. Racism is implicit in a number of ways such as confusing two people for the same one, assuming that two black people know each other, believing that all black people share the same ideology, viewing black people as unfortunate, or suspecting black students of being thieves.

His main point, though, is that racism is everywhere because it is promoted through the media; therefore, he presents that point as his first one.

Sometimes you might wish to save your most important point for last. In an essay titled, "Four-Letter Words Can Hurt You," Barbara Lawrence makes the point that the reason four-letter words are considered taboo is not simply because of sexual hang-ups, but because they refer to women as body parts, thereby denying them their humanity. However, before she states that point, she discusses the origin of many of these forbidden words and, therefore, establishes their origin in violent sadistic acts. In that essay, the author has built up to her most important point, saving it for last.

SIGNPOSTING IDEAS

No matter what order of presentation you decide on, your essay will not hold together unless you link each point to your main thesis through signposts or "cueing devices." Signposts remind your reader of how each point supports the main point of the essay, review where the essay has been, indicates where it is going, and keeps the reader from getting lost. Most readers can focus on only a limited amount of information at any one time; therefore, signposts or cueing devices help readers understand how the essay is structured so they will not become confused.

The simplest method of signposting is to say simply, "this is my first point; this is my second; etc." Less obvious signposts do not announce their presence so explicitly, but instead smooth the transition between ideas. Alfee Enciso uses a signpost by beginning his fourth paragraph with a reference back to an idea from his third paragraph, in which he discussed his own background in race relations. Here is how Enciso moves into his fourth paragraph:

> *Despite my race-relations credentials,* none of these particulars, whether isolated or bunched together, can stand up to one undeniable fact: I am an American, born and raised. To be an American is to be racist.

Signposting can be achieved through transitional words and phrases such as *however, nonetheless, therefore, moreover, additionally, nevertheless,* and many others. Here are some transitional devices that are frequently used for signposting:

- To establish cause and effect: Therefore, thus, as a result, consequently
- To show similarity: Similarly, in the same way
- To show difference: However, on the contrary, but, despite that
- To elaborate: Moreover, furthermore, in addition, finally
- To explain or present examples: For example, for instance, such as, in particular

Signposting can also be achieved through transitional paragraphs that act as a link between two ideas and prepare the reader for a new topic or indicate a forthcoming order of ideas. Here is an example of a transitional paragraph:

> But too many of those who are worried about health care have let our fear overshadow our reason. In particular, I believe four major issues should be considered in decisions about this important issue . . .

The essay would then discuss each of these issues.

USING A FUNCTION OUTLINE

A useful way to ensure that your essay is well-structured is to analyze a text using a *function outline*. A function outline consists of brief statements about how each paragraph functions within an essay in terms of its relationship either to the thesis or to one of its supporting points; its purpose is to focus on thesis development and coherence and to initiate revision. Function outlines may be written either on a separate sheet of paper, such as a Function Outline Worksheet, or in the margins of the text itself.

For an example of how a function outline works, read the article "Brother, Don't Spare a Dime" by L. Christopher Awalt. It can be found online at http://www.newsweek.com/brother-dont-spare-dime-203574. Then note how the article can be analyzed using a Function Outline.

FUNCTION OUTLINE WORKSHEET

Steps for Writing a Function Outline

1. Number all the paragraphs in your essay.
2. Highlight or underline the thesis statement. Write the thesis statement below.
    Thesis Statement: The group most responsible for the homeless being the way they are is the homeless themselves.
3. Skim the essay, highlighting the main supporting points. Briefly summarize these points below.

    First Main Point: There are many people who are only temporarily homeless. They work hard to get off the street and are usually homeless only for a short time.

    Second Main Point: The real problem are the homeless who actually choose the streets. They "enjoy the freedom and consider begging a minor inconvenience. These people may suffer from mental illness, alcoholism, poor education, or laziness."

    Third Main Point: Cites the example of a man the author tried to help. Despite the best of help, the man was back on the street a month later.

    Fourth Main Point: Suggests that those who don't believe him offer work to those who are begging.

    Fifth Main Point: The solution to homelessness must include some notion of self-reliance and individual responsibility.
4. Go through the essay, paragraph by paragraph, noting how each one functions to support the main point of the essay. Does the paragraph develop a main supporting point? Does it provide background material? Is it an example? Does it present a counter argument? Locate specific words or cueing devices in the paragraph that

refer back to the thesis and remind the reader of the main point to be developed. If cueing devices do not appear, think about what material you might want to add.

Paragraph #1 Establishes that homelessness is a problem, a danger to public safety.

Paragraph #2 Discusses various explanations for homelessness and establishes a thesis.

Paragraph #3 Establishes the credibility of the writer based on his own experience.

Paragraph #4 Qualifies that not every homeless person is on the street because he or she wants to be. There are exceptions.

Paragraph #5 Establishes that the homeless who try to get off the street are not the real problem.

Paragraph #6 Makes the point that many of the homeless actually prefer to be on the street.

Paragraph #7 Cites example of the man he tried to help.

Paragraph #8 Refers to his example to emphasize his point that society was not to blame for this man's failure. He had only himself to blame.

Paragraph #9 Anticipates objection that his experience was merely anecdotal. Advises readers to try to offer a homeless person work.

Paragraph #10 Points out that solutions are not easy. Indicates the implications of the thesis—any solution must include some notion of self-reliance and individual responsibility.

5. Are there places in the paragraph that seem to head in another, perhaps related, direction? If so, can these sections be refocused or do you wish to modify the thesis to accommodate a potential new direction?

   The author skips over the effect that drug and alcohol addiction and mental illness can have on a person's ability to take responsibility for him or herself. The idea of blame usually is associated with that of choice. These people may not really have a choice.

6. Having worked through the entire essay, note which areas of the paper need modification or elaboration. Do you feel that the thesis statement should be modified in any way? If so, what new cueing and support would be needed?

   The author needs to define more carefully what he means by "blame." He also should discuss the problems posed by alcohol and drug addiction as well as mental illness. Basing the argument on only one example also weakens the argument.

ANALYZING A TEXT USING A FUNCTION OUTLINE

A well-known document that adheres almost perfectly to the classical form of argumentation is *The Declaration of Independence.* Use a function outline to analyze that text. Then respond to the following questions:

1. What is the thesis or claim?
2. How does Jefferson establish credibility?
3. What form of reasoning is used?
4. In which sections does Jefferson address the opposing viewpoint?

THE USE OF NARRATIVE AND DESCRIPTION IN ARGUMENTATION

Narrative and description are sometimes viewed as unimportant in writing an argument essay because they are more often associated with fiction. However, if you consider the goal of argumentative writing, you will recognize that narration and description can also be used to fulfill an argumentative purpose. Certainly, when you are writing a formal argument, you can use narrative and description to enliven your writing and attract the attention of your reader. Specific narrative examples and lively descriptions provide far more interesting reading than do broad generalizations.

Narrative or descriptive examples are also useful for introducing a topic. Remember, though, to link such examples firmly to your thesis and to do so within the first few paragraphs. Anticipate the reaction of impatient readers who might be tempted to say "Okay. Get to the point already." Do not become so enthralled with the narrative itself that you forget about establishing and supporting a position.

USING "I"

In some disciplines, it is absolutely forbidden for students to use the pronoun "I" in formal argumentation, and this restriction may pertain to the writing you do for some of your college courses. You may, in fact, be under the impression that the rule is absolute, which it isn't. Actually, the prohibition against using "I" in academic writing has undergone considerable modification over the past several years and continues to change.

Whether you should use "I" will depend on what is required in your particular discipline or for a specific assignment. But like all writing, it depends on your purpose. If the use of "I" enhances the effectiveness of your essay, then you should certainly use it. For example, if you have had personal experience with the topic you are writing about, the use of the first person can lend vividness and immediacy to your writing by enabling the reader to experience the incident through your own eyes. You might also want to use the first person if you are writing about a subject in which your own firsthand experience renders you an expert. Topics concerned with the experiences of a college student, for example, are often based on personal experience, so it would be perfectly appropriate for you to use the first person in writing about them. If you decide to use the first person, be able to explain your reason for doing so. Do not, for example, use it in your thesis statement stating simply, "I do not think this is right," or "In my opinion, this idea is false." A reader might respond by saying, "Why should I listen to your opinion?" or "Why should I care what you think?" Unless you are an expert on your topic because you, yourself, have firsthand experience that supports your main point, the fact that you have a particular opinion or endorse a particular idea will have little impact on a reader.

Here is an example of how first person narrative can be used to introduce a topic and establish the writer's credibility. In this case, the writer has had direct personal experience that renders him qualified to use it:

> I am a writing teacher at a university. I teach courses in writing and rhetoric to both graduates and undergraduates. I write books and articles, and I present papers at academic conferences. However, I do not own a red pen; I refuse to mark grammatical errors on students' papers, and I am not horrified by incorrect punctuation. And yet, whenever I meet new people and mention my profession, someone invariably says, "Uh oh. I better watch my grammar!"

> We who teach college writing need to help people (and especially students) understand that good writing is not just "correct" writing—that writing is about communicating ideas, and that when teachers put too much emphasis on grammatical correctness, students' ideas die an early death. Fearing the dreaded red pen, students sit frozen at their computer screens, afraid to write anything more complicated than a simple sentence. This is not what writing is.

EXERCISE

INFORMAL VERSUS FORMAL ARGUMENTATION

Using the first person, write an informal two-page essay about some aspect of college life that you think needs to be changed—some suggestions: The parking area, the registration system, the computer facilities, the food in the cafeteria, the condition of the residence halls. Then rewrite your essay as a formal argument addressed to a university official. What differences can you detect between the two essays in terms of narrative and description?

WRITING ASSIGNMENT

Read "A Culture of Cruelty" and "Brother, Don't Spare a Dime" in Chapter 5 and decide which point of view you agree with most. Then respond to the following questions:

1. What strategies for introducing the topic are used in each essay?
2. What strategies for concluding are used in each essay?
3. Write an essay of 3–5 pages that responds to one or another of these essays. In your introduction, you might lead into your thesis by referring to the position with which you *disagree.*

The Declaration of Independence, Thomas Jefferson

1. What is the thesis of the Declaration?
2. What reasons are cited for the thesis in the Declaration?
3. How do the authors of the Declaration establish credibility?
4. How is the Declaration similar to the classical form of argumentation? How is it different?

IN CONGRESS, JULY 4, 1776
The Unanimous Declaration of the Thirteen United States of America

When in the Course of human events it becomes necessary for one people to dissolve the political bands which have connected them with another and to assume among the powers of the earth, the separate and equal station to which the Laws of Nature and of Nature's God entitle them, a decent respect to the opinions of mankind requires that they should declare the causes which impel them to the separation.

We hold these truths to be self-evident, that all men are created equal, that they are endowed by their Creator with certain unalienable Rights, that among these are Life, Liberty and the pursuit of Happiness.—That to secure these rights, Governments are instituted among Men, deriving their just powers from the consent of the governed,—That whenever any Form of Government becomes destructive of these ends, it is the Right of the People to alter or to abolish it, and to institute new Government, laying its foundation on such principles and organizing its powers in such form, as to them shall seem most likely to effect their Safety and Happiness. Prudence, indeed, will dictate that Governments long established should not be changed for light and transient causes; and accordingly all experience hath shewn that mankind are more disposed to suffer, while evils are sufferable than to right themselves by abolishing the forms to which they are accustomed. But when a long train of abuses and usurpations, pursuing invariably the same Object evinces a design to reduce them under absolute Despotism, it is their right, it is their duty, to throw off such Government, and to provide new Guards for their future security—Such has been the patient sufferance of these Colonies; and such is now the necessity which constrains them to alter their former Systems of Government. The history of the present King of Great Britain is a history of repeated injuries and usurpations, all having in direct object the establishment of an absolute Tyranny over these States. To prove this, let Facts be submitted to a candid world.

He has refused his Assent to Laws, the most wholesome and necessary for the public good.

He has forbidden his Governors to pass Laws of immediate and pressing importance, unless suspended in their operation till his Assent should be obtained; and when so suspended, he has utterly neglected to attend to them.

He has refused to pass other Laws for the accommodation of large districts of people, unless those people would relinquish the right of Representation in the Legislature, a right inestimable to them and formidable to tyrants only.

He has called together legislative bodies at places unusual, uncomfortable, and distant from the depository of their Public Records, for the sole purpose of fatiguing them into compliance with his measures.

He has dissolved Representative Houses repeatedly, for opposing with manly firmness his invasions on the rights of the people.

He has refused for a long time, after such dissolutions, to cause others to be elected, whereby the Legislative Powers, incapable of Annihilation, have returned to the People at large for their exercise; the State remaining in the mean time exposed to all the dangers of invasion from without, and convulsions within.

He has endeavoured to prevent the population of these States; for that purpose obstructing the Laws for Naturalization of Foreigners; refusing to pass others to encourage their migrations hither, and raising the conditions of new Appropriations of Lands.

He has obstructed the Administration of Justice by refusing his Assent to Laws for establishing Judiciary Powers.

He has made Judges dependent on his Will alone for the tenure of their offices, and the amount and payment of their salaries.

He has erected a multitude of New Offices, and sent hither swarms of Officers to harass our people and eat out their substance.

He has kept among us, in times of peace, Standing Armies without the Consent of our legislatures.

He has affected to render the Military independent of and superior to the Civil Power.

He has combined with others to subject us to a jurisdiction foreign to our constitution, and unacknowledged by our laws; giving his Assent to their Acts of pretended Legislation:

For quartering large bodies of armed troops among us:

For protecting them, by a mock Trial from punishment for any Murders which they should commit on the Inhabitants of these States:

For cutting off our Trade with all parts of the world:

For imposing Taxes on us without our Consent:

For depriving us in many cases, of the benefit of Trial by Jury:

For transporting us beyond Seas to be tried for pretended offences:

For abolishing the free System of English Laws in a neighbouring Province, establishing therein an Arbitrary government, and enlarging its Boundaries so as to render it at once an example and fit instrument for introducing the same absolute rule into these Colonies.

For taking away our Charters, abolishing our most valuable Laws and altering fundamentally the Forms of our Governments:

For suspending our own Legislatures, and declaring themselves invested with power to legislate for us in all cases whatsoever.

He has abdicated Government here, by declaring us out of his Protection and waging War against us.

He has plundered our seas, ravaged our coasts, burnt our towns, and destroyed the lives of our people.

He is at this time transporting large Armies of foreign Mercenaries to compleat the works of death, desolation, and tyranny, already begun with circumstances of Cruelty & Perfidy scarcely paralleled in the most barbarous ages, and totally unworthy the Head of a civilized nation.

He has constrained our fellow Citizens taken Captive on the high Seas to bear Arms against their Country, to become the executioners of their friends and Brethren, or to fall themselves by their Hands.

He has excited domestic insurrections amongst us, and has endeavoured to bring on the inhabitants of our frontiers, the merciless Indian Savages whose known rule of warfare, is an undistinguished destruction of all ages, sexes and conditions.

In every stage of these Oppressions We have Petitioned for Redress in the most humble terms: Our repeated Petitions have been answered only by repeated injury. A Prince, whose character is thus marked by every act which may define a Tyrant, is unfit to be the ruler of a free people.

Nor have We been wanting in attentions to our British brethren. We have warned them from time to time of attempts by their legislature to extend an unwarrantable jurisdiction over us. We have reminded them of the circumstances of our emigration and settlement here. We have appealed to their native justice and magnanimity, and we have conjured them by the ties of our common kindred to disavow these usurpations, which would inevitably interrupt our connections and correspondence. They too have been deaf to the voice of justice and of consanguinity. We must, therefore, acquiesce in the necessity, which denounces our Separation, and hold them, as we hold the rest of mankind, Enemies in War, in Peace Friends.

We, therefore, the Representatives of the united States of America, in General Congress, Assembled, appealing to the Supreme Judge of the world for the rectitude of our intentions, do, in the Name, and by Authority of the good People of these Colonies, solemnly publish and declare, That these united Colonies are, and of Right ought to be Free and Independent States, that they are Absolved from all Allegiance to the British Crown, and that all political connection between them and the State of Great Britain, is and ought to be totally dissolved; and that as Free and Independent States, they have full Power to levy War, conclude Peace, contract Alliances, establish Commerce, and to do all other Acts and Things which Independent States may of right do.—And for the support of this Declaration, with a firm reliance on the protection of Divine Providence, we mutually pledge to each other our Lives, our Fortunes, and our sacred Honor.

—John Hancock

New Hampshire:
    Josiah Bartlett, William Whipple, Matthew Thornton

Massachusetts:
    John Hancock, Samuel Adams, John Adams, Robert Treat Paine, Elbridge Gerry

Rhode Island:
    Stephen Hopkins, William Ellery

Connecticut:
    Roger Sherman, Samuel Huntington, William Williams, Oliver Wolcott

New York:
William Floyd, Philip Livingston, Francis Lewis, Lewis Morris

New Jersey:
Richard Stockton, John Witherspoon, Francis Hopkinson, John Hart, Abraham Clark

Pennsylvania:
Robert Morris, Benjamin Rush, Benjamin Franklin, John Morton, George Clymer, James Smith, George Taylor, James Wilson, George Ross

Delaware:
Caesar Rodney, George Read, Thomas McKean

Maryland:
Samuel Chase, William Paca, Thomas Stone, Charles Carroll of Carrollton

Virginia:
George Wythe, Richard Henry Lee, Thomas Jefferson, Benjamin Harrison, Thomas Nelson, Jr., Francis Lightfoot Lee, Carter Braxton

North Carolina:
William Hooper, Joseph Hewes, John Penn

South Carolina:
Edward Rutledge, Thomas Heyward, Jr., Thomas Lynch, Jr., Arthur Middleton

Georgia:
Button Gwinnett, Lyman Hall, George Walton

FUNCTION OUTLINE WORKSHEET

A Function Outline consists of brief statements about how each paragraph functions within an essay in terms of its relationship either to the thesis or to one of its supporting points; the purpose of writing a Function Outline is to focus attention on thesis development and coherence and to initiate revision. Function outlines may be written either in the margins of the essay itself or on a separate sheet of paper, such as the Function Outline Worksheet below:

Steps for Writing a Function Outline

1. Number all the paragraphs in your essay.

2.   Highlight or underline the thesis statement. Write the thesis statement below.

Thesis Statement:

_____

_____

3.   Skim the essay, highlighting the main supporting points. Briefly summarize these points below.

First Main Point _____

Second Main Point _____

Third Main Point _____

Fourth Main Point _____

Fifth Main Point _____

4.   Go through the essay, paragraph by paragraph, noting how each one functions to support the main point of the essay. As you read, think about the following questions: Does the paragraph develop a main supporting point? Does it provide background material? Is it an example? Does it present a counter argument? Locate specific words or cueing devices in the paragraph that refer back to the thesis and remind the reader of the main point to be developed. If cueing devices do not appear, think about what material you might want to add.

Other questions to consider: Are there places in the paragraph that seem to head in another, perhaps related, direction. If so, can these sections be refocused or do you wish to modify the thesis to accommodate a potential new direction?

In the space below, indicate the function of each paragraph in your essay.

Paragraph #1 _____

_____

Paragraph #2 _____

_____

Paragraph #3 _____

_____

Paragraph #4 _____

_____

Paragraph #5 _____

_____

Paragraph #6 _____

_____

5. Having worked through the entire essay, note which areas of the paper need modification or elaboration. Do you feel that the thesis statement should be modified in any way? If so, what new cueing and support would be needed?

8

CHAPTER

The Nature of Proof

The advertisement for Hibiscus Haze at the beginning of this book makes a number of claims that need further clarification and substantiation. The phrase, "made with natural ingredients," doesn't define what the word "natural" means or explain why natural ingredients are better, and the sentence, "If you haven't used it, ask someone who has and you will understand" also raises questions, one of which might be "who" one should ask and what sort of understanding will result. Hibiscus Haze, of course, is an advertisement, and claims of this type are often used in this genre, because their goal is to call attention to a product and generate an emotional response. However, the goal of most college essays is to have an impact on a rational audience, people who base their decisions on reliable information, on ideas that seem believable and logically presented, and on the credibility of the writer. Although we now recognize that what is considered credible and logical may vary according to culture and that rational response is often entwined with emotional factors, most college writing will require you to support or prove your claim using credible evidence. Even if you have a fluent writing style and have developed an effective structure, your essay will not achieve its purpose if you do not support your thesis or claim with compelling reasons.

This chapter is concerned with several strategies used in college writing to support a claim, focusing on three types of appeal: Appeal to logic and reason (logos), appeal to the character of the writer (ethos), and appeal to the feelings of the audience (pathos). It will emphasize the importance of appealing to people's understanding and common sense through logic and reason (logos) and discuss Aristotelian and Toulmin logic. This chapter also includes a section on logical fallacies.

THE IMPORTANCE OF REASON

Because academic argument is written for an audience that is presumed rational, reason is an important element in an argumentative essay. We would like to clarify, however, that we used the phrase "presumed rational" in the last sentence because even rational people are not rational all the time and don't always make rational decisions. For instance, if, during a school election, someone makes the claim that Jennifer is a good candidate for school president but cites no reasons in support of that statement, the rational response would be for no one to vote for her. But some students, even those who are usually rational, might not base their choice of candidate completely on rationality and might decide to vote for Jennifer anyway—maybe because she has long hair or because she can whistle tunes through a straw or just because they like her.

You may be wondering, then, why you should appeal to your reader primarily on the basis of reason, rather than emotion, if people are not always rational. Wouldn't a well-crafted emotionally charged appeal be more effective in convincing an audience? The response is that arguments written in college, *by definition,* are intended for a rational audience. This assumption means that you must use good reasons to support your thesis, even if you think you could write an equally convincing essay simply on the basis of your own expertise on the topic or because the topic lends itself to some emotionally charged examples that are likely to appeal to your readers' feelings.

This requirement that a writer must include well-developed reasons in support of a thesis is a primary characteristic of college writing genres that distinguishes them from other genres, even those with the similar goal of having an impact on an audience. For example, a famous runner might write a letter to a school coach endorsing a particular brand of running shoes without citing any reasons for his choice, and the coach might decide to buy that brand for the school team, simply on the basis of the credibility, or ethos, of the writer. Or a concerned member of a community might address a letter to a charitable organization describing a lonely puppy, whimpering for its mother in an animal shelter, and the organization might decide to donate money to the shelter, simply on the basis of that emotional appeal (pathos). But even though both letters might achieve their desired goals of affecting an audience, neither the letter to the team nor the appeal to the charitable organization can be considered appropriate academic arguments if they don't include clearly stated reasons. In fact, a coach who thinks critically might want to know why a particular brand of shoe is supposed to be "better" for a school team, even if it is endorsed by a famous runner. Similarly, there are a number of shelters that care for abandoned puppies. Before sending money, a donor might wish to find out something more about the particular shelter—who is in charge, how it is maintained, how the money is spent. Some charities allot large salaries to administrators and don't use much of its donations for the cause for which the charity is intended. College writers are critical thinkers, and critical thinkers base their decisions on logical reasons.

Here are some examples of how reasons are used to support a claim in the genre of argument:

Jon's claim:	Jon is a college student who wishes to transfer from State College to Northern College.
Claim:	Northern College is a better choice for me than State.
	Reason 1: Northern College offers programs in environmental studies.
	Reason 2: Northern College offers small classes.
	Reason 3: Northern College fosters close interaction between professors and students.
Opposing Claim:	State College is a better choice for Jon than Northern. (This is Jon's Aunt Maria's idea)
	Reason 1: State College offers a good program in business.
	Reason 2: State College has a good reputation.
	Reason 3: Aunt Maria has a degree from State College and has had a successful professional life.
Claim:	Colleges should have speech codes restricting sexist or racist speech.
	Reason 1: Unlimited free speech can be devastating to those injured by it.
	Reason 2: Speech codes are needed to prevent racist and sexist remarks.
	Reason 3: It is the function of higher education to help students refrain from hurtful remarks about other groups.
Opposing Claim:	Colleges should not have speech codes restricting sexist or racist speech.
	Reason 1: Speech codes are an infringement on First Amendment rights.
	Reason 2: Speech codes cannot prevent racist or sexist thinking.
	Reason 3: Colleges should be concerned with learning not with dictating codes of behavior.

EXERCISE

Read "The Case for Torture" by Michael Levin at the end of this chapter. What is Levin's claim? What reasons does Levin cite in support of his claim?

THE TRADITION OF REASON

In his *Rhetoric,* the Greek philosopher, Aristotle, defined three approaches to argumentation: *Ethos* (Greek for "character"), which refers to the trustworthiness or credibility of the writer or speaker; *pathos* (Greek for "emotion"), which refers to the emotional appeal of an argument so that it affects the reader's feelings; and *logos* (Greek for "word"), which refers to the internal consistency of the argument, in particular the logic of its reasons and the quality of the supporting evidence. Aristotle claimed that all three of these components are important, but he gave particular emphasis to the role of reason.

THE RELATIONSHIP BETWEEN INDUCTIVE AND DEDUCTIVE REASONING

Inductive and deductive reasoning are both used in college writing genres which aim to convince readers that an idea is worth considering. They are often distinguished from one another, but they are also closely related. An inductive argument is based on a number of examples from which the writer has drawn a conclusion. For example, suppose you had made several trips to a tropical island and each time had gotten sick when you had eaten a yellow fruit with purple spots. Later on, you learn that other travelers have also gotten sick from this fruit. Based on this information, you would probably conclude that this fruit can make people sick. Induction thus moves from **specific examples** to a **generalization** based on examples. Therefore, if you say, "Yellow fruit with purple spots makes people sick," you have made a claim based on induction.

Having drawn this conclusion, let us now suppose that you travel once again to the same tropical island. But this time, when someone offers you a piece of yellow fruit with purple spots, you immediately turn it down, based on the idea that it will make you sick. In this case, you have applied a general principle (yellow fruits with purple spots make people sick) to a specific example (this particular piece of yellow fruit with purple spots will make me sick), thereby making a claim based on deduction. A deductive argument is based on a **general principle that is applied to a specific case**. But the general principle *originated* through inductive reasoning.

INDUCTIVE REASONING

Both inductive and deductive reasoning are used in college writing genres. If your thesis or claim is based on a generalization from examples, you have used inductive reasoning. The following interchange is an example of inductive reasoning:

Sandra:	I am going to make a fruit salad for the Fourth of July party.
David:	Don't buy your fruit at Fruitful Farms Supermarket. They have a terrible selection and every time I go in there, the fruit is dried out and wilted looking.

In this interchange, David indicated that he has had experience with fruit at Fruitful Farms Supermarket. His conclusion was reached inductively, in that it was based on several specific instances in which he had frequented the store. Actually, a lot of what we know about the world and most of what we have been told about the world, has been obtained through induction—that is, by generalizing from a few examples. For example, if you grew up in a large city, such as New York, Los Angeles, or Chicago, you probably have never seen a leopard roaming the streets (luckily) and have probably not encountered a live leopard, except in a zoo. However, you have probably seen leopards in pictures or films, and those you have seen have spots and look like large cats. You can, therefore, presume that the few you have seen were typical leopards and believe that most leopards have spots and look like large cats. Similarly, although none of us have heard every dog bark or seen every fish swim, we would feel safe predicting that, in general, dogs bark and fish swim.

Inductive reasoning is often associated with a question to be answered, either a casual question, such as "How good is the fruit at Fruitful Farms Supermarket?" or, in scientific writing, "Does a particular decongestant clear stuffy sinuses?" In science or social science writing, the tentative answer to the initial question is called the *hypothesis*. Once the writer has framed a question and postulated a hypothesis, then he or she gathers all the evidence available that pertains to the question and may contribute to the answer. Finally, on the basis of this evidence, the writer draws a conclusion, sometimes called an inference, which provides an answer to the question. Here is an example:

Question:	How did this glass on the kitchen floor get broken?
Evidence:	We own a gray cat.
	There is gray cat hair on the counter.
	There are small paw prints on the counter.
Conclusion:	The cat jumped onto the counter knocking the glass onto the floor.

This conclusion seems obvious because it takes all the evidence into account. But if it turns out that we did not own a cat, the rest of the evidence would be quite mysterious. Also, even if the conclusion seems believable, it is not necessarily true. Perhaps the cat did jump on the counter, but it is also quite possible that someone else knocked the glass onto the floor.

Inductive arguments are usually more complex than this example, and because conclusions in induction are not usually certain but only probable, writers who use inductive reasoning must make an *inductive leap* to move from evidence to a sound conclusion. Valid conclusions in inductive reasoning must be based on samples that are **sufficient** and **typical** (this, of course, also pertains to statistics or examples) or else you will be generalizing from too few examples. If you say, "The dangers of smoking are greatly exaggerated. I know *a person who* smoked three packs a day and lived to be one hundred," you are basing a conclusion on only one person, which constitutes an insufficient sample. If you use inductive reasoning to support a thesis or claim, you must check that your sample has been adequate. Otherwise, you will be drawing a hasty conclusion from an unrepresentative example.

Generalizing from an insufficient sample is often the cause of unfair stereotyping. If you say, "Don't hire this person. I once knew someone from his country and that person was dishonest," you are assuming that all people from a particular country have the same degree of honesty, an idea that is unlikely to be true and which a rational audience would not accept.

EXERCISE

In small groups choose a facility or situation associated with your college from which you have drawn a conclusion based on induction. Some possibilities include the food in the cafeteria, lines at registration, using the library, or the computer center. Cite as many examples as you can and draw a conclusion based on those examples. Share your work with other students in the class.

INDUCTION AND PROBABILITY: THE NECESSITY TO QUALIFY

An inductive argument usually moves from a series of specific instances to a generalization that represents a degree of probability. Before Dr. Jonas Salk could claim that his vaccine prevented polio, he had to test it on a group that was both typical and of adequate size. He then concluded that it was probable that his vaccine could prevent polio in anyone. But for issues concerned with human behavior or opinion, it is not as easy to generalize from specific instances, as there are bound to be many exceptions. It is, therefore, necessary to qualify your statements to indicate that you are aware of possible exceptions. If you survey a number of businesses and discover that female employees cite problems of finding adequate child care as their most pressing concern, that does not mean that every female employee will necessarily feel the same way. However, you can qualify statements you make about this subject by using qualifying words such as *many, a number of,* or *most* so as to avoid simplistic and hasty conclusions. For instance, you can state that for *many* employees, child care represents a significant problem in the workplace.

In another example, suppose that your roommate, Sophia, throws her clothes on the floor every day. You might assume that she will continue to do so throughout her college years, but this assumption is based only on probability. Even though Sophia has thrown her clothes on the floor every day of the semester, it is possible that she may change her habits and start to put her clothes away neatly. Induction is involved with probability, not with certainty, so it is important to use expressions such as "it is likely that," "to a certain extent," or "for the most part" to qualify your statements.

DEDUCTIVE REASONING: THE SYLLOGISM AND THE ENTHYMEME

Although a rational audience will not accept a claim without support, no thesis or claim will be convincing unless the writer and the audience share assumptions, beliefs, or principles that can serve as a common ground between them. An assistant manager might say to his boss:

> We should have an office Christmas party because it will generate a sense of friendship among employees.

This statement is based on the assumption that it is desirable for employees to feel friendly toward one another. The boss, however, may not share this assumption and be concerned only with how much money such a party is likely to cost. She would thus not be in favor of the Christmas party on the basis of this reason. However, if the assistant manager could convince his boss that employees who are friendly with one another feel a sense of allegiance to a company and thus are likely to work harder, she might be convinced to hold the party.

THE SYLLOGISM

As a way of making explicit the connections between a statement, its support, and its underlying assumptions, Aristotle created a three-part structure called a *syllogism,* which consists of three statements: A major premise, a minor premise, and a conclusion. Here is an example of a famous syllogism:

> Major premise: All people are mortal.
> Minor Premise: James is a person.
> Conclusion: James is mortal.

In this example, the major premise is an assumption or a belief about the world that every rational person shares, a truth that is self-evident and obviously true. The minor premise is a related but more specific statement, and the conclusion is a claim that is drawn from these premises. In the previous example, the major premise "All people are mortal" is self-evident, and because the minor premise follows from it, any person reading this three-part statement will have to accept the conclusion or claim. When an audience accepts the major premise as true, and if the minor premise and conclusion follow consistently from it, then the argument is said to be *valid* and the audience must accept the conclusion.

The idea that all people are mortal is generally regarded as a truth. However, it is now recognized that what is accepted as absolutely true, good, or right varies according to culture and that individual perspectives are influenced by the identity of the speaker or writer. Factors such as gender, race, ethnicity, income level, age, sexual identity, or physical/mental/ emotional ability can intersect and influence concepts that are considered absolute. To justify an argument, then, whether structured formally as a syllogism or informally as an enthymeme, it is necessary for a writer to consider the assumption on which the argument is based, will be accepted by its intended audience.

Syllogisms are associated with deductive arguments, which proceed from a general premise or assumption to a specific conclusion, and it is deductive logic that people often mean when they use the term *logic.* In terms of form, deductive arguments imply that if a minor premise follows from the major premise and that if all the statements in the syllogism are true, then the argument is valid and the conclusion is true. If the syllogism is not logical, however, then the argument is not valid and the conclusion will not be true. Here is an example of a syllogism that is not logical and, therefore, does not compel the acceptance of the conclusion as valid:

> Major premise: All canaries are birds.
> Minor premise: All parakeets are birds.
> Conclusion: Therefore, all canaries are parakeets.

This conclusion is, of course, ridiculous. But how did such a silly conclusion derive from two premises that are true? The explanation is that although both canaries and parakeets are birds, the term *parakeets* does not appear in the major premise. This error arose, then, because the form of the syllogism was incorrect and the conclusion is therefore not valid.

Sometimes, the form of the syllogism is logically correct, but the conclusion will still not be true because the major premise is not true. Here is an example:

Major premise: All birds are red.
Minor premise: Carol's parrot is a bird.
Conclusion: Therefore, Carol's parrot, Finnegan, is red.

Of course, we know that not all birds are red. In fact, Finnegan happens to be green; not all birds, including parrots, are red. This conclusion is not true because the major premise is false. Although the form of the syllogism is correct, the conclusion is not true. For an argument to be convincing, a syllogism must be both logical and true.

THE ENTHYMEME

A shortened version of a syllogism, which leaves the major premise unstated is the *Enthymeme*, which consists of a claim with a "because" clause. The expanded thesis we referred to in Chapter 6 was actually an Enthymeme, which may be defined as an incomplete logical statement that presumes the acceptance of the unstated major premise and will not be valid without it. Here is how a syllogism may be stated as an enthymeme:
James is mortal because he is a person.
This claim is both valid and true because all logical people accept the major premise or underlying assumption that "All people are mortal."
Aristotle's concept of the syllogism is based on the notion that there are well-established truisms and, for some topics, these truisms are still considered valid. However, there are also many assumptions that are not shared by all. For example, the following syllogism could be applied to Jon's decision to change his major to environmental studies:

Major premise: Students should choose a major based on interest.
Minor premise: Jon is interested in environmental policy.
Conclusion: Jon should major in environmental policy.

As an enthymeme, this argument can be stated as follows:

Jon should major in environmental policy because this major interests him.

Many of us would share the assumption that students should choose a major based on interest, but not everyone does. Jon's Aunt Maria, for example, might not think that interest in a major is important at all, and, therefore, that basis for a claim would not convince her.

Because your audience must share the **underlying assumptions** behind your claim in order for your argument to be convincing, it is important to be aware of those assumptions as you develop your ideas and draft your argument. By focusing on the assumptions that both he and Aunt Maria might share, Jon might be able to make a more convincing case about his choice of environmental studies as a major. He might, for instance, focus on Aunt Maria's concern with making a living and emphasize that an Environmental Studies major could lead to a professional position after graduation. Jon might then reframe his argument as follows:

Major premise: Students should choose a major that will lead to a professional position after graduation.

Minor premise: Environmental studies is a major that will lead to a professional position after graduation.

Conclusion: Jon should major in environmental studies as a major.

Or, stated as an enthymeme:

Jon should major in environmental studies because it is a major that will lead to a professional position after graduation.

EXERCISE

For the audience cited in each situation, work in small groups to decide which of the following reasons are most likely to be convincing. Support your decision by describing what you believe are the values of each particular audience.

1.   Audience: Your composition teacher
     A.   I need an extension on my research paper because I need extra time for studying chemistry this week.
     B.   I need an extension on my research paper because I want to locate some additional materials in the library.
2.   Audience: An administrator at your school
     A.   Students should sit in on university curricular committees because they need to know what sort of changes are being planned.
     B.   Students should sit in on university curricular committees because they can provide school officials with important insight into student needs.
3.   Audience: Parents of teenagers at a local high school
     A.   The school should fund an end-of-year retreat for students because they worked hard and deserve a treat.
     B.   The school should fund an end-of-year retreat for students because it will enable them to discuss important cultural and ethical issues and plan for the following year.

EXAMINING SYLLOGISMS AND ENTHYMEMES

Because Aristotle's concept of formal logic pertains only to the structure of the argument, not necessarily to its truth, it is important to question whether or not the major premise in an enthymeme or syllogism is actually and unconditionally true or whether it simply expresses an idea that most people **feel** is true. The enthymeme *Frank is mortal because he is a person* contains the unstated assumption that "All people are mortal," which is a statement that all rational people believe is true. But in the enthymeme *Jon should major in environmental policy because it interests him,* the unstated assumption that students *should choose a major based on interest,* is one that only some people might agree with. Some people might feel that it is too soon for college freshmen to know what interests them since their interests might change as they become aware of new courses and fields. Others might feel that students should choose a school based on its reputation, not on whether a school offers any particular major. Or, like Aunt Maria, they might feel that the choice of major should be determined by professional opportunity, not necessarily by interest.

EXERCISE

FOR GROUP DISCUSSION

For the following enthymemes, identify the unstated major premise. Rewrite each enthymeme as a syllogism. Then discuss whether or not you believe these assumptions are true.

1.   Buy this beauty product because it will make your skin look younger.

2.   Mrs. Smith is a wonderful teacher because she is patient.

3.   *Jurassic World* is a terrific movie because it has unusual special effects.

4.   The political correctness movement is dangerous to society because it threatens freedom of speech.

5.   The women's movement has threatened the stability of the family because it took women out of the home.

6.   Studying a musical instrument is good for kids because it involves discipline.

7.   Participating in sports is good for kids because it teaches coordination.

8.   Ted is a bad manager because he always thinks he is right.

EXERCISE

THINKING ABOUT INDUCTION AND DEDUCTION

Examine the following statements and decide which are based on inductive reasoning and which on deductive. Then decide whether or not these statements are well reasoned. Discuss your observations in small groups.

1. Peter is one of our most punctual employees. In fact, he has never been late to work in the past five years since he joined the firm. Since he didn't come on time today, I assume that something serious must have happened to him.

2. People who collect snakes usually like other reptiles as well. Lisa has a large snake collection, so I think she will also like this iguana.

3. Mexican women are very warm and loving with babies, so I suggest that you hire Consuelo as a nanny because she comes from Mexico.

4. Students in the United States have not been given adequate preparation in geography. Seth was educated in the United States, so it is unlikely that he knows anything about geography.

5. Louisa is very athletic and works out at the gym every day, so she will probably be able to learn mountain climbing techniques easily.

6. Justin is especially interested in electronics, so if you wish to interest him in your product, you should demonstrate its technical applications.

7. Clifton successfully negotiated a number of mergers in his previous job, so I suggest that you consult him about the upcoming acquisition.

ERRORS IN REASONING

Statements based on poor logic and mistaken belief are called *fallacies,* and although numerous attempts have been made to categorize them, many of them overlap with one another. In writing college arguments, it is not necessary that you study an exhaustive list of fallacies, but it is useful to become at least somewhat familiar with some of them so that you can avoid using them in your own writing and detect them in the sources you use. The following is a list of the more common fallacies.

SLIPPERY SLOPE REASONING

This is an argument that assumes that one action will lead to another similar action, which in turn will lead to another and to another, ultimately resulting in something quite undesirable. An example of a slippery slope argument is the following:

> Doctor-assisted euthanasia will ultimately lead to mass suicide. In the beginning, only people with incurable, painful illnesses will request to die. Then others with less drastic conditions will request it. Before you know it, people with even minor illnesses will begin thinking of assisted death as a viable option.

Slippery slope arguments are used quite frequently in the context of a variety of social or policy situations. "Smoking marijuana will ultimately lead to heroin addiction" is a popular version. Another is "If you forbid people to smoke in restaurants, they soon will not be able to smoke at all." The essence of a slippery slope argument is that once a first step is taken, a descent all the way down is inevitable.

BLACK AND WHITE THINKING

This is a form of reasoning that presumes an "either-or" situation, such as the following:

> Either we enroll in that painting course, or we will never learn to paint.

This statement does not consider that we might learn to paint through some other means.

HASTY GENERALIZATIONS

Hasty generalizations are caused by drawing conclusions from insufficient evidence.

Hasty generalizations are often used to condemn a whole group of people on the basis of an inadequate sample, such as in the following statement:

> Let's invite Stewart to be a club member. He's Jewish and all Jews are rich.

Hasty generalization leads to stereotyping.

FALSE CAUSE

Related to the fallacy "hasty generalization" is the false cause, which assumes causal connections where none may exist, as in the following statement:

> As soon as mandatory school busing was instituted in the town of Rockport, many families began moving out of town.

This statement presumes that it was mandatory school busing that caused people to move, when, in actuality, the move also coincided with the closing of one of the town's major industries.

FALSE AUTHORITY

Authorities from one field are sometimes cited as if they were authorities in another, a fallacy that is used commonly on television when movie stars are used to endorse particular products on television that they may know little about. If a famous person endorses a particular ideology, you should not immediately assume that it is then worthwhile.

RED HERRING

The name "red herring" is derived from the idea that a pack of dogs would be distracted from a scent if a herring with a strong odor were dragged across the trail. In argumentation, a red herring means that the writer has brought in a point that has little or nothing to do with the issue being discussed. An example of a red herring would be as follows:

> Jon should not enroll in State College because it doesn't offer a major in environmental studies.

> Anyway, State College places too much emphasis on sports.

ATTACK ON THE PERSON RATHER THAN THE ISSUE (AD HOMINEM ARGUMENTS)

Arguments that attack the person rather than the issue are extremely common in controversies concerning social issues. An example of a statement using this form of fallacious reasoning is as follows:

Don't listen to what Angela has to say. She's just a typical dumb blond.

A CAUTION ABOUT FALLACIES

Some textbooks provide a long and detailed list of fallacies, and by doing so, they imply that all fallacies can be easily classified and that by identifying them, you will be able to write a convincing argument. Our intention here, however, is simply to alert you to the possibility that reasoning can be false in a number of ways so that you scrutinize your own arguments more carefully and approach those of others with a critical perspective.

TOULMIN'S SYSTEM OF INFORMAL LOGIC

In *The Uses of Argument,* the British philosopher, Stephen Toulmin has adapted formal logic to focus more directly on audience, anticipating the possible reactions of readers. Toulmin postulates an audience that might initially be in opposition to the claim, an audience that might question and weigh the argument, but which can be convinced of its merit if the writer establishes common ground. Unlike formal logic, which is based entirely on the structure of the syllogism, Toulmin's system acknowledges that most major premises are not as easily accepted as the classic "All people are mortal." He, therefore, includes another term, called the *backing* which, as its name implies, provides a backup even for the major premise in an argument. His system thus focuses greater attention on the underlying assumptions behind all claims and acknowledges the importance of clarifying and qualifying an argument to suit particular situations. Toulmin's system thus is well suited for the genre of argument, which presumes a diverse readership in which not everyone will share underlying assumptions.

THE ELEMENTS OF TOULMIN'S SYSTEM

Toulmin's system conceives of argument as consisting of six elements, the first three corresponding to the major premise, minor premise, and conclusion of a syllogism. In Toulmin's system, the major premise is called the *warrant,* the minor premise is called the *grounds,* and the conclusion is called the *claim.* Let us examine here how Toulmin's system differs from the syllogism and how writers of academic argument can utilize this system in framing and evaluating ideas. In Toulmin's system, the claim is pretty much the same as the conclusion in a syllogism. To use one of the examples discussed previously, a claim would be *Jon should major in environmental studies.* The grounds in Toulmin's system is similar to the minor premise in a syllogism, except that they consist not only of one statement, but of all the evidence, facts, and information that can be used in support of the claim. Thus, for the claim that *Jon should major in environmental studies,* the grounds might consist of all of the information about what opportunities are actually available, statistics on job possibilities, projections of future trends, etc. The grounds thus include not only the reasons for a claim, but all the evidence that can be used in support of those reasons.

The warrant in Toulmin's system is similar to the major premise of a syllogism—that is, it consists of a general statement from which the grounds and the claim follow logically. An example of a warrant is the statement, "Students should choose a major based on professional opportunity." However, Toulmin acknowledges that most warrants are not as easily accepted or as self-evident as the syllogism of formal logic presumes. He therefore, provides a fourth element to the list of elements called a *backing,* which provides support for the warrant. For the warrant that "Students should choose a major based on professional opportunity," the writer might provide information from professional organizations substantiating that their employees majored in the subjects they are now working in professionally or statements from people working in the field indicating that their major was of importance in establishing a career, etc.

The other additional elements in Toulmin's system are concerned with limiting the claim. These are called *qualifiers* and *conditions of rebuttal. Qualifiers* limit the absoluteness of a claim by indicating the extent to which it is true. By being aware of qualifiers, the writers of academic argument may modify their claims by using expressions such as *probably, possibly,* or *very likely.* Or else they may indicate specific instances that limit the claim. Jon's claim might thus be modified as follows: "Jon should major in environmental studies assuming that his academic goal is to choose a career" or "Jon should major in environmental studies at this point in his studies" (he might be exposed to other courses that give him new career opportunities).

Conditions of rebuttal point out instances in which the claim or warrant might not be true, or other ways in which the audience might object to what the writer is arguing. In the example we have been working with, an audience might argue that professional opportunity is not the only basis on which to select a major. Therefore, the claim might be modified as follows:

> Jon should major in Environmental Studies, as long as his interest in the subject continues.

This statement anticipates that some readers might say: "Professional opportunity is a good basis for choosing a major, assuming the student is interested in the field." These people feel that professional opportunity alone is not enough of a rationale for making this kind of decision.

The strength of Toulmin's system is that it anticipates the reaction of the audience and acknowledges the importance of using qualifiers to modify assertions. The other advantage is that it acknowledges that readers are likely to bring up exceptions to both the warrant and the claim and recognizes that writers of argumentation must anticipate these exceptions.

The six elements of Toulmin's system are shown in the following model:

Enthymeme: Jon should major in environmental studies because it offers professional opportunities.

Claim:	Jon should major in environmental studies.
Qualifier:	At this point in his life.
Grounds:	Information about the professional opportunities in the field.
Warrant:	Students should choose a major based on professional opportunity.
Backing:	Successful professionals who were polled indicated that it was beneficial for them to have majored in a subject that was directly related to the field they entered.
Conditions of Rebuttal:	Unless he is no longer interested in the field.

COMPARING THE SYLLOGISM AND THE TOULMIN MODEL

The syllogism, developed over two thousand years ago, and Toulmin's more recent model of argument are similar in many ways and both are useful for understanding the reasoning that is involved in the argument based genres. In both the syllogism and the Toulmin model, the three main elements of an argument correspond to one another. The major premise, minor premise, and conclusion of the syllogism are similar to the warrant, grounds, and claim of Toulmin's model. However, there are notable differences between them as well. Whereas the *major premise* in a syllogism is usually an accepted assumption that does not need to be proved (all people are mortal), the warrant in the Toulmin model (Students should choose a major based on professional opportunity) is not nearly as well established. The Toulmin model recognizes that the validity of the warrant needs to be established in order to link the claim and the grounds. The *backing,* therefore, provides the necessary support for the warrant.

Toulmin's model also suggests the necessity for qualifying the claim. The *qualifier,* which is sometimes manifested in words such as *probably,* or *at this time,* indicates that claims are not static, and the *conditions of rebuttal* further limit the absoluteness of the argument. Toulmin's model thus reflects the complexity and flexibility of the genre of argument intended for a modern audience.

EXERCISE

1. Restate and define the three major elements in Toulmin's system. In writing, explain why warrants are important in convincing an audience. For the following claims and grounds, find the implied warrants:

    A. You should send your child to summer camp. It will enable him to participate in sports.

    B. You should take Professor Johnson's political issues class. It will enable you to understand current controversies.

    C. You should not use Styrofoam cups. They pollute the environment.

    D. You should hang around at the Polo Lounge. You'll be able to meet rich people there.

2. Read an article in a newspaper or magazine and respond in writing to the following questions:

    A. What is the argument concerned with?

    B. What is the writer's thesis or claim?

    C. What grounds does the writer use?

    D. What is the warrant implied in the claim?

    E. What strategies does the writer use to convince his or her audience?

THE ROLE OF ETHOS

Chapter 1 emphasized the importance for the writer of a college essay to demonstrate that he or she is knowledgeable, trustworthy, logical, and fair because audiences are most likely to accept the ideas of those with good character, or *ethos*. Ethos is also important when you refer to authorities and experts in their fields within your own essay. Unless the person is extremely well-known, or unless you are writing to a specialized audience that is familiar with the names of the experts in the field, it is a good idea to include information that testifies to the expertise of your reference. For example, in an essay concerned with fairy tales, you might wish to indicate to your reader that someone whose ideas you are using to support your own position is a well-known child psychologist. You might, therefore, present this information as follows:

> Dr. Richard Smith, Director of the Stanford Institute of Child Development, asserts that fairy tales are very important in early childhood.

By including information about those you quote, you are maximizing the likelihood that your audience will accept what they have to say.

THE ROLE OF PATHOS

Pathos is used to arouse the emotions of the audience, primarily through emotional language that includes vivid descriptions and moving narratives and anecdotes. All of us are familiar with the use of emotional appeals in advertising; similarly, an essay discussing the need for a homeless shelter will be more effective if it includes moving examples depicting the misery of people who are homeless than one that simply cites statistics about homelessness. Remember, though, that when you appeal to your audience using emotional language, the references should be appropriate to the tone and purpose of college writing. Overly sentimental or hysterical language will detract from the effectiveness of your essay, as will appeals to emotion that may tug at your audience's heartstrings but are extraneous to your thesis.

THE THREE APPEALS

By Cesar Soto

These are the three appeals and (some of) their distinguishing features:

Ethos: Appeal to Ethical Sense

- Presentation of the author as a good person, a likeable person, a believable person.
- Presentation of the author as a knowledgeable person, personally experienced in the area and/or well studied in it.
- Does the author use credible sources? Do the sources have any biases? How persuasive are the sources?
- Does the author present him/herself as somewhere in-between an objective observer and an impassioned advocate? Look at tone and language: Dry and academic or overly personal with a (too) conversational tone?

Logos: Appeal to Reason: Construction of Argument

- Clear, coherent presentation of the thesis: Where is the thesis located? Does it appear too late or too early in the text?
- Clear, though less forceful, presentation of the opposing view ("although" clause usually preceding thesis presentation).
- The organization of evidence is sound, logical.
- Supporting material/evidence is logical and consistent.
- Do topic sentences accurately reflect paragraphs' content(s)? Does the essay do what it promises to do in the thesis statement?
- Argument is partly based on facts, statistics, authority, logic.

Pathos: Appeal to Emotion/Identification

- Does the text indirectly, or directly, establish a sense of common values and ways of seeing the world? May use second person to do this: We, us, you, etc.
- Does the text use literary/poetic techniques, such as imagery, repetition, narrative, dramatic dialogue and rhythmic, emotion-heightening language?
- Look at the introduction and see if it contains a scenario that invites you to identify with the topic: is it fear-based, etc. The use of personal experience is also an appeal to pathos.

EXERCISE

HOW ARE ADS SIMILAR TO AND DIFFERENT FROM ARGUMENT ESSAYS?

1. Bring an ad to class and answer the following questions:
   A. What is the purpose of the ad?
   B. What is the claim made by the ad?
   C. How does the ad appeal to reason (logos)?
   D. How does the ad appeal to authority (ethos)?
   E. How does the ad appeal to the emotions of its audience (pathos)?
   F. What features of the ad are similar to those in the genre of argument?
   G. How is the ad different from an argumentative essay?

2. Choose one ad and rewrite it as an argumentative essay. Which features carry over easily? Which features do not? What sort of material did you have to add?

The essay, "The Case for Torture" was published in 1982. Write an essay evaluating the relevance of this essay in the context of recent events.

Levin, Michael. "The Case for Torture." *Newsweek, 7* June 1982. Print

It is generally assumed that torture is impermissible, a throwback to a more brutal age. Enlightened societies reject it outright, and regimes suspected of using it risk the wrath of the United States.

I believe this attitude is unwise. There are situations in which torture is not merely permissible but morally mandatory. Moreover, these situations are moving from the realm of imagination to fact.

Death: Suppose a terrorist has hidden an atomic bomb on Manhattan Island which will detonate at noon on July 4 unless . . . here follow the usual demands for money and release of his friends from jail. Suppose, further, that he is caught at 10 a.m. on the fateful day, but preferring death to failure, won't disclose where the bomb is. What do we do? If we follow due process, wait for his lawyer, arraign him, millions of people will die. If the only way to save those lives is to subject the terrorist to the most excruciating possible pain, what grounds can there be for not doing so? I suggest there are none. In any case, I ask you to face the question with an open mind.

Torturing the terrorist is unconstitutional? Probably. But millions of lives surely outweigh constitutionality. Torture is barbaric? Mass murder is far more barbaric. Indeed, letting millions of innocents die in deference to one who flaunts his guilt is moral cowardice, an unwillingness to dirty one's hands. If you caught the terrorist, could you sleep nights knowing that millions died because you couldn't bring yourself to apply the electrodes?

Once you concede that torture is justified in extreme cases, you have admitted that the decision to use torture is a matter of balancing innocent lives against the means needed to save them. You must now face more realistic cases involving more modest numbers. Someone plants a bomb on a jumbo jet. He alone can disarm it, and his demands cannot be met (or if they can, we refuse to set a precedent by yielding to his threats). Surely we can, we must, do anything to the extortionist to save the passengers. How can we tell 300, or 100, or 10 people who never asked to be put in danger, "I'm sorry you'll have to die in agony, we just couldn't bring ourselves to . . . "

Here are the results of an informal poll about a third hypothetical case. Suppose a terrorist group kidnapped a newborn baby from a hospital. I asked four mothers if they would approve of torturing kidnappers if that were necessary to get their own newborns back. All said yes; the most "liberal" adding that she would like to administer it herself.

© 1982 by Michael Levin, Professor of Philosophy, CCNY and GC-CUNY. Reprinted by permission.

I am not advocating torture as punishment. Punishment is addressed to deeds irrevocably past. Rather, I am advocating torture as an acceptable measure for preventing future evils. So understood, it is far less objectionable than many extant punishments. Opponents of the death penalty, for example, are forever insisting that executing a murderer will not bring back his victim (as if the purpose of capital punishment were supposed to be resurrection, not deterrence or retribution). But torture, in the cases described, is intended not to bring anyone back but to keep innocents from being dispatched. The most powerful argument against using torture as a punishment or to secure confessions is that such practices disregard the rights of the individual. Well, if the individual is all that important, and he is, it is correspondingly important to protect the rights of individuals threatened by terrorists. If life is so valuable that it must never be taken, the lives of the innocents must be saved even at the price of hurting the one who endangers them.

Better precedents for torture are assassination and pre-emptive attack. No Allied leader would have flinched at assassinating Hitler, had that been possible. (The Allies did assassinate Heydrich.) Americans would be angered to learn that Roosevelt could have had Hitler killed in 1943, thereby shortening the war and saving millions of lives, but refused on moral grounds. Similarly, if nation A learns that nation B is about to launch an unprovoked attack, A has a right to save itself by destroying B's military capability first. In the same way, if the police can, by torture, save those who would otherwise die at the hands of kidnappers or terrorists, they must.

Idealism: There is an important difference between terrorists and their victims that should mute talk of the terrorists' "rights." The terrorist's victims are at risk unintentionally, not having asked to be endangered. But the terrorist knowingly initiated his actions. Unlike his victims, he volunteered for the risks of his deed. By threatening to kill for profit or idealism, he renounces civilized standards, and he can have no complaint if civilization tries to thwart him by whatever means necessary.

Just as torture is justified only to save lives (not extort confessions or incantations), it is justifiably administered only to those known to hold innocent lives in their hands. Ah, but how can the authorities ever be sure they have the right malefactor? Isn't there a danger of error and abuse? Won't "WE" turn into "THEM"?

Questions like these are disingenuous in a world in which terrorists proclaim themselves and perform for television. The name of their game is public recognition. After all, you can't very well intimidate a government into releasing your freedom fighters unless you announce that it is your group that has seized its embassy. "Clear guilt" is difficult to define, but when 40 million people see a group of masked gunmen seize an airplane on the evening news, there is not much question about who the perpetrators are. There will be hard cases where the situation is murkier. Nonetheless, a line demarcating the legitimate use of torture can be drawn. Torture only the obviously guilty, and only for the sake of saving innocents, and the line between "US" and "THEM" will remain clear.

There is little danger that the Western democracies will lose their way if they choose to inflict pain as one way of preserving order. Paralysis in the face of evil is the greater danger. Some day soon a terrorist will threaten tens of thousands of lives, and torture will be the only way to save them. We had better start thinking about this.

ADDITIONAL TOPICS FOR DISCUSSION AND WRITING

The list of references below can be used for discussion and are also well suited for writing a college argument. Choose one of these articles and locate the full text online. Then think about the following questions:

What is the main idea being advocated in this article?
Can you present this idea as an enthymeme?
What sort of support does the author use?
Is personal experience relevant for this topic?

Summarize and write a response to this article. What sort of support will be relevant in your response?

1. "Does Cosmo Deserve a Plain Brown Wrapper?" by Megan Daum (*Los Angeles Times Opinion*/op-Ed Column, 6 August 2015)

    A new campaign is trying to put the magazine, *Cosmopolitan,* behind a concealing wrapper and warning label prohibiting its sale to minors.

2. "Should Female Athletes Have to Prove They are Women?" by Alice Dreger (*Los Angeles Times Opinion*/Op-Ed 30 July 2015)

    The International Olympic Committee and the International Association of Athletics Federation argue that decisions about who can compete as a woman should be based on testosterone levels. But some women, although identifying as women and raised as women, do have high levels of testosterone. Should they be allowed to compete?

3. "We're Making Life Too Hard for Millennials" by Steve Rattner (*Los Angeles Times Opinion*/op-Ed Column, 31 July 2015)

   Americans between the ages of 18 and 34 are doing more poorly financially than the baby boomers who have been irresponsible in their fiscal policies. What can be done to ease the burden on today's young people?

4. "Congress and Obama Are Too Timid on Marijuana Reform" The Editorial Board (Editorial from *The New York Times*, 8 August 2015)

   Recently, a number of states have legalized marijuana for medicinal purposes. Should it be legalized in all states and removed from the Controlled Substances Act?

9

CHAPTER

Types of Support

Sitting in the student cafeteria, you might have the following conversation with a friend:

You:	My roommate, Sylvester, is impossible to live with. He is driving me crazy!
Friend:	Why?
You:	Because he's sloppy and inconsiderate.

Your friend might then nod in sympathy, convinced that Sylvester is indeed impossible to live with. But suppose you were trying to convince the members of the Housing Bureau on your campus that you need to change roommates. In that case, you might construct your position more formally. You might decide to write your statement as follows:

> My roommate, Sylvester, is difficult to live with because he is sloppy and inconsiderate.

Or you might analyze your claim as follows:

Claim:	My roommate, Sylvester, is difficult to live with.
Reasons:	He is sloppy.
	He is inconsiderate.
Warrant:	Sloppy, inconsiderate people are difficult to live with.

However, although the reasons cited would probably be sufficient for your friend in a casual conversation, some members of the Housing Bureau might require additional support for your reasons, raising questions, such as "In what way is he sloppy? How is he inconsiderate? Can you give examples of his sloppiness and lack of consideration?" Or they might raise a question about your warrant or the underlying basis of your claim, such as "Why do his sloppiness and lack of consideration make him impossible to live with?" In other words, you may have to provide further support in order for your audience to be convinced.

Support is a key component in college writing. Sometimes you may need additional support for your reasons; at other times, you may need to bolster your underlying assumptions or warrants as well. This chapter is concerned with various strategies for providing support; in particular, statements from experts, examples, statistics and information from surveys and interviews.

DEFENDING YOUR WARRANT

The claim "My roommate, Sylvester, is difficult to live with" was supported by the warrant "sloppy, inconsiderate people are difficult to live with"—an assumption that many people probably share. Not everyone, however, will accept this warrant as absolutely true. Learning of Sylvester's irritating habits, some members of the Housing Bureau might say, "As far as I'm concerned, sloppiness and lack of consideration cause only minor difficulties. A grouchy, angry roommate with a foul temper—now these are more serious problems. But if Sylvester is cheerful and pleasant, his sloppiness and lack of consideration should be regarded as only minor character flaws."

In this case, if you wished to convince the Housing Bureau that Sylvester should be exchanged for another roommate, someone you found easier to live with, you would have the obligation of defending your warrant. You might then decide to provide the additional support that college students are particularly disadvantaged when they must contend with sloppy, inconsiderate people. This additional support might be stated as follows:

> For college students, people who are sloppy and inconsiderate are especially difficult to live with because **their habits interfere with other students' ability to study.**

This additional information would provide additional support for your warrant because it specifies that sloppiness and lack of consideration interfere with an important component of education—the ability to study—thereby establishing that such qualities are particularly unsuitable for a college roommate. Phrased as a syllogism, this additional support might appear as follows:

Major premise:	People whose habits interfere with study are unsuitable roommates for college students.
Minor premise:	Sylvester's habits interfere with study (he is sloppy and inconsiderate).
Conclusion:	Sylvester is an unsuitable roommate.

The claim that a roommate's habits interfered with your ability to study would then probably be regarded as serious by members of the Housing Bureau and might, indeed, get Sylvester out of your room. It is, therefore, important for you to scrutinize your warrants as well as your reasons to decide whether or not you need to provide additional support.

SUPPORTING YOUR REASONS

Additional support might occur in the form of examples or specific details that lend specificity and concreteness to your writing and help the reader understand your ideas more clearly. For example, support for reason number 1 (Sylvester is sloppy) might consist of the following examples:

1. Sylvester throws his dirty clothes everywhere. His filthy socks and dirty underwear are draped over chairs, on the beds, and all over the floor. His stuff is draped all over my own desk, making it hard for me to keep my notes organized.
2. Sylvester never throws away his own trash—all available surfaces in the room are littered with pizza boxes, containers from McDonald's, candy bar wrappers, etc. The mess in the room upsets me so much that I have difficulty concentrating on my work.
3. Sylvester never cleans up any mess he makes. If he spills soda, the spill remains until the ants get to it. There's always something sticky on the dresser because Sylvester has knocked something over. Once, he spilled soda all over a paper I was writing.

Support for reason number two (Sylvester is inconsiderate) might consist of the following:

1. Sylvester plays his music loudly until very late at night, even when I am studying.
2. Sylvester invites his noisy friends in every night to argue, sing, and party until the early hours of the morning so that I can't get any sleep.
3. Sylvester's idea of a joke is to sneak up on my pet canary, Tweety, and scare her half to death. In fact, Tweety has become so traumatized that she has started to pluck her own feathers. I have had to spend time bringing Tweety to the vet, taking time away from my studies.

These examples substantiate the reasons you cited in support of the claim, "Sylvester is difficult to live with," and they significantly strengthen your argument because they are specific and concrete. Certainly, the members of the Housing Bureau would be more likely to take your complaint against Sylvester seriously if you cited these specific examples of his difficult behavior.

EXERCISE

For a situation in your own life, write a claim supported by at least two reasons. Then, for each reason, cite evidence that provides support. If you have difficulty thinking of claims, here are some ideas you can use:

1. My parents are very old fashioned because they think_____.

2. My children are unappreciative of whatever they have because they complain that _____.

3. Mr. Gradgrind is a terrible teacher because _____.

4. _____ is a film worth seeing because _____.

5. My roommate is difficult to live with because _____.

6. My (husband, wife, sister, brother, mother, father) is difficult to live with because _____.

For each claim, indicate the warrant on which it was based.

EXAMPLES AS EVIDENCE

Examples provide an important form of support. If you wish to argue that some children's toys reinforce gender stereotypes, you might cite examples of the toys displayed in toy stores. If you wish to argue that a particular business charges extremely high prices, you can cite numerous examples to indicate that this is so. If you are examining the trend of many motorists to equip their cars as if they were homes and offices, you can cite examples of people who not only have phones, computers, and fax machines in their cars, but also video cameras, television sets, changes of clothes, and coffee makers. In the essay titled, "How to Give Orders Like a Man," Deborah Tannen uses the example of a university president who gives indirect orders to her assistant to illustrate an important theme in her essay—that women frequently speak differently than men do, even when they are in a position of power.

In selecting examples, be sure to use those that are concrete and pertinent; you should also make sure to include enough of them to be convincing. The following paragraph has little impact because it cites only a few general examples:

> Working parents are concerned about a number of problems associated with child care. Often, child care facilities are dirty and poorly supervised.

More specific examples and additional information, however, can improve this paragraph:

> Working parents are concerned about a number of problems associated with child care. Daycare is hard to find, difficult to afford, and often of distressingly poor quality. Having toured over a dozen facilities, one working mother tells appalling stories of what she found. In one place the children were all lined up in front of the TV like a bunch of zombies. In another, the place was so filthy that she was unable to find a clean spot in which to seat her child during the interview. Because of the scarcity of good facilities, waiting lists for established daycare centers are so long that parents apply for a spot months before their children are born, and, in some cases, before the child is even conceived.

HYPOTHETICAL EXAMPLES

Real examples or examples from your own life can be effective, but you can also cite hypothetical examples if they seem sufficiently illustrative of the point you are attempting to develop. For example, an illustration that has been used to support bilingual education is as follows:

> Suppose you were planning to visit another country for a long period of time. Certainly, you would find it easier to maneuver in that country if you had access to someone in the country who spoke your language, could answer your questions,

and provide an overview of what you would need to know. Now imagine what it would be like if you did not have access to such a person. Without that form of assistance, your adjustment to your new country would most likely take much longer.

Hypothetical examples can be especially useful if the concept you are explaining is difficult to understand or abstract. The essay "The Case for Torture" in Chapter 8 points out that in some instances, torture would be considered a moral act, and it uses the example of a terrorist who has refused to reveal the whereabouts of a deadly virus that will destroy civilization unless found immediately. The essay points out that in this instance, the use of torture might be considered morally justifiable.

AUTHORITY AS SUPPORT

Statements from authorities in the field provide another important form of support for many genres of college writing. Even in casual conversation, the question "Who says so?" is frequently posed when someone offers an unsupported opinion, and the strength of your position will be greatly enhanced if you can say, "Several authorities on this subject say so," or perhaps, "I myself am an expert on this topic, and I say so."

The Authority of Personal Experience

Personal experience or the experiences of people you know can be an important source of support. For the topic of whether fairy tales are helpful or harmful for children, for example, most, if not all, of you will be able to recall fairy tales from your childhood, remember some of the feelings they evoked in you, and use these recollections to support your position on this topic. Many other topics also lend themselves to support through personal observation. If you were writing a paper about the role of resident advisors in the college residence halls, you might discuss the role your own advisor played in helping you adjust to college life. If you were writing about the necessity for public schools to provide after-school care, you might cite difficulties you have had finding adequate after-school activities for your own children. Topics relating to school, work, or travel are particularly likely to be within the realm of your personal experience, which can be used to support your position.

Personal Experience and Appeal to the Reader (Pathos)

Short narratives and descriptions based on personal experience can be very appealing to readers, enabling them to share experiences with you that serve as support for your ideas. L. Christopher Awalt in his essay "Brother, Don't Spare a Dime" uses an example from his own experience to help readers understand how he arrived at his position on helping the homeless. He discusses an older man who had been on the street for about ten years due to alcoholism, and because his story sounded believable, Awalt enrolled him in a detoxification, wrote him monthly checks, and attempted to find a job for him. At first, all went well and the man seemed to be making remarkable improvement. However, sixth months later, Awalt "found him drunk again, back on the streets" (Awalt, L. Christopher. "Brother, Don't Spare a Dime," *Newsweek* 30 Sept. 1991).

When you read about Awalt's fruitless efforts to help this man, you may find yourself agreeing with him that helping the homeless is not easy. On the other hand, you may be wondering if this example is really representative of all or even of most of the homeless, which raises the important issue of when personal experience is appropriate to use in a college essay. Some examples are not typical and if you use those, you will be undermining, rather than supporting your main idea or claim. Unfortunately, there is no hard and fast rule about this, but our recommendation is based on how typical it might be and how relevant it is to the topic. The well-known writer, Richard Rodriguez, for example, used his own experience as the major source of evidence in his book, *Hunger of Memory*. Rodriguez recounts his experience with learning English and of adjusting to American society to argue against bilingual education policies; in essence, Rodriguez is claiming that his own experience has greater validity than the claims of the "experts" in the field of language acquisition who may not have actually gone through the experience of learning a second language as a child.

Personal experience, then, can enhance your own credibility (ethos) and have an impact on your reader (pathos). Keep in mind, however, that most writing you do in college requires you to supplement personal experiences with material from other sources, so unless the assignment specifically asks to narrate one particular experience, you should not plan to base your entire essay solely on your own experiences, even if they are typical and representative.

WRITING ASSIGNMENT

In a 1–2 page narrative, recount an experience you have had since you have enrolled at your college or university. The experience may be concerned with registration, an incident occurring in a class, the cafeteria, a club or team, etc. Then read your narrative aloud to a group of three classmates. Do they feel that your experience is typical? Would you be able to use this experience as an example in an argumentative essay?

AUTHORITIES FROM PUBLISHED WORKS

Even if you have had a great deal of personal experience with your topic, the inclusion of acknowledged authorities will enhance your credibility. Those who have published books and articles about the topic bring the weight of publication to their assertions and may have familiarity with aspects of the topic you may not have thought of; sometimes, they have been involved in the controversy a long time and can provide a historical perspective that you cannot have. Remember, though, that the publication of a book or article on an issue does not make that person an "authority." As a critical thinker, you should find out as much as possible about the author so that you can assess whether or not to include him or her in your essay. Chapter 2 in this book suggests several approaches for assessing a published work with a critical perspective.

Opinions of authorities can be included in a number of ways, such as:

- to support a statement of yours, thus enhancing your authority
- to contradict someone else's opinion
- to indicate that an example you have cited is typical
- to provide another example
- to interpret facts
- to analyze the causes of a problem
- to offer a solution
- to predict a consequence

Note the use of information from an authority in the following paragraph:

> Over the past several years, many American parents are being forced to make room for their adult children, who are returning to the nest in increasing numbers. "There is a naive notion that children grow up and leave home when they're 18, and the truth is far from that," says Sociologist Larry Bumpass of the University of Wisconsin in Madison. "Today, according to the U.S. Census Bureau, 59% of men and 47% of women between 18 and 24 depend on their parents for housing, some living in college dorms, but most at home."
>
> **Toufexis, Anastasia. "Show Me the Way to Go Home: Expected Numbers of Young Adults Are Living With Their Parents."** *Time* **4 May 1987. Print.**

In this paragraph, the use of the sociologist and the citation of statistics from the U.S. Census Bureau indicates that the tendency of adult children to return home was typical at that time. It thus helps establish the credibility of the writer who is examining this trend.

OTHER TYPES OF EVIDENCE

In addition to examples and the statements of authorities, two other effective forms of support that can be used to support a claim are *analogies* and *evidence provided by statistics.*

Analogy as Evidence

An analogy is an extended comparison between two "things" (processes, ideas, actions, objects, events, etc.), a strategy that is especially useful for helping readers understand something unfamiliar by presenting it in terms of a parallel more familiar example. When used appropriately, analogy can be a helpful device for convincing an audience that if two things, ideas, or policies are similar in one way, then they are also similar in other ways and what is true for one is, therefore, true for the other.

In the following paragraph, Alfee Enciso uses an analogy to make his point that America tends to deny that it is racist:

> America's denial of its racism is tantamount to an alcoholic refuting his illness. And like an addict, if my students, city, or country continue to insist on being "colorblind" or judging all people by the content of their character, then the specter of racism will continue to rear its terrifying head
>
> **Enciso, Alfee. "Living Under 'a Veil of Denial'."**
> *Los Angeles Times* **Dec. 1992. Print.**

The analogy here attempts to establish that if America continues to deny that it is a racist country, it will never be able to improve, as is the case when an alcoholic denies his alcoholism.

Sometimes, however, an analogy may *seem* to strengthen a position, but when scrutinized more carefully, it breaks down. For example, look at the following paragraph, which uses an analogy to argue in favor of mandatory drug testing:

> Any of us who has ever gone for a medical examination has had to submit to a blood test. Blood tests are required for many jobs, entrance into schools, and even marriage licenses, and even if we think that they represent an invasion of privacy, we recognize their necessity because we feel that they are good for society. Drug testing, which involves the testing of urine, is similarly used for the good of society. However, many people object to mandatory drug testing because they consider it an invasion of privacy. But if we allow blood testing, surely we can allow urine testing for drugs, since drug abuse is such a tremendous societal problem.

In this paragraph, the writer is arguing by analogy that blood testing is similar to urine testing, in that both may be considered invasions of privacy, but both are necessary for the good of society. However, if you examine this analogy carefully, you will see that in certain ways, it doesn't completely support the case for mandatory drug testing because of the purposes for which these tests are used. Blood tests are used to diagnose diseases that usually can be cured, and thus the tests are used *for* the benefit of the person being tested. Urine tests for drug abuse are usually used to identify a drug user to his or her employer, and the information is often used *against* the person being tested. Moreover, people usually choose to have blood tests voluntarily as part of routine physical examinations, whereas urine tests for drugs are usually mandatory. The effectiveness of the analogy, then, is undercut by some of these differences.

Statistics

Showing what statistics indicate is another forceful way of supporting a position. However, statistics can also be misleading if they are not current, if they are not typical of the population they are intended to describe, or if they do not reflect what the author claims they reflect. Moreover, statistics are problematic not only for the average person, but sometimes even for those who are familiar with statistical methods. In deciding on the credibility of a source that uses statistics, the Three-Pass Approach to critical thinking can help you figure out if the writer has a particular agenda that he or she is using statistics to support. Pay particular attention to the following:

Factors to Consider in Examining Statistics

The source of the information
The size and representativeness of the sample
Percentages versus actual figures
Associative versus causal connections

The Source of the Information

In deciding whether or not to include statistical information, examine the source of the information and try to figure out how the numbers were obtained. Did the information come from a study that used a questionnaire? If so, do you have access to the sorts of questions that were asked and do you feel that these questions elicited the information that they claim they did? Would people be likely to misrepresent, either deliberately or unintentionally?

The most reliable reports are those that are published in peer-reviewed journals. A particularly reliable source of statistics is a government organization, since the government is unlikely to award money for research without seriously evaluating its importance.

The Size and Representativeness of the Sample

For a statistic to be valid, it should mean what the author says it is representative of the population of which it is a sample. Yet often a sample is drawn from only a small segment of the population and it may not be representative at all. For instance, if you asked men in a pet store if they liked dogs and cats and most answered "yes," it would not be valid to conclude that most men liked dogs and cats, since the population was self-selecting. Similarly, if you stood outside the cafeteria with a sign saying, "please use this form to express your feelings about the food," it is likely that only students who felt very strongly about the food would bother to respond—probably, the students who disliked the food would respond most frequently. You might then conclude that most of the students disliked the food, when that might not be the case at all. Some studies are actually conducted in this way, but in examining their results, you should think carefully about how the information was obtained.

Percentages Versus Actual Figures

The other point to notice is whether the statistic cites percentages or actual numbers and to reflect on the significance of what is being claimed. Both percentages and actual figures may not be significant if the number is fairly small, as in the following examples:

> Twice as many college women are looking to marriage as their major goals in life, a study conducted at the University of Crockerville suggests. When questioned about their plans after college, 40% of respondents indicated that their primary goal after graduation was to find a husband, as opposed to only 20% of respondents questioned two years ago.

Of course, this paragraph does not state that only twenty women participated in the study. A critical reader might also ask who conducted the study and how the question was phrased.

Here is another example of how statistics can misrepresent information:

> More college men expect their wives to stay at home and take care of the house in 2005 than they did in 1995, a study conducted at the University of Crockerville suggests. Whereas in 1995, only five hundred college men responded to a survey that they expected their wives to stay at home, in 2005, 750 college men answered the same survey in the affirmative.

What this paragraph does not state is how many people were questioned, nor does it mention that the enrollment at the University of Crockerville increased extremely rapidly during these years, from two thousand students in 1995 to twenty thousand students in 2005. Therefore, the figure cited may actually indicate a *decline* in the proportion of college men who say that they expect their wives to stay at home.

Associative Versus Causal Connections

An important point to keep in mind in deciding whether or not to include statistics is that a link between two events or situations does not necessarily imply cause and effect. For example, an article might claim that there is an association between the number of computers in a region and death rates from heart attacks. But it doesn't mean that the computers, themselves, caused the heart attacks. Instead, the association might mean that people who spend a great deal of time sitting at a computer get little exercise or perhaps eat fattier foods, both of which might be responsible for the increase in coronaries.

If you are writing about social issues, which are commonly used as subject matter in writing classes, it is particularly difficult to use statistics to make definitive statements, because human behavior tends to be imprecise and difficult to measure. For example, one of the difficulties of assessing the effect of new educational programs in a classroom is that the effect of a particular teacher's personality is difficult to measure, so that the success or failure of a particular program might be due to the teacher, not to the program itself. Similarly, in measuring the success of programs teaching basic skills, such as reading and writing, improvement sometimes is not readily reflected on tests and often does not manifest itself immediately after instruction. The worth of any particular educational program is thus extremely difficult to assess objectively.

Interviews, Surveys, Questionnaires

An additional source of evidence for argument essays are interviews or surveys that you have conducted yourself. Interviews can be especially useful because they not only provide expert opinion and important information, but also can help you understand alternative or opposing viewpoints. The important point to remember about conducting an interview, though, is to plan for it carefully. Before the interview, find out as much as you can about the person you will be interviewing and be prepared to explain its purpose. It is also important to write out your questions in advance so that you don't waste time trying to formulate them during the interview and keep them consistent in each interview. Of course, it goes without saying that you will receive a more favorable reception if you are punctual, courteous, and respectful. Do not argue with the people you are interviewing, even if you strongly disagree with them. Remember that the function of the interview is for you to gain material for your essay, not to engage in a debate.

In recording information from an interview, it is a good idea to record it. If that is not possible, be sure to take good notes. Then as soon as the interview is over, rewrite your notes while the information is fresh in your mind.

An informal survey can also be an effective use of evidence. At a local school, an enterprising member of the Parent Teachers Association polled eighty-six parents about whether they wanted an after-school program for the children of working parents, and whether they would be willing to contribute a small amount to it. Overwhelmingly, the response was positive, and as a result, the school now has an afternoon child care facility.

Questionnaires also provide useful information, but developing and distributing them can be more challenging than writing an informal survey. In fact, those who write questionnaires as part of their research—social scientists, for example—must take special courses to learn how to do it properly. Writing a questionnaire may seem simple on the surface, but if the questions are confusingly worded or if the possibilities for response do not allow for enough flexibility, the questionnaire will bias the response and not provide accurate information. If you plan to write a questionnaire, you should include the following elements:

Working with Questionnaires

1. Explain its purpose.
2. Keep your questions simple.
3. Try it out on a friend to work out problematic sections before making multiple copies.
4. Make sure it is neatly printed and easy to read.

ANTICIPATING THE OPPOSITION: THE NEED FOR ADDITIONAL REASONS

The final support strategy discussed in this chapter involves anticipating the objections your audience might have to your reasons and then providing additional support. For example, Jon, the college student who wishes to change his major, might make the following argument:

Students should major in subjects that interest them.
Environmental studies interests me.
Therefore, I should major in environmental studies.

This line of thinking, however, might not be sufficient to convince Aunt Maria, who might then pose the following objection to Jon's claim:

I don't believe that students should major in a subject just because it interests them. I, myself, am interested in a lot of things, like sports, for example. That doesn't mean that I should have been a Recreational Studies major or tried to become a professional baseball player. Your cousin majored in creative writing because it interested him, but now he can't earn a living. Choosing a major just out of interest is a luxury that only wealthy people can afford, and you, Jon, aren't wealthy.

Having considered Aunt Maria's objections, Jon might then respond with the qualification that one should major in subjects that interest them, providing that these subjects lead to employment after college. He could then point out the professional opportunities that exist in the field. Anticipating Aunt Maria's objections, Jon could also point out the differences between pursuing a sport such as baseball and majoring in a subject like environmental studies. He could argue that baseball is a highly competitive sport, at which only a few talented athletes succeed, whereas environmental studies is a growing field, which requires students to learn many transferable skills such as statistics and mathematics, and is likely to provide diverse career opportunities in the future. By anticipating Aunt Maria's objections, Jon would thus be able to provide additional support.

ARTICLES THAT USE STATISTICS AS SUPPORT

Topic: College and Financial Success

Each of the articles below use statistical information from graphs and charts to support an argument concerned with the topic of whether a college education will ultimately be worthwhile financially. Access both of these articles and analyze how each uses statistical data. Which do you find most convincing?

1.   In "Should Everyone Go to College?" Stephanie Owen and Isabel Sawhill argue that "telling all young people that they should go to college no matter what may be doing them a disservice" They point out that although "on average, college graduates make significantly more money over their lifetimes than those with only a high school education. . . . what gets less attention is the fact that not all college degrees or college graduates are equal. There is enormous variation in the so-called return to education depending on factors such as institution attended, field of study, whether a student graduates, and post-graduation occupation."

(Brookings, May 8, 2013
www.brookings.edu/.../08-should-everyone-go-to-college-owen-sawhill)

2.   In "Maybe College Isn't for Everyone. But It's Probably for You." Dylan Matthews uses statistical information to counter Owen and Sawhill's article "Should Everyone Go to College?" Matthews argues that despite the major a student chooses, all college graduates report "higher lifetime earnings than the average high school graduate."

Dylan Matthews "Maybe College Isn't for Everyone. But It's Probably for You."
http://www.washingtonpost.com/news/wonkblog/wp/2013/05/10/
maybe-college-isnt-for-everyone-but-its-probably-for-you/

Topic: College Majors and Jobs

Read the article by Brad Plumer titled "Only 27 Percent of College Grads Have a Job Related to their Major" (*Washington Post Wonkblog*).

>   How does the author use information from the U.S. Bureau of the Census to support his position?

Topic: Teens and Social Media

Amanda Lenhart "Teens, Social Media & Technology." (Pewresearchcenter April 9, 2015)

>   How are statistics used in this article to support the author's main point?

10

CHAPTER

Organizing and Incorporating Information

Imagine a college student emerging from the library, her backpack stuffed with all sorts of potentially useful materials she has downloaded and printed from the Internet or found in articles and books. She walks jauntily, pleased with the success of her visit to the library, and when she arrives home, she fixes herself a snack, sits down at her desk, and piles all of her materials around her, ready to begin to work. But then, she looks at all the "stuff" she has found, and her euphoria suddenly evaporates. "Now that I have found it, what do I do with it?" she thinks to herself. "How can I learn all the information in these materials? What should I do to understand it? How should I organize it so that I will really be able to use it in my essay? How much of it should I use? How can I create order out of all of this chaos?"

Gathering information from the library or online is an important part of the research and writing process. But once you have found materials you can use, you need to be able to take notes, figure out how you might use the information you have found to support your thesis or main idea, and incorporate it smoothly into your essay using proper documentation conventions—in other words to "create order out of chaos." Organizing, synthesizing, and documenting information is particularly important in college writing because you need to demonstrate to your reader that you have thoroughly researched and considered necessary information, background, and viewpoints. Whereas personal information is sufficient for some genres, such as a personal narrative or an exploratory essay on a personal topic, when you write an argument essay on a complex and/or controversial issue, you will need to incorporate other perspectives.

This chapter is concerned with various strategies for managing information. It discusses methods for taking notes, including summaries and direct quotations, and suggestions for organizing and incorporating information smoothly into your text.

BEING ACTIVE IN THE RESEARCH PROCESS

To thoroughly engage with your topic, it is important to assume an active role in all stages of the research process. Before you even begin to search for sources, it is a good idea to do some preliminary exploration of the topic, perhaps responding to exploration questions or thinking about possible directions you might want to investigate. You might write an outline or even a preliminary draft of your essay so that you can consider a possible thesis and think about the type of information you will need. With at least some idea of your thesis, you will be more focused in searching for information, although it is likely that your ideas will change, at least somewhat, as you discover new possibilities.

As you read and take notes, you should not simply be trying to "learn" or memorize; rather, you should be thinking about how new information or a particular perspective corresponds to what you already know about the topic, whether or not you are convinced by it, and how you might be able to use it in your essay. If you simply record information mechanically, without thinking seriously about it, or if you print a great deal of information from the Internet or photocopy many articles and selections from books, and then sit down with a highlighter, you will spend a great deal of time doing mechanical activities such as printing or highlighting. But when you have finished, you may not have reflected deeply on what you have read.

If this picture describes your own method of working with information, you might consider whether it really is the most effective one to use. On the surface, it appears quite easy and efficient, but unless you become involved with what you read, either by taking notes by hand or on the computer, you can breeze through an entire essay without really reading it at all—you simply cast your eye over the page and move your highlighter deftly over what seem to be important sentences. But then, when you are in the process of actually writing your essay and want to incorporate information from outside sources, you may discover that you have forgotten completely what these sources are about and that you are unable to remember where a piece of information you want to use is located. Then you will have to spend considerable time rereading. In many instances, the quick highlighting job is not really efficient at all.

THE ROLE OF OUTSIDE SOURCES

The argument essays written for college classes often use information from published works to support the thesis and to indicate that the writer has adequately researched the topic. Because you are probably not an authority on the topic you are writing about, your argument will probably need the support of credible experts who have worked and/or been published in the field. For example, in the following excerpt from an essay concerned with the death penalty, Steve cited information he found in a report published by the National Research Council published by the National Academy of Sciences, a very prestigious organization.

For the death penalty to work as a deterrent, it must be allowed to instill fear in the criminals—that is, to act as a deterrent. However, according to a report by the committee on Deterrence and the Death Penalty, research as of 2012 "is not informative about whether capital punishment decreases, increases, or has no effect on homicide rates." Moreover, as the report further notes, from 1973 to 2009, although "8,115 people were sentenced to death in the United States," only "about 15 percent of those sentenced—had been executed by the end of 2009." This lack of definitive research on the issue of deterrence and the fact that few executions actually occur, suggests that the deterrence argument is questionable.

(Committee on Deterrence and the Death Penalty 2012)

Because Steve could not know this information on the basis of his own experience, he obtained them from a report written by the Committee on Deterrence and the Death Penalty, which is associated with the National Academy of Sciences, a highly respected and prestigious organization. Notice, also, that after Steve quoted the information, he indicated in the last sentence of the paragraph why the quote was significant.

COMMON KNOWLEDGE

In working with information obtained from published work, students often are confused about what kind of information should be documented. Some kinds of information are considered "common knowledge." This is information that most people know and, therefore, does not require a reference. For instance, the statement that the Los Angeles riots occurred in the spring of 1992 is common knowledge, but any commentary on that incident, such as the number of arrests, or the extent of the damage, would require a reference. Similarly, the fact that Malcolm X was a civil rights leader who was assassinated is common knowledge; however, if you referred to a social historian who claimed that Malcolm X did not condone racial violence, as is commonly assumed, then it is important that you acknowledge that point of view through a citation. Sometimes it is difficult to determine whether something is common knowledge, since for one person it may be new information and another it may not. In general, though, well-known facts are considered common knowledge; opinions and observations on these facts must be documented.

DISTINGUISHING BETWEEN PRIMARY AND SECONDARY SOURCES

When you are citing your sources, you need to be aware that there is a difference between primary and secondary sources. A primary source provides first hand or "primary" knowledge of your topic. It is the original work or document upon which your paper is based. Primary sources would include such items as the Declaration of Independence, a novel, or a poem. If you are writing about a particular person, a statement made by that person would constitute a primary source, and it is possible for you to obtain primary source material from interviews published in the newspaper.

A secondary source is any type of commentary on the primary source. For instance, an article that analyzes the Declaration of Independence is a secondary source. A critical commentary on a work of literature is a secondary source. A statement made about the person who is the subject of your paper is a secondary source. For instance, if you are writing a paper about President Obama's economic views, his own statements are a primary source, but newspaper articles commenting on his statements would be a secondary source.

It is important to differentiate between primary and secondary sources so that you do not misrepresent or distort in any way. For instance, the following sentence was written by an observer and is, therefore, a secondary source:

> The President was obviously troubled by the arrest of Professor Henry Louis Gates.

This statement reflects the *opinion* of someone who observed the President, and it may only indicate that, to the observer, the President appeared to be troubled. However, when someone uses the word "obviously" in this way, the statement can be viewed as interpretive. In this context, the phrase "obviously troubled" suggests that the President's feelings were so apparent that they could be discerned by everyone. Keep in mind that all secondary sources are interpretive to some degree, and it is important to be aware of that when you decide to use them in your essay.

In contrast, an actual statement made by the President is a primary source. If you were listening to the President speak and he said, "This incident with Professor Gates is troubling to me," his statement is a primary source.

HOW MANY SOURCES TO USE?
HOW DO THESE SOURCES FUNCTION WITHIN THE ESSAY?

You may be under the impression that the more sources you use the better your essays will be. However, it is the *quality*, rather than the number, of sources that is important and it is the *function* these sources fulfill within the text that determines an essay's quality. In deciding to use a source, the main consideration, after critically evaluating it, is to consider what role it will play in your essay. Sources can provide factual data, and can be used as **examples and expert support.** They can also represent **an opposing viewpoint**, against which the essay will then argue.

In trying to decide how many sources to use, a great deal depends on the genre in which you are writing and on the topic being addressed. A long research paper will include more sources than a short one and a topic about which a great deal has been written will necessitate more sources than one that is new or limited in some other way. Depending on the assignment, you should include enough to show that you have "done your homework" and fulfilled the requirements of the assignment. If you include too many sources without commenting on them or considering why you are using them, the paper will read like a long list of quotations and your own position will be overwhelmed. The key is to use enough sources to support your position, but not so many that your own perspective is lost.

A SUGGESTED METHOD FOR TAKING NOTES: USING WORKSHEETS

In order to work with information effectively and efficiently, it is important to construct a method of taking notes that works for you. In the past, students were sometimes taught to use index cards for this purpose, and if you have been successful in using them, you should continue to do so. Note cards, though, don't leave very much room in which to write and they sometimes fragment ideas so that it is hard to retain the main point of the article or book section as a whole.

Those who prefer to take notes in the context of a whole work or those who like to take a lot of notes and jot down ideas for how they might use them may prefer to use worksheets, pads of paper, or the computer. If you are interested in using note sheets for the purpose of recording information from outside sources, we suggest that you create note sheets from a long pad of lined paper or make copies of the sheets included in this chapter. You can also replicate the form of this sheet on your computer. Then, we suggest that you use the following procedure:

SUGGESTIONS FOR TAKING NOTES

1. Select your sources

Using the Three-Pass Approach discussed in Chapter 2, select those sources you want to read for the purpose of taking notes. If it is possible, photocopy each selection that you think will be particularly useful so that you will be able to refer to it again. When you photocopy, be sure to include the page that contains the bibliographical information, as this can be a valuable resource for locating additional material if you need it.

2. Record bibliographical information at the top of a note sheet

At the top of a note sheet, copy down all relevant bibliographical information—the author's name, the title of the book or article, the copyright or journal information, and the page numbers of the selection. Even if you have a photocopy of the material, it is still important to record this information in your notes because you do not want to lose track of your sources. All of us who write have had the experience of rereading our notes and finding a statement that we really want to use, but for which we cannot locate the source. Many a frantic last minute scramble around the library has been due to carelessness about recording a source.

3. Briefly summarize the main point of the selection at the top of the sheet

After recording the bibliographical information at the top of the sheet, try to get an overview of the work so that you can write a brief summary of it (introductory paragraphs, abstracts, and book introductions are useful for this). A summary of the selection or article will help you understand your notes more fully when you look them over at a later time. Without that summary statement, you may not remember how the notes you took fit into the author's main idea and they will then be less meaningful to you. Of course, you may not be able to discern the main point of the selection as a whole until you have read it through, so leave a few lines blank for this purpose.

4. Record notes

Read the selection carefully, and when you come upon an idea that you think is important or that you may want to use in your essay, **write down the number of the page** on which it occurs and then either copy the quotation directly, using quotation marks, or summarize or paraphrase the ideas it expresses. As you write down your notes, ideas may come to you about how you would like to use that note in your essay. As they occur, write these ideas down so that you don't forget them, and mark each one with a symbol such as a star (*) so that it will attract your attention later on when you reread your notes.

To illustrate how this method can be used to write an actual essay, let us look at how Tyrone took notes for his essay, which is concerned with potential dangers associated with genetic research. He found an article written in 1990 that discusses some of the issues that are still being addressed today and he thought that a reference to this article would be useful as a comparison with other, more recent articles on this topic. The article he took notes on was titled "Genetics and Human Malleability," published in *The Hastings Center Report*, January/February 1990, pp. 67–73. The author was W. French Anderson. Here is how Tyrone recorded some information from that article using a note sheet:

EXAMPLE OF A NOTE SHEET

Bibliographical Information:

Anderson, W., French. "Genetics and Human Malleability." *The Hastings Center Report* (January/February 1990): 67–73.

Summary: The article distinguishes between *somatic* cell gene therapy used to cure diseases and *enhancement* genetic engineering, which would enable scientists to engineer away characteristics that those in power consider abnormal or undesirable. The main position of the article is that genetic engineering should be restricted to medical therapy.

Notes:
        * Information provided on W. French Anderson who has pioneered research on gene therapy. Shows his credibility.

68   " . . .successful somatic cell gene therapy also opens the door for enhancement genetic engineering, that is, for supplying a specific characteristic that individuals might want for themselves (somatic cell engineering) or their children (germline engineering), which would not involve the treatment of a disease."

        * use in defining differences between somatic and enhancement therapy

70   Raises a number of ethically questionable scenarios.

        "Should a pubescent adolescent whose parents are both five feet tall be provided with a growth hormone gene on request?"

        * Could be used as an example of possible dangers of unrestricted genetic testing.
        This example also raises the question about how to distinguish a serious disease from a "minor" disease from cultural "discomfort."

        Important to make this distinction.

In this example of a note sheet, the author's last name appears first in the bibliographic information, enabling Tyrone to alphabetize his sheets very easily when he is compiling his bibliography. Notice that Tyrone has distinguished direct quotations from paraphrase by enclosing the direct quotation in quotation marks and that he used an ellipsis in the first note (marked with three spaced dots like this . . .) to show that some of the quotation was left out. Distinguishing direct quotation from paraphrase or summary is very useful when you reread your notes, because it will enable you to document properly if you decide to include that particular note in your paper. If you take notes on the computer, you will be able to paste them directly into your essay, saving you some time. Note also that Tyrone has made notes for himself about how he might want to use information from this article in his paper.

RECORDING INFORMATION IN THE FORM OF DIRECT QUOTATION

In recording information on a note sheet, there are many instances in which you would prefer direct quotation rather than paraphrase or summary. These may be summarized as follows:

USE DIRECT QUOTATIONS IF . . .

1. The style is so unusual that you wish to retain its flavor.
2. The passage was spoken by a particular authority or famous person and you wish to use the actual words of that authority to support your own position.
3. You are discussing someone's first-hand experience and you wish to capture that immediacy through using the speaker or writer's actual words.
   A. Use direct quotation if the style is so unusual that you wish to retain its flavor. Here is an example:

   > One of the most famous scenes in the history of film is the moment in *Gone With the Wind* when Rhett says to Scarlett, "Frankly, my dear. I don't give a damn."

   It would be much less effective if this were summarized, as in the following example:

   > One of the most famous scenes in the history of film is the moment in *Gone With the Wind when* Rhett tells Scarlett that he is completely indifferent to what happens to her.

   B. Use direct quotation if the passage was spoken by a particular authority or famous person and you wish to use the actual words of that authority to support your own position.

   For example:

   > The well-known physician, Lewis Thomas, argues that "the only solid piece of scientific truth about which I feel really confident is that we are profoundly ignorant about nature" (321).

C. Use direct quotation if you are discussing someone's firsthand experience and you wish to capture that immediacy through using the speaker or writer's actual words.

For example:

> John Burns, eye witness to the accident, said that "the Mercedes was speeding down the street at about seventy miles an hour."

In this instance, the use of direct quotation enhances the reliability of the statement.

PUNCTUATING DIRECT QUOTATIONS IN YOUR TEXT

If you decide to quote your source directly using direct quotation, be sure to enclose all quoted material within quotation marks and punctuate as follows:

1. Place commas and periods *inside* quotation marks. Thus:

> On the astrology page of the *Star Gazette,* the well-known astrologist, Fifi Moonbeam stated that "Jupiter will ally itself with Mars in two weeks," and that "the Moon will be in its seventh house."

However, if you are including a page reference in parenthesis, then the comma or period goes after the quotation marks. Thus,

> On the astrology section of the *Star Gazette,* the well-known astrologist, Fifi Moonbeam stated that "Jupiter will ally itself with Mars in two weeks" (7), and that within the month "the Moon will be in its seventh house" (8).

2. Place semicolons and colons outside of the quotation marks. For example, here is a passage from a book by Roland Smith about the habits of cats:

> Many cats sleep at least sixteen hours a day, their favorite spot usually being a chair or some place relatively high off the ground such as an ironing board. Even a comfortable fluffy rug will not usually attract them because it lies on the floor.
>
> **Roland Smith, *The Lion at the Hearth: The Way of the Cat***

If you wished to quote from this passage in a sentence that had a semicolon, this is how you would do it:

> Smith discusses the tendency that cats have of sleeping "relatively high off the ground"; he notes that they will avoid even a soft, fluffy rug because it "lies on the floor" (49).

If you wished to quote from this passage in a sentence that had a colon, this is how you would do it:

> Smith notes two favorite sleeping places for cats: "a chair or some place relatively high off the ground" (49).

3. Question marks and exclamation marks are kept **within** quotation marks if they are part of the original quotation. For example:

> Speaking to her nephew, Aunt Maria asked, "What's so interesting about environmental studies?" (Because the question mark is part of the original quotation, the question mark is kept inside.) However, when the sentence itself is in the form of a question, the question mark is placed **outside** the quotation marks as in the following example:

> Didn't Jon have an answer prepared when Aunt Maria asked what was "so interesting about environmental studies"? (Because the question mark is part of the whole sentence, it is placed outside of the quotation marks.)

4. Single quotation marks are placed inside double quotation marks for a quote within a quote.

> Jon said, "I needed some more time to respond to Aunt Maria's question about what was 'so interesting about environmental studies.'"

5. If you omit part of a quotation, use an ellipsis (three spaced dots). For example, here is a paragraph from Roland Smith's book about cats:

> The cat remains a mysterious animal. Although it is a popular domestic pet, it never really loses its wildness, and one can always sense the throb of the jungle behind an inscrutable pair of cat eyes. Watch a cat as it stalks its prey, its body motionless, its whole being intent on the chase, and it is clear that the deep feline nature of the lion lies just beneath the skin of even the most domesticated tabby sleeping by a fire.
>
> **Roland Smith, *The Lion at the Hearth: The Way of the Cat*, 57**

Here is an example of a sentence that quotes from this paragraph using an ellipsis:

Roland Smith maintains that the cat "never really loses its wildness and . . . that the deep feline nature of the lion lies just beneath the skin of even the most domesticated tabby" (57).

6. Use brackets whenever you need to substitute or add words to a quotation. For example:

Roland Smith maintains that when a cat "stalks its prey, its body [becomes] motionless [and] its whole being [becomes] intent on the chase" (57).

EXAMINING AND EVALUATING WEB SOURCES

Your ability to read critically and evaluate what you see also pertains to evaluating the credibility of webpages. Today, almost anyone can create a webpage using an HTML code-based page, a WYSIWYG editor, or a Wiki page. It is possible for someone with very little experience to create and post a webpage with information that may not always be correct. For this reason we need to be careful and analyze where this information is coming from and who is posting it. Following are some strategies you can use to determine their quality:

1. The Source

Look at the URL carefully. Is it someone's personal page? Often you can tell if there is a personal name, such as "bjones" followed by a tilde (~) or a percent sign (%). A personal page may not mean that the source isn't credible. Sometimes you will find the personal webpage of an author or scientific expert in the field you are studying. But it is important to know something about the person who wrote it. Is this person qualified to do so? Is there information provided about this person, such as an e-mail address or phone number?

2. The Domain

Look at the extension at the end of the URL, which will indicate where it came from. Preferred sites are .edu (associated with educational institutions), .gov (associated with local, state, or federal government), .org (associated with non-profit or for profit organizations), or .net (associated with networks and businesses). Commercial organizations tend to use ".com." Now remember that although the domains can give you a clue on who may be behind the Website, it does not mean that you can trust it. For example, if a religious group receives federal funding, then they can use a .gov domain for their Website. Another example could be a for profit organization that may have a school and thus use a .edu domain. Always make sure you know who is behind that domain.

3. *Clues That Provide Additional Information*

Background and Qualification
Look for links that indicate where the information is coming from. Often there is a link that says "background" or "about us." If you do not see any of these links, most likely the site is not reputable. These links provide key information that allows you to reach the people who created the site. If they are not there, there is a reason why the creators do not want to be reached which is usually not a good one. Once you go into these links, think about the following: Does the author provide credentials about his or her qualifications to construct this page? Because anyone can post a webpage, it is important to get a sense of whether the page was posted by someone who really knows about the subject. Perhaps it was written by someone who has a very strong opinion on the subject and is unable to be objective. Many webpages are opinion pieces and may not include credible evidence.

Date
Find the date that the page was updated and who did the updating. For some topics, a recent date is very important. For others, it might not matter as much. There are several ways for you to check for the date.

- Usually there is a date on the top left side of the page. If it is an article, the date should be at the top after the name of the article.
- Scroll all the way to the end of the page and there should be a date at the bottom of the page.
- In the "About Us" page, there should be a date when the page was created.

4. *The Quality of the Information*

Once we find a Website, we need to look at the quality of the information. Just because it is online does not mean that the information is accurate or up to date. Remember that unlike books and articles that go through an extensive editing and fact-checking process, Websites do not, and thus we must be very careful and question everything we read in them. Here are a few questions that may help you decide if the information presented is valid and useful:

What is the purpose of this Website?
How detailed is the information?
Does the information seem objective?
Can you figure out where the author obtained the information?
Are there links to other sources of information? Are these links current?
What sources are cited? Are there footnotes posted?
Does this information make sense to you? Is it consistent with what you think and believe about the world?

University libraries often provide excellent guides for evaluating web sources, and I suggest that you supplement the advice provided by accessing these sources. The library at Cornell lists five criteria:

Accuracy—the author and institution that published the page and a way of contacting him or her

Authority—the author's credentials and the domain

Objectivity—the accuracy of the information and a balanced presentation

Currency—up-to-date information and current links

Coverage—the ability to view the information in its entirety, without having to pay fees

Another excellent series of pages on evaluating a Website can be found at http://www.library.jhu.edu.researchhelp/general/evaluating/ (from the Milton Library at Johns Hopkins University).

The ability to evaluate a source, whether it is an article, a book, or a webpage is crucial to being able to write an effective college argument. The suggestions in this chapter will help you scrutinize sources with greater insight.

EVALUATING VISUAL ARGUMENTS

Developed by Emmanuel Sabaiz-Birdsill

When looking at visual arguments, we need to look at every single part of the argument in order to understand the connections that have been created. It is through this connection that the argument is being made. This is a two-part worksheet that will help you gather information and begin analyzing the arguments made in visual texts.

First Part

1. Where did you find the visual argument? Magazine, TV, Internet, side of a bus?
2. How big is it?
3. What is the company behind it?
4. What is the product/service or idea in the visual argument?
5. List all the images in the visual argument, from the main one, which is usually the main product, to the very small one.
6. Is there a background? If so, what is it? Can you tell if the image takes place outdoors/ indoors?
7. List the colors used in the visual argument, including the one used for the text.
8. Text: does the visual argument have any text, and if so what kind and how big is it? Where is the visual argument? How much text is there in relation to the images?

Second Part

After you have listed all this information, here are a few questions you should be able to answer in order to start making the connection:

1. What is the main purpose of the visual argument? To sell something, to inform, to make a point?
2. Who is the intended audience? Men, women, teens, politicians?
3. Is this a new visual argument or an old visual argument? Can you date it? If so how?
4. Does it rely on your previous knowledge of the brand, product, ideas, or topic?
5. Is there a Website, phone number, or address where you can look up more information? If so, what is it?
6. If we were to remove certain images, or the text, would the visual argument be as effective? Explain.
7. Do you think the visual argument is successful at what it is supposed to do? If so, why?

EVALUATING WEB SOURCES

Developed by Emmanuel Sabaiz-Birdsill

When we look at a Website, we need to be very careful about how we use the information that we find. Since not all Websites go through a review or editing process, we must gather as much information as we can to decide if we will use them or not. Use the following worksheet to gather as much information as you can.

1. What is the name of the Website?
2. What is the URL of the Website?
3. Who wrote the content? What type of credentials do they have?
4. Is the information provided in text form, audio, or images?
5. What year was the content created or updated?
6. Is it associated with a particular organization or group?
7. What references are used in the site? Are they in-text references, or are they links to other Websites?
8. Can you reach the creators of the site in case you have a question? If so, how?
9. Is this a blog or a personal Website?
10. Is this an informative site or an opinion site?

By gathering as much information as possible in the early stages, we will be able to determine if the site is appropriate to use, and we will have all the information we need for our in-text citations and works cited page.

WRITING A SUMMARY

A summary, defined as a restatement of a piece of writing in a compact form, is an important strategy for working with information because it helps you to understand the major point, important ideas, and structure of a source. Summaries are very useful for condensing a longer piece of writing and helps you gain a clear sense of the author's purpose and the major direction of the piece.

THE PURPOSE OF A SUMMARY

The type of summary you write depends on the purpose for which it is intended. If you are writing the summary for yourself, and you have retained the full copy of the text, the summary can be much shorter and less detailed than one written for a reader who has not read the original and has no access to it. But whether you write a summary for yourself or for someone else, it is important to note the author and/or the article's title and to include sufficient details so that any reader, including you at a later time, will be able to understand it without confusion.

Following is an example of a summary of the introduction to Michael Crichton's best selling book, *Jurassic Park*.

> In his introduction to *Jurassic Park,* Michael Crichton notes three ways in which the current biotechnology differs from "past scientific transformations." The first is that it is "broad-based" in that it is conducted in over two thousand laboratories. The second is that it sometimes is geared toward unimportant areas of investigation and often follows the "vagaries of fashion," and third, it is not subject to consistent government regulation. But what Crichton identifies as of most concern is that there are no "watchdogs" among the scientists themselves because most have a commercial stake in their research.

Note that in this summary, quotation marks are used whenever the author's exact words are included. This is very important to remember in order to avoid inadvertent plagiarism.

WRITING A SUMMARY: SOME SUGGESTIONS

Writing a summary means understanding the overall meaning of the text and making decisions about what is important. Here are some steps you might find helpful for writing a summary:

1.   Scan for the main point

A summary represents the essence of a book or article and it is, therefore, necessary to understand the main point the author is trying to make before you write. To find this main point in an article, scan the first paragraph or two since this is often where the main point or thesis may be found. Then look over the conclusion where you may find an overview of the results or a rephrasing of the main ideas in the text. Once you feel that you understand the main point, look for sub-points that might be related to it. If you are writing a summary of a book, you should read the introduction as if it is an article. See if you can identify the main ideas that the book is addressing. Most introductions provides an overview of each chapter, and if so, you might include some of that information in your summary.

2.   Determine the structure

By locating sub-points, you will gain insight into the structure of the text. If you are working with a photocopy of the work you are summarizing, underline the sub-points and be sure to include them in your summary. Try to distinguish main points from examples. Decide whether you need to include any examples in your summary.

3.   Condense lists and eliminate extraneous detail

In most published works, there is at least some repetition and superfluous detail. In selecting material to eliminate, look for repetition and unnecessary elaboration. Pay attention to words or even whole paragraphs that may simply repeat previously stated information or link two paragraphs together.

4.   Use synonyms and rephrase

Finding synonyms and rephrasing can help you understand what you read and develops your writing style. Avoid copying too much material from the text, particularly if you plan to include it in your essay.

5.   Rewrite the summary so that it reads well

Particularly if you plan to include the summary in your essay, you should rewrite it so that it reads easily.

EXERCISE

Choose one of the following passages and write a summary of it.

1. Today, huge television audiences watch surgical operations in the comfort of their living rooms. Moreover, thanks to the animated cartoon, the geography of the digestive system has become familiar territory even to the nursery school set, and the satisfaction of curiosity about almost all matters is a national pastime. Obviously, then, the secrecy surrounding embalming can, surely, hardly be attributed to the inherent gruesomeness of the subject.

   (Adapted from Jessica Mitford, "Behind the Formaldehyde Curtain,"
   The American Way of Death)

2. The koala, all 10 to 30 pounds and two to three feet of it (there is an amazing range in size among adults), is a beast of tall trees. Koalas live most of their lives high up in any one of 35 species of eucalyptus, or gum tree. They subsist on eucalyptus leaves, which they can't digest on their own. They rely on microorganisms in their digestive tract to do it for them. They can also handle some mistletoe leaves and some leaves from a tree known as the box.

   (Roger Caras "What's a Koala?")

3. As much as America is joined in a common culture, Americans are reluctant to celebrate the process of assimilation. We pledge allegiance to diversity. America was born Protestant and bred Puritan, and the notion of community we share is derived from a seventeenth-century faith. Presidents and the pages of ninth-grade civics readers yet proclaim the orthodoxy: We are gathered together—but as individuals with separate paths, distinct destinies. Our society is as paradoxical as a Puritan congregation: We stand together, alone.

   (Richard Rodriguez "Does America Still Exist?")

4. My concern is that, at this point in the development of our culture's scientific expertise, we might be like the young boy who loves to take things apart. He is bright enough to disassemble a watch and maybe even bright enough to get it back together again so that it works. But what if he tries to "improve" it? Maybe put on bigger hands so that the time can be read more easily? But if the hands are too heavy for the mechanism, the watch will run slowly, erratically, or not at all. The boy can understand what is visible, but he cannot comprehend the precise engineering calculations that determined exactly how strong each spring should be, why the gears interact in the ways that they do, etc. Attempts on his part to improve the watch will probably only harm it. We are now able to provide a new gene so that a property involved in a human life would be changed, for example a growth hormone gene. If we were to do so simply because we could, I fear we would be like that young boy who changed the watch's hands. We, too, do not really understand what makes the object we're tinkering with tick. . . .

Anderson, W. French "Genetics and Human Malleability."
The Hastings Center Report January/February 1990: 67–73. Print.

SAMPLE SHEET FOR TAKING NOTES

Bibliographical Information:

Summary:

Page #:   **Note:**

AVOIDING PLAGIARISM

The term *plagiarism* is derived from the Latin word *plagiarius* or, kidnapper, and to plagiarize means to steal, to take what is not yours. In current usage, to plagiarize is to take the ideas of another writer and to pass them off as one's own. It is the unacknowledged borrowing of sources.

Today, plagiarism is considered a serious academic offense (often resulting in a failing grade, or worse), but in earlier times the unacknowledged borrowing of sources was not considered a problem. In fact, in the middle ages, to mimic or echo another author's ideas, style, or actual words was considered the highest compliment. Originality was not valued, nor were authors considered the owners of their work. Shakespeare never even published his own plays, and those who did felt free to amend them as they wished. (At one point *King Lear* was even given a happy ending!) It was not until the eighteenth century that an author's writing was seen as a personal expression, and thus as something that someone could "own."

In using information from published works in college writing, an author's words and ideas are considered a form of permanent property that must be acknowledged, even if these words were downloaded directly from a webpage. When you use another writer's words or ideas and acknowledge that you have used them, it is as if you are borrowing that property. But if you use another writer's words or ideas and do not acknowledge your source, it is as if you have stolen something that does not belong to you. And the theft of words and ideas in all genres of college writing is regarded very seriously. At the present time, when so much information is readily available via the Internet, people are paying very close attention to the acknowledgment of sources. It is therefore very important that you learn to document the information you have found in outside sources.

The two types of documentation styles that are most commonly used are the MLA (Modern Language Association) and the APA (American Psychological Association), and the method of documentation varies according to discipline, both of which are discussed in the appendix.

A useful Website that discusses both systems can be found on the Purdue University OWL (online writing lab). Here are two Websites that explain this information:

MLA   *http://owl.english.purdue.edu/owl/resource/747/01/*
APA   *http://owl.english.purdue.edu/owl/resource/560/01/*
Chicago Manual of Style   *http://www.chicagomanualofstyle.org/tools_citationguide.html*

This method uses a system of footnotes inserted into the text. It is often required for research papers in history and for some humanities publications.

Before deciding which system you should use, you should check with your instructor.

WRITING ASSIGNMENTS

Assignment #1 (this assignment was created by Jennifer Welsh at the University of Southern California)

Our culture's attitude toward science and technology has its roots in the Enlightenment, a period in which reason and observable fact were believed to hold the answers to any questions we could think up. Being steeped in these beliefs, we have difficulty imagining any other way of thinking: questions about the limitations and risks of scientific knowledge seem to threaten our most fundamental principle that to know more is always better. But the controversies surrounding new discoveries and technological developments, from the atomic bomb to gene splicing, computers to threshing machines, suggest that we are not as comfortable with this principle as we thought. Certainly, in the introduction to *Jurassic Park,* Michael Crichton suggests the need for scientists to be monitored. He points out that a major problem associated with current research in biotechnology is that there are no "watchdogs" among the scientists themselves because most have a commercial stake in their research.

Writing Topic

Choose one area of scientific research that has the potential for having a profound impact on humanity (genetic engineering and prenatal testing lend themselves well to this topic). Use various resources to find out more information about it. Then write a 4–6 page essay that addresses the following question:

> Are there dangers inherent in this type of research that scientists ought to consider?

Assignment #2

Choose two movies that use the theme of science or technology running amok. *Frankenstein, Back to the Future, The Fly* and, of course, *Jurassic Park* are good possibilities. Examine the attitude toward scientific research expressed in these movies and note that in all of them, the "creator" is blamed or holds himself responsible, at least in part, for the ensuing events. Then write an argumentative essay of 4–6 pages addressing the following topic:

> Should scientists be responsible for the consequences of their work?

SAMPLE STUDENT PAPER USING INFORMATION FROM OUTSIDE SOURCES

Genetic Testing

Genetic testing is the fastest-growing area in medical research and can be used to diagnose illnesses in children and adults. Researchers have already found genes associated with Alzheimer's disease, Huntington's Chorea, Breast Cancer, colon cancer, and many other diseases, and, in many instances, it is now possible for people to have genetic testing and learn about possible genetic risks. Used with therapies that replace defective genes with working ones, genetic tests might soon lead to cures. However, the rapid growth of genetic testing is raising ethical questions for which there are no simple answers. Some of the information obtained from this research can easily be misinterpreted and lead to discriminatory employment and insurance practices. Moreover, the potential danger that genetic testing will lead to genetic "improvements" cannot be overlooked.

Genetic illness is often understood in terms of the single-gene model, in which a defect in a gene causes a particular health effect. Some diseases work this way (such as sickle cell anemia and Tay-Sachs disease), and interpretations of the single-gene model invite people to think that genes equal fate. However, it is now recognized that because many conditions arise from both genetic and environmental factors, this model is turning out to be an oversimplification. No more than 3% of all human diseases are caused by defects in a single gene (Rennie), and for most illnesses, genetic tests can never by themselves predict the course of a patient's health.

Moreover, the misperception that genes determine health on a one-to-one ratio can have serious social and ethical repercussions. In fact, screening programs aimed at detecting genetic diseases in large groups of people have already been attempted with often less-than-desirable results. In the early 1970s the federal government funded a screening program to detect carriers of the sickle cell gene, which is prevalent in the African American community. Characteristics of the disease, for which there is no cure, include fever, anemia, and pain in the joints and abdomen (Harkavy). However, instead of providing insight into the disease, the testing became a weapon to justify long-standing prejudices. Some insurance companies began to deny coverage to black carriers on the grounds that they had a preexisting medical condition or that their children were bad risks. Some scientists even suggested that the best solution to the anemia problem would be for blacks carrying the gene not to breed. Eventually, this misinformation was corrected and the test began to be useful, but the problems caused by widespread testing for sickle cell anemia indicate the potential harm that could arise from uncritical use of genetic screening.

Of course, in some instances, genetic screening has done a great deal of good, as is the case involving screening for Tay-Sachs disease, which is prevalent among Jews of eastern European descent. Children born with this disease suffer from a gradual deterioration leading to mental retardation, paralysis, and blindness, usually dying before the age of four (Harkavy). However, with the advent of genetic testing, couples who are both carriers of the mutation can choose to have preimplantation genetic testing, which enables scientists to analyze the DNA of cells taken from pre-embryos and implant in the mother those genes that do not carry the deadly Tay-Sachs disease (Rennie). The tests set at ease the minds of fearful couples who might otherwise never risk having children.

Unlike the screening for sickle cell anemia, the Tay-Sachs program was always voluntary, which means that people had the opportunity to prepare for the consequences of the testing. Genetic testing should always be voluntary, and the results should be kept confidential to prevent misuse. Moreover, patients undergoing such testing should be provided with access to genetic counseling, so that they can understand the results and their implications.

Much of the potential harm associated with genetic testing concerns discrimination by insurance companies. Community rating is a system in which a customer's premiums are determined by the health profile of his or her community. Genetic information about individuals does not matter. Insurers claim that individual risk rating serves the public welfare more equitably at less expense, and therefore that genetic information is needed to set fair rates for all policy holders. It would be wrong, they argue, to make healthy people pay higher premiums because they had been lumped in with those at higher risk (Rennie). The problem, however, is that everybody is genetically defective in some way. According to most estimates, everyone carries at least five to ten genes that could make that person sick under the wrong circumstances or could adversely affect children (Rennie). The ability of insurers and others to interpret genetic information wisely is questionable, and as the circumstances surrounding the testing for sickle cell anemia suggests, such information has the potential for fueling discrimination.

Moreover, an additional potentially harmful issue associated with genetic testing concerns the difficulty of distinguishing between a genetic disease and an undesirable trait. As genetic researcher W. Anderson French points out:

> . . . successful somatic cell gene therapy also opens the door for enhancement genetic engineering, that is, for supplying a specific characteristic that individuals might want for themselves (somatic cell engineering) or their children (germline engineering) which would not involve the treatment of a disease. (68)

Scientists are showing that genes influence many aspects of human behavior such as intelligence, alcoholism, overeating, anger, and murderous aggression (Horgan). Would it be ethically appropriate to use genetic testing and genetic therapies to enhance height or intelligence? Suppose a memory-enhancing gene were discovered, on what basis would a decision be made "to allow one individual to receive the gene but not another" (Anderson, 70)? Although some argue that all scientific discoveries are useful and that research should not be inhibited, we need to ask ourselves a question: will we know what to do with all this information about a human's genetic map?

Presuming technological feasibility, parents may someday be able to select their children's sex, height, or other cosmetic features and the consequences of those choices may be hard to predict. In order to minimize its potentially adverse effects, genetic testing should be restricted to those conditions for which there is some urgency and for which some beneficial intervention is possible, either as therapy or as reproductive planning. We should try to stay out of those areas where genetic diseases and undesirable traits are blurred and focus on those that can prevent illnesses and death.

WORKS CITED

Anderson, W. French. "Genetics and Human Malleability." *The Hastings Center Report* (January/February 1990): 67–73. Print.

Harkavy, Michael. *The American Spectrum Encyclopedia.* Uitgeverij Het: Spectrum B.V. 1991. Print.

Horgan, John. "Eugenics Revisited." *Scientific American* June 1993: 122–128+. Print.

Kolata, Gina. "If Tests Hint Alzheimer's, Should a Patient Be Told?" *New York Times.* 24 October 1995: A11. Print.

Rennie, John. "Grading the Gene Tests." *Scientific American* June 1994: 88–92. Print.

Siebert, Charles. "At the Mercy of Our Genes." *New York Times* 5 January 1996: All. Print.

Vines, Gail. "How Far Should We Go?" *New Scientist* February 1994: 12–13. Print.

EXERCISE

The student paper just shown incorporates outside sources for a variety of purposes. Note each instance and then in small groups discuss the form each one has taken (quotation or summary) and the purpose of each one within the essay.

11

CHAPTER

Two Important Strategies in College Writing: Establishing Causality and Defining Terms

Standardized tests improve student learning.
Secondhand smoke causes lung cancer.
Affordable health care in the United States will benefit the middle class.
Obesity is caused by the fast food industry.
Music education contributes to brain development.

All of these statements are concerned with connections between cause and effect, and many college writing assignments frequently require you to consider these connections, sometimes to predict possible effects and sometimes to trace possible causes. For example, if you were writing about the topic of whether to legalize marijuana, you would have to address the potential effects of that legalization, and if you were writing about the rise in terrorist organizations in the early twenty-first century, you would have to examine what are considered to be possible causes. Moreover, college writing assignments are also frequently concerned with definitional issues. For example, an essay that advocates a particular policy justify it because it is "fair," or a particular hiring practice might be dismissed because it is sexist. Because theses or positions are often justified with value-laden words, such as "fair" or "just," "sexist," "humane," or "appropriate," they need to be defined in the context in which they are being used, particularly since we now recognize that cultures vary a great deal in how they view these terms.

Establishing causality and defining terms are two strategies for developing and supporting ideas that appear frequently in college writing. Both can be used within an essay as a means of supporting a thesis, and both are sometimes used as a theme for an entire essay. This chapter explores various possibilities for using these strategies in college writing assignments.

THE NATURE OF CAUSAL ARGUMENTS

Statements that are concerned with cause and effect claim that a particular event, condition, or situation is going to *cause* a specific effect or effects, or that a particular effect or effects was *caused* by a particular event, condition, or situation. Here are some examples:

- An increase in the minimum wage will *cause* harm to small business
- Eating genetically enhanced vegetables will *not cause* harmful side effects
- Violence in children is an *effect* of watching violent cartoons

Causation is an important strategy in the college writing because it often addresses the cause or effect of existing or potential societal problems, such as immigration, crime, technology, racism, and sexism. In dealing with topics such as these, an argumentative essay will frequently identify a problem and then

- examine its causes
- call attention to potential consequences or effects
- suggest possibilities for solving it, based on what predicted effects are likely to be

Causal arguments are based on a relationship between one event or situation and another. If high school student, Farley, decides not to study for his math final and he then receives a failing grade on it, the *cause* is his failure to study and the *effect* is his failing grade. If his failing grade on the test causes him to fail the course, the poor grade on the test then becomes the cause of his failure. Thus, an event or situation can be both a cause and an effect, depending on *when* it occurs. Causes come *before* effects; effects come *after* causes.

Causation involving physical actions is usually easy to determine. If Bart Simpson throws a brick at a window and the window breaks, it is obvious that the breakage was caused by the brick, no matter what excuse Bart might offer. But causation as a topic for argumentative writing is usually concerned with more complex human behavior than breaking a window with a brick (and if you try to figure out *why* Bart decided to throw the brick, this action becomes more complex as well). For example, one might ask why Farley didn't study for his math final. Was it simply laziness or lack of interest? Did something happen in Farley's personal life that so distracted him that he couldn't study? Was Farley so intimidated by math that he felt that he had no chance of passing? Maybe Farley has a full-time job or family responsibilities that leave him no time to study. These questions (and no doubt you can think of several others) about what seems to be a simple issue, the failing of a math exam, show how difficult it is to determine causality, especially when you are writing about political, social, and ethical issues.

Causality is difficult to understand because human behavior often seems inexplicable and unpredictable. For example, it is generally acknowledged that children raised in poverty in the inner city are often educationally disadvantaged. Yet there are a number of instances in which some of these children rise above their circumstances and become quite successful students. Why can some children accomplish this while others cannot? Some factors, such as family stability, offer a partial explanation, but they don't explain everything. Conversely, it is also true that not all educationally advantaged children succeed in school. The literature is stuffed with possible explanations for why this might be so, but no one can either predict or explain human behavior with absolute certainty.

IMMEDIATE VERSUS REMOTE CAUSALITY

Causality is often discussed in terms of a chain, which means that one cause leads to an effect that becomes the cause of another effect, and so on. The *immediate cause* is the one that is closest in time to the event or situation being analyzed. *Remote causes* are those that occurred in the past.

To distinguish between immediate and remote causes, note the following example:

1. Farley did not study for the math exam.
2. Farley failed the math exam.
3. Farley's failing grade on the math exam caused him to fail the math course.
4. Farley's failure of the math course caused him to drop out of school.
5. Because Farley did not have a high school diploma, he could not get a job to support himself.
6. Farley's failure to get a job caused him to become unable to meet his expenses.
7. Unable to meet his expenses, Farley began shoplifting small items from the supermarket.
8. Farley then began stealing items from department stores.
9. Farley eventually met an underworld character named Felix, a notorious cat burglar, who stole expensive jewelry from hotel rooms.
10. Felix made Farley his apprentice.
11. Eventually Farley became an internationally known jewel thief.

In this obviously absurd example, Farley's meeting with Felix and becoming his apprentice is the *immediate cause* of his becoming a notorious jewel thief. But as in most instances, a number of earlier events or factors led to the one in the present—Farley's dropping out of school and being unable to get a job, for example, are certainly important factors. Sometimes, though, it is difficult to determine the role that remote causes play in contributing to a present event. It would be nonsensical, for example, for someone to claim that Farley's career as a jewel thief was caused by his failure to study for a math exam in high school. But every causal event can be traced backward through the chain into the past, often indefinitely. Philosophers know that it is difficult, if not impossible, to determine the first cause of anything.

EXERCISE

Choose an event or condition in your own life and trace as many causes for it as possible. What causes have contributed, for example, to the fact that you are reading this book?

PRECIPITATING VERSUS CONTRIBUTING CAUSE

Similar to the distinction between immediate and remote causes is that between a *precipitating* and a *contributing* cause. A precipitating cause is an event or situation that triggers a particular effect. A contributing cause is a set of conditions that give rise to the precipitating cause. For example, Farley may have had poor experiences in math classes all of his life, and these poor experiences are the contributing causes of Farley's failure to study for his math exam. But then, in his junior year in high school, Farley had a particularly poor math teacher, Mr. Smith, who came to class unprepared and gave Farley the impression that he would never succeed in math no matter how hard he tried. Mr. Smith's poor teaching, then, might have been the precipitating cause of Farley's failure to study for his math final.

THE DANGER OF OVERSIMPLIFICATION

A common problem for all writers who address causality is to assume that there is only one cause for a particular consequence. Because human nature is complex, most issues suitable for argumentation can be traced to multiple causes, so in writing an argumentative essay that deals with causality, you should be careful not to oversimplify. It would be ridiculous to claim, for example, that if only Farley had not had Mr. Smith for math, he would never have become a notorious jewel thief.

EXERCISE

Working in small groups, identify the immediate cause, remote cause, precipitating cause, and contributing cause for the following events or situations:

1. Why a particular television program is popular.

2. How you chose the college you are attending.

3. How you chose your major.

4. Why women choose particular professions.

5. Why certain brands of running shoes or cell phones are so popular.

TYPICAL WEAKNESSES OF THE CAUSATION ARGUMENT

Arguments that address causality typically can be weakened by the following features:

1. Oversimplification
    In analyzing causation, it is tempting to try to find one discreet cause when, in reality, most events or situations have many causes. If you are analyzing why a candidate lost an election, the loss was most likely due to a number of factors, not to just one. Certainly, complex social problems, such as an increase in crime, unemployment, or divorce must be analyzed in terms of multiple causes.
2. Mistaking correlation for causation
    When one event occurs immediately after another, they are correlated, but not necessarily connected. The fallacy known as "false cause" assumes causal connections where none may exist. The increase in crime in big cities has been paralleled by the growth of the television industry, but that doesn't necessarily mean that watching television causes people to commit crimes.

CAUSATION IN THE PROPOSAL ARGUMENT

Determining causality and predicting consequences are particularly important in arguments that may loosely be labeled "proposal arguments." Proposal arguments tend to focus on the future and may suggest a course of action, such as instituting a sports club at a local school or expanding parking facilities on campus. Often, they begin by analyzing a problem or situation and then suggest solutions based on predicted consequences or effects. Writers who argue in favor of speech codes on campus, for example, predict that they will have the effect of eliminating racist or sexist speech. Writers who argue against speech codes on campus predict that they will have the effect of stifling free speech.

The proposal argument consists of two main components:

1. Identifying that a problem or exigence exists.
2. Showing that the proposal represents a reasonable solution or a way of addressing the problem.

To demonstrate to your readers that a problem or exigence exists, you may need to discuss its background or cite evidence, such as examples or statistics. To convince them that they should accept your perspective on the problem, you will have to cite reasons and evidence, just as you would in any argumentative essay.

POLICY OR ACTION PROPOSALS

Proposal arguments may be concerned either with questions of policy or with specific actions or behaviors. *Policy* proposals aim to address major social, political, or economic problems, such as discrimination, allocating resources within a particular population, controlling crime, or providing equal opportunity in education and employment. Frequently, they are broad in scope and may be based on philosophical and ethical concerns. The other type of proposal, sometimes designated an *action* proposal, advocates a specific action to solve a particular problem and is usually more narrow and concrete. Proposals to change the registration system at your university or to institute recycling in a particular community are examples of an action proposal. Often, proposal arguments will address both policy and action because the justification for a particular action may be based on philosophical and ethical values. A policy providing maternity leave for mothers as well as paternity leave for fathers, for example, is based on the idea that both parents need to bond with a child and that the early months of a child's life are when this important bonding occurs. On the other hand, a policy that provides maternity leave only for the mother is based on the idea that mothers should assume the primary responsibility for caring for a newborn and that the father should provide monetary support. In the course of your professional and academic life, you will probably write proposals of both kinds.

THE STRUCTURE OF PROPOSAL ARGUMENTS

Proposal arguments usually consist of three parts: 1) describing the problematic situation or exigence and convincing the audience that it is important, 2) proposing a way of addressing or solving the problem (predicting consequences), and 3) indicating why your proposal is better than other possibilities. Here is a suggestion for structuring a proposal argument:

Introduction:
—introduces the exigence, problem, or situation concerning a person, situation, issue, or concept
—provides relevant background
—indicates why the exigence, problem, or situation is important to address
—presents the writer's proposal for addressing or solving the problem

Body:
—examines the cause or causes of the problem
—presents justification for the proposal
—shows that the proposal can help solve the problem
—provides evidence in support for the proposal
—acknowledges that the problem is complex and may not be easily solved (particularly in policy proposals)

—indicates awareness of alternative viewpoints
—refutes the opposing viewpoint

Conclusion: —sums up the argument
—reiterates the importance of accepting the proposal

CONVINCING YOUR AUDIENCE THAT A PROBLEM EXISTS: ARGUING FROM PRECEPT, EFFECT, AND SIMILARITY

Because proposal arguments aim to solve or at least address a problem or exigence, an important goal for the writer is to convince the audience that a problem exists and this requirement, of course, requires you to think about the needs and values of your intended audience. What may be considered a "problem" for some people may not be considered a problem for others, and many people are surprisingly unaware of some of the major problems in society—many are so busy with their own lives that they simply do not know about them. Others deliberately avoid thinking about anything that will disturb their concept of a safe and ordered world. If your readers do not understand that there is a problem, or if they believe that the problem is not serious enough to warrant concern or change, they will be unlikely to pay much attention to your proposal. To convince your readers to recognize that a problem exists or to consider the problem seriously, you might wish to present it in terms of one or all of three useful strategies: precept, effect, and similarity. All of these strategies have the goal of persuading your audience to pay attention to the problem you are addressing through an appeal to emotion and values. Here is an example of how precept, effect, and similarity might be used in a proposal argument:

Proposal: The University should not mandate political correctness.
Arguing from Precept: because political correctness is a form of censorship. (Censorship is a precept that most people condemn. However, some people are less concerned about it and think that some form of censorship is desirable.)

Arguing from Effect: because laws mandating political correctness cannot control sexist or racist thinking and can lead to a repressive environment on campus. (However, some people think that legislating what people can say can actually influence how people think.)

Arguing from Similarity: because laws that mandate political correctness are like mind control in the novel *1984*. (However, some people may not acknowledge this similarity.)

ARGUMENTS BASED ON PRECEPT

Arguing on the basis of a precept involves showing that a particular situation or policy is either wrong or right according to a generally accepted value, principle, definition, or belief that your reader is likely to take seriously. For example, one common argument against the use of racial quotas in the workplace is that they are "unfair." This strategy argues from the principle that "unfairness" means that something is "bad" and presumes that most readers would reject racial quotas on that basis. Of course, someone in favor of racial quotas might argue that they are not "unfair" at all, but are, in actuality, aimed at redressing the unfairness that occurred in the past. This person might feel that racial quotas actually contribute to "fairness" in the workplace. Similarly, a popular argument against school policies that mandate political correctness is that they are actually a form of censorship, which in the United States is considered "bad." An opponent to this claim, however, might argue that the laws against censorship never were designed to include offensive racial or sexual slurs and that controlling this form of speech cannot be considered censorship.

ARGUMENTS BASED ON EFFECT

Proposal arguments can also claim that if a problem is not solved or a problematic situation is not addressed, that an undesirable effect or consequence will occur. One might argue, for example, that unless affirmative action policies are enacted, women and minorities will not be given a fair chance. Or one might make the claim that unless political correctness laws are passed on campus, students will make racist remarks that will result in a hate-obsessed, divided university community. On the other hand, one might also argue that political correctness mandates do not solve the problem at all but rather might cause other undesirable effects, such as discouraging students from engaging in honest debate on emotionally charged issues.

ARGUMENTS BASED ON SIMILARITY

A writer who argues from similarity will compare the situation he or she is addressing to another situation that an audience might relate to with greater force or emotion. The aim of this strategy is to transfer the audience's attitude from one emotionally charged topic to another. For example, if you were arguing that there should be serious penalties for plagiarism, you might discover that many people do not view plagiarism as a serious crime. You might then compare plagiarism to stealing, which your readers would probably view more gravely. Similarly, a proposal to institute stronger penalties for littering in the local park might argue that destroying the environment is like burning down your own house. If you decide to argue from similarity, it is important to remember its function—that is, to generate a strong response in your reader and to call attention to the seriousness of the issue you are addressing. Similarities that don't produce this impact will not enhance the effectiveness of your essay.

EXERCISE

Working in small groups, think of potential support for each of the following claims, using one of the three methods of justification noted—precept, effect, and similarity. If possible, use "because" clauses to indicate the kind of support you would provide. Here is an example:

Claim: Teenagers should be required to do community service.
Precept: Because community service teaches young people to care about others.
Effect: Because community service will help them become concerned citizens.
Similarity: Because living in a community without taking any interest in it is like living in a house about which you have no concern. You are unlikely to do anything to improve it.

1. Young people should be required to do public service.
    Precept: because public service is_____
    Effect: because performing public service will have the effect of_____.
    Similarity: because doing public service is like_____

2. Smoking should be forbidden in restaurants.
    Precept: because smoking in restaurants is_____.
    Effect: because smoking in restaurants will have the effect of
    _____.
    Similarity: because smoking in restaurants is like _____.

3. Grading in Composition courses should be eliminated.
    Precept: because grading in Composition classes is _____.
    Effect: because grades in Composition classes can have the effect of
    _____.
    Similarity: because grades in Composition classes are like _____.

QUALIFICATION IN THE PROPOSAL ARGUMENT

In writing the proposal argument, it is especially important to use qualifying words and to acknowledge the existence of alternative viewpoints because the topics for a proposal argument are often concerned with complex problems that are extremely difficult, if not impossible, to solve easily. Although you may feel strongly that your proposal is superior to others and you may predict that only the most positive consequences will result, you will appear more credible to your audience if you acknowledge the possibility that events may take an unusual turn, that people may behave unpredictably, or that people have differing ideas about what is good, desirable, or just. Thoughtful writers of proposal arguments indicate the tentativeness of their observations by using qualifying terms such as *seems, suggests, indicates, to some degree,* or *to a certain extent.* See Chapter 1 for further discussion on the importance of qualification.

WRITING ASSIGNMENT

Working either individually or in small groups, make a list of problems affecting your community, culture, ethnicity, or society. Then choose one and write an argumentative essay of four to six pages in which you (1) identify the problem, (2) indicate why it is a problem that ought to be addressed, (3) propose a solution or way of addressing the problem, and (4) indicate your awareness of the complexity of this problem by discussing alternative perspectives. If appropriate, use one or more of the strategies discussed in this chapter: precept, effect, and similarity.

Use the following exploration questions to generate material for this topic:

1. Is there a controversy associated with this problem?
2. Is this a problem that you were aware of when you were growing up?
3. Is this a problem that has affected you personally in some way?
4. Can you think of at least two people who hold differing views about this problem? If so, describe these people and summarize what you believe were their points of view.
5. Has your opinion changed about this problem in any way? Why or why not?
6. Do you think that this problem is important for everyone to think about? Why or why not?

ADDITIONAL QUESTIONS

1. What is the cause of this problem?
2. Who is affected by this problem?
3. Who has the power to do something about this problem?

4. Why hasn't it been addressed or solved up until now?
5. Why would it be useful to address or solve this problem?
6. What costs would be incurred by addressing or solving this problem?
7. Who would pay for these costs?
8. Have other solutions to this problem been proposed?
9. Why is your solution better than others?

AN EXAMPLE OF AN ESSAY THAT ADDRESSES CAUSALITY

The report below discusses the result of a study that examined the effects of legalizing medical marijuana. Note how the author of this essay uses evidence to support its thesis. Do you find this essay convincing? Why or why not?

Consequences of Legalizing Marijuana

Legalization increased both marijuana use and marijuana abuse/dependence in people 21 or older.

Marijuana use is illegal under federal law. Despite this, an estimated 18 million people were current marijuana users in 2011. As of June 2014, 23 U.S. states had legalized the use of marijuana for medical purposes in response to growing awareness that the active ingredient in the drug may be useful as an analgesic for chronic pain, an antiemetic, and an antispasmodic. Two states, Washington and Colorado, had legalized recreational use as well.

In "The Effect of Medical Marijuana Laws on Marijuana, Alcohol, and Hard Drug Use" (NBER Working Paper No. 20085), Hefei Wen, Jason M. Hockenberry, and Janet R. Cummings use individual survey data from seven states to examine the effect of legalizing medical marijuana. They find that legalization increased both marijuana use and marijuana abuse/dependence in people 21 or older. It was also associated with an increase in adult binge drinking, defined as the number of days on which an individual had five or more drinks on the same occasion in the last month. People 12 to 20 years old were 5 to 6 percent more likely to try marijuana for the first time when medical use was legalized. Legalization was not associated with an increase in adolescent drinking, or with increased cocaine or heroin use in either group.

The data are drawn from the 2004 to 2011 National Survey on Drug Use and Health. The survey data include self-reported information on respondent drug use, the frequency of use, and questions designed to assess drug abuse or dependence with respect to criteria in the *Diagnostic and Statistical Manual of Mental Disorders,* 4th edition. The authors controlled for age, gender, race/ethnicity, cigarette smoking, urban residence, family income, marital status, educational attainment, college enrollment, and employment status. They also controlled for state beer taxes, unemployment rates, average personal income, and median household income.

The survey data do not distinguish between legal medicinal and illegal recreational use. In practice, many state laws are vague about the medical conditions that qualify for legal medical use. "Chronic pain" is not medically verifiable, and the authors explain that allowing people with chronic pain to qualify for medical use makes it difficult to separate medical users from recreational users posing as medical users.

For adults, the baseline predicted probability of an individual having used marijuana in the last month was 8.6 percent. Legalization increased it by 1.37 to 1.40, an increase of 16 percent. The number of marijuana use days per month rose by 0.14 to 0.21 days a month, or 12 to 17 percent. Legalization increased the probability of adolescent initiation of marijuana use in the last year by 0.32 to 0.46 percent, a 5 to 6 percent increase. While this suggests that more adolescents experimented with marijuana, the data do not suggest that regular use increased in this group.

The authors note that the 6 to 9 percent increase in frequency of adult binge drinking, along with an estimated increase in the probability of simultaneous use of marijuana and alcohol of 15 to 22 percent, suggests that legalization could result in "considerable economic and social costs from downstream health care expenditures and productivity loss."

-- **Linda Gorman**
National Bureau of Economic Research
http://www.nber.org/digest/oct14/w20085.html
The Digest is not copyrighted and may be
reproduced freely with appropriate attribution of source.

THE IMPORTANCE OF DEFINING TERMS

Whether your essay is concerned with causality or is focused on another idea, it is important that you define your terms so that the reader will understand their meaning. For example, in statements such as:

"Affirmative action programs are not *fair.*"

"That movie is not *suitable* for children."

The terms *fair* and *suitable* require definition because what is "right," "good," "fair," or "suitable" for one person may not be suitable for another and may depend a great deal on the context or culture that is being discussed. Similarly, if you decide to support a particular candidate for president of the student government because he or she is a "good leader," it will be necessary for you to define what you mean by this. Or if you have decided that a particular television program is not "appropriate" for children, you would have to define what you mean by "appropriate."

A number of topics typically assigned in writing classes will require you to define how you are using particular terms—for example,

Freedom of speech
Pornography
Cruel and unusual punishment
Obscenity
Patriotism
Conservative
Liberal
Sexual harassment
Hate crime

And there are many others.

TYPES OF DEFINITIONS

Ordinary Versus Stipulative

There are a number of ways that a term may be defined. One common method is to define a word in terms of its ordinary or customary usage; often the source of that definition will be a dictionary. A "hero," for example is defined in several ways by *The American Heritage Dictionary:*

> **1.** In mythology and legend, a man, often of divine ancestry, who is endowed with great courage and strength, celebrated for his bold exploits and favored by the gods. **2.** A man noted for feats of courage or nobility of purpose—esp one who has risked or sacrificed his life: *a war hero.* **3.** A man noted for his special achievements in a particular field: *the heroes of medicine.* **4.** The principal male character in a novel, poem, or dramatic presentation. **5.** Slang. A large sandwich consisting of a roll that is split lengthwise and contains a variety of fillings, as lettuce, tomatoes, onions, meats and cheese.

If you were writing an essay in which the term *hero* was important, you might wish to clarify for your reader that you conceived of a hero in terms of its customary usage as defined in a dictionary. Or you may wish to cite the customary or ordinary definition in order to show that a public figure or celebrity wasn't really a hero at all.

Another form of definition that you might wish to use in an argumentative essay is the *stipulative definition,* which involves assigning a term a special or particular meaning that limits the way it will be defined within a specific context. In his essay titled "From Hero to Celebrity," Daniel Boorstin stipulates the following definition:

> The traditional heroic type included figures as diverse as Moses, Ulysses, Aeneas, Jesus, Caesar, Mohammed, Joan of Arc, Shakespeare, Washington, Napoleon, and Lincoln. For our purposes it is sufficient to define a hero as a human figure— real or imaginary or both—who has shown greatness in some achievement. He is a man or woman of great deeds.

In this stipulative definition, Boorstin has indicated how he is defining the term *hero,* and he cites the attributes that he feels are most important. For Boorstin, a hero is a human figure, one who has reached greatness in some achievement, someone who has performed great deeds. He also indicates that a hero can be either a man or a woman, and in this way he distinguishes his definition from that in the dictionary, which uses the term to refer only to a man.

Below are other examples of a stipulative definition. Note how each uses a counter example to define the term.

> 1. Although a child who has a roomful of expensive toys is sometimes referred to as "spoiled," that child may not exhibit the behavior of a spoiled child. A child who is spoiled is one who believes that he or she is better than other children, is generally rude and inconsiderate, demands that his or her every wish be granted, and sulks if this does not happen. Thus the term "spoiled" is more indicative of an attitude and mode of behavior than it is of the possession of material goods.

> 2. What does the "end of work" mean, exactly? It does not mean the imminence of total unemployment, nor is the United States remotely likely to face, say, 30–50 percent unemployment within the next decade. Rather, technology could exert a slow but continual downward pressure on the value and availability of work— that is, on wages and on the share of prime-age workers with full-time jobs. Eventually, by degrees, that could create a new normal, where the expectation that work will be a central feature of adult life dissipates for a significant portion of society.
>
> **Thompson, Derek."A World Without Work."**
> ***The Atlantic* July/August 2015: 53. Print.**

EXERCISE

Working in small groups, create a stipulative definition of the following terms:

1. A good dog

2. A satisfying job

3. An effective teacher

4. A car worth buying

5. A computer for daily use

ESSENTIAL VERSUS INCIDENTAL CHARACTERISTICS OF A DEFINITION

The simplest way to define a term is to provide either a dictionary definition or a synonym and then present those characteristics that make the term what it is. The definition of a "vest," for example, is stated in the dictionary as "a short sleeveless collarless garment, either open or fastening in front, worn over a shirt or blouse and often under a suit coat or jacket." This definition is stated in the most common format, which places the term within the next larger class or category and then cites the particular features that distinguish it from other terms in the same category. Thus, a "vest" is first of all an article of clothing.

However, in defining terms, it is also important to distinguish characteristics that are essential from those that are merely incidental. Essential characteristics are those that must be present in order for the article to be what it is. Incidental characteristics are those that may be present but are not absolutely necessary. An essential characteristic of a vest, for example, is that it is sleeveless; otherwise, it would be considered a blouse or a shirt. Therefore, the characteristic "sleeveless" is essential for defining the term *vest*. However, although current fashion suggests that a vest be worn over a shirt or a blouse, it is sometimes worn on its own and yet would still be considered a vest. In this instance, then, the characteristic "being worn over a shirt or blouse" would be considered "incidental," meaning that it is not absolutely essential to the definition.

EXERCISE

Find the dictionary definition for the following terms. Then, working in groups, examine the definition of each term and decide which characteristics are essential and which are incidental.

1. a salad

2. a party

3. a pet

4. a sandwich

5. a game

6. computer nerd

7. a nosy person

8. a best friend

STRATEGIES OF DEFINITION

Many words can be defined fairly easily by noting their essential characteristics or providing a synonym. The word *honor*, for example, may be defined as "homage," "reverence," or "deference." Terms used in academic argument, however, often require a more expanded definition beyond a simple one-word or one-sentence explanation. Several strategies that are useful for this purpose are the following: defining by example, defining by negation, defining by classification, and defining by operation.

DEFINING BY EXAMPLE

It is often useful to provide an illustration or example to help your reader understand what you mean. If you are discussing an educational television program that you think is suitable for young children, you might mention *Sesame Street*. If you refer to a "suspenseful" book, it would be useful for you to illustrate that concept by mentioning a few titles. Citing examples, however, does not provide a complete definition, so it is important to include other methods of definition as well. The following passage, concerned with defining a leader, begins with a simple definition and then uses several examples for clarification:

> Great leaders are always great simplifiers, who cut through argument, debate, and doubt to offer a solution everybody can understand and remember. Churchill warned the British to expect "blood, toil and sweat"; FDR told Americans that "the only thing we have to fear is fear itself"; Lenin promised the war-weary Russians peace, land and bread. Straightforward but potent messages.
> **Korda, Michael. "How to Be a Leader." *Newsweek* 5 January 1981**

DEFINING BY NEGATION

Defining by negation means to explain what something *is* by showing what it *is not*. "Freedom of speech" does not mean "permission to make racist remarks," "liberty" does not mean "license," "a greeting card rhyme" is not "poetry" are all examples of defining by negation. Related to this method of definition is that of defining by contrast—that is, a particular thing or concept is defined by contrasting it with something else. In the following paragraph, the writer defines "mystery" books by contrasting them with "thrillers":

> A mystery is concerned with understanding—giving the reader the pleasure of figuring things out. A thriller is about resolution—about making sure that the villain is caught. You may not know who the villain is in a mystery, and the pleasure is in following the author to find out. In a thriller, you probably know who the villain is, but you read along to find out how he or she will be apprehended.

DEFINING BY CLASSIFICATION

When you define by classification, you situate the term within a class of things—people, animals, birds, tools, subjects, ideas, etc.—and then indicate how that term differs from other terms in that class. In the following excerpt, Patty McEntee situates the word *obscenity* within the class of pornography in order to show that obscenity is not protected by the first amendment:

> "Pornography" is a generic term that includes both hard-core and software porn. "Obscenity" is the legal term for "hard-core" pornography, and obscenity is not protected by the First Amendment. . . .
>
> **McEntee, Patty. "Is Pornography a Matter of Free Expression?"**
> ***America* 10 August 1991.**

DEFINING BY OPERATION OR FUNCTION

An effective way to define is to state what something does or to explain how it works. The word *debate* can be defined as "a formal contest of argumentation in which two opposing teams defend and attack a given idea." A *tutor* may be defined as "a private instructor who gives additional, special, or remedial instruction." A *Writing Center* may be defined as "a facility where writers of all kinds can receive individualized assistance in writing through the help of a knowledgeable, well-trained tutor."

EXERCISES

1. Working in small groups, write a definition for the following terms. Try to include all of the strategies noted: Synonym, example, negation, classification, and operation.

   A.   Competition
   B.   Political correctness
   C.   "Working out"
   D.   Sports car
   E.   Guilt
   F.   Sexual harassment
   G.   Art
   H.   Anxiety

2. Write a definition of a term from a profession, sport, or hobby that you know a great deal about but which may be unfamiliar to most people. Use at least one of the strategies discussed.

THE ESSAY OF DEFINITION

In some instances, the entire premise of an argumentative essay may be based on a problem involving definition—that is, the purpose of the essay is to establish that a problematic situation, concept, or issue either does or does not fit a particular definition. For example, the famous case of Rodney King that became the catalyst for the Los Angeles riots in 1992 involved the question of whether the police were guilty of brutality or whether they were just "doing their jobs." If you were to write an essay with the goal of establishing that the police were, indeed, guilty of brutality to Rodney King, you would first have to define "brutality," establish criteria for labeling an action as "brutal," and then show how the actions of the police on that day fit that definition.

Because most definitions are not straightforward, argumentative essays that focus on definition contain the implicit question "to what extent?" or "to what degree?" Here are some examples of how the element of "degree" and "extent" help shape the definition essay:

Topic	Question
heroism	To what extent is a particular action "heroic"?
marriage	To what extent is marriage for women a form of slavery?
political correctness	To what extent is political correctness a form of repression?
after-school sports	To what extent is participation in after-school sports educationally beneficial?

CHARACTERISTICS OF THE DEFINITION ESSAY

An argumentative essay that focuses on a definition retains the primary characteristics of the genre of argument; that is,

1. It focuses on a problem or controversy. In a definitional essay, the problem concerns the extent to which a particular person, situation, issue, or concept fits a particular definition.
2. It advocates a position, thesis, or claim about a complex issue or subject about which there are at least two views. In a definitional essay, the position, thesis, or claim concerns the extent to which a given person, situation, issue, or concept possess the necessary attributes of the definition.
3. It aims to have an effect on its readers—to move readers to think about the criteria for the definition and acknowledge the extent to which the person, situation, issue, or concept possesses this necessary criteria.

4. It explores its subject in sufficient depth so as to acknowledge an opposing viewpoint; that is, it recognizes that the person, situation, issue, or concept may have characteristics that confound easy definition and so is not easily classified.

5. It presents convincing evidence utilizing a variety of support strategies.

STRUCTURE IN THE DEFINITIONAL ESSAY

The structure of the definitional essay similarly retains the generic components of academic argument. Here is a model you can apply:

Introduction:
—introduces the problem or controversy concerning a person, situation, issue, or concept
—provides relevant background
—indicates that the problem or controversy is concerned with definition
—states position, thesis, or claim

Body:
—presents the definition in terms of necessary and sufficient criteria
—illustrates the definition using a variety of strategies
—establishes that the person, situation, issue, or concept possesses the necessary criteria for the definition
—addresses the opposing viewpoint by acknowledging that the person, situation, issue, or concept may have characteristics that confound easy definition, making it difficult to classify
—refutes the opposing viewpoint

Conclusion:
—sums up argument

WRITING ASSIGNMENTS

Causality

1. Read "Why Johnny Can't Read, But Yoshio Can"

(http://www.thefreelibrary.com/Why+Johnny+can't+read,+but+Yoshio+can. -a06745944) The article discusses three characteristics of Japanese schools that seem to be responsible for their students' superior performance. Then write an argumentative essay of 4–6 pages responding to the following question:

Should these characteristics be adopted in American schools?

In responding to this question, you might also wish to include those characteristics that you wouldn't like to see included.

DEFINITION: THE TOPIC OF HEROISM

Find several articles concerned with the topic of heroism. Then respond to one of these writing prompts:

1. Using the culture with which you are most familiar, choose a contemporary figure that might be considered heroic. Write an argumentative essay of 5–6 pages discussing how and why this person ought to be considered a hero. Be sure to formulate a clear definition on which to base your argument.
2. Develop a clear definition for a "hero" and write an argumentative essay addressing the following question:
   Do you think it is possible for a hero to exist in modern society?

ADDITIONAL QUESTIONS

To access some additional ideas on the topic of heroism, write responses to the questions that follow. You might also wish to discuss these questions in small groups.

1. Should any person who performs a heroic deed be considered a hero? Or is it important to separate the deed from the person who performed it?
2. Does the intention count in defining a hero—that is, if a soldier is running away from a battle and, in the course of doing so, discovers a hidden mine field thereby saving thousands of men, is he a hero?
3. Does a hero have to be perfect?
4. Does the private life of a hero have an impact on whether that person can be considered heroic?
5. Is it possible for anyone to be a hero in the modern world, in which intense media scrutiny reveals every flaw?
6. How would you distinguish a hero from a celebrity?

CHAPTER

12

Revising a College Argument

Some students have the idea that competent writers should be able to produce a profound, interesting, compelling, creative, perfectly constructed, cohesive, and grammatically correct text without doing any revision. This idea is a myth and can be very discouraging for people whose initial drafts need to be revised again and again. The truth is that very few people, if any, can turn out a perfect draft without a lot of hard work. Good writing is *revised* writing, whether you are writing for academic or professional purposes—in fact, even shopping lists are usually revised.

Some writers revise as they write, reconceptualizing and editing while they complete a first draft. Others finish a draft, put it aside for a while, and then revise it. Many do both, revising and editing a first draft, then engaging in additional revisions afterward. Whatever strategy you prefer (waiting until ten minutes before class before correcting a few spelling mistakes does *not* count as a revision strategy), it is important to understand that true revision, as opposed to surface "editing," involves rethinking and sometimes altering the thesis, structure, and support. A common misconception is that revising an essay means simply correcting the punctuation and spelling—that is, cleaning up the surface. Of course, ultimately your essay should be error free, rhetorically and stylistically effective, and, if possible, eloquent and graceful. But before you focus on error correction and style, you should address conceptual and structural issues.

SUGGESTIONS FOR REVISION

The following suggestions are aimed at helping you revise effectively:

1. Leave Sufficient Time to Revise

Even if you revise as you compose, it is a good idea to allow at least some time between completing a draft and revising it. If you begin to revise your essay immediately after you

275

have completed a first draft, you will probably not be able to view your work objectively and will consequently miss many areas that need improvement. This is the disadvantage of "last minute jobs"—they don't enable a writer to acquire sufficient distance from the text. However, if you let the essay alone for a while (even an hour is better than nothing), you will return to it with fresh eyes, viewing it almost as if you were the audience, rather than the writer, and you will be in a better position to notice where revision is needed. To begin the revision process, print a copy of your paper and then leave it for a little while before beginning your revision.

2. Think about the Thesis, Claim, or Central Point by Reading Introductory Paragraphs Aloud

Early drafts often need additional work on the thesis, claim, or central point. A first draft, in particular, may contain a lot of information discussing the topic but lack a main point; sometimes a thesis in a first draft is too broad to be addressed adequately. To begin revising an early draft, read your first few paragraphs aloud, paying particular attention to your main point or thesis. Then see if you can answer the following questions:

What is the purpose or goal of your essay?
Do you have a statement that contains your thesis? Does the assignment prompt suggest that you have one?
Does your essay address a problem or exigence?
Have you considered who would care about this problem or exigence?
Would someone disagree with your ideas? In what way?
If you have a specific thesis statement, do you use the word "because"?
Is the word *because* necessary for this particular thesis?
Have you qualified your position sufficiently?

A useful way to look at thesis, claim, or central point is to consider the impact you wish to have on your audience. Here are some points to consider related to audience:

What does your audience already know or believe about the topic?
Is the aim of your essay to change your audience's thinking or enlighten your audience in some way?
Which aspect of your thesis, claim, or central point is your audience least likely to agree with?

To examine your essay in terms of audience, write your main point on a separate piece of paper. Then see if you can answer the following questions:

Before my audience reads my essay, what beliefs or attitudes toward this topic are they likely to have?
After my audience reads my essay, how do I wish their beliefs or attitudes to change or at least be reconsidered?
What would someone say who disagrees with my essay?

CLARIFYING THE THESIS, CLAIM, OR CENTRAL POINT: AN EXAMPLE OF REVISION

In his composition class, Paul wrote an essay in response to the following essay prompt:

> It is generally acknowledged that the various women's movements over the past fifty years have had a positive impact on important social and political issues, such as employment equality, reproductive rights, maternity leave, and sexual harassment. However, some people feel that as a result, men have been disadvantaged in a number of ways, losing not only employment advantages but also their sense of masculine "identity." These people think that men also need a "movement."

Locate several articles or essays concerned with various possibilities for a men's movement and consider whether such a movement would be beneficial in some way. Then choose one of these movements and write an essay in which you address the following question:

> ### To what extent is this movement likely to be beneficial?

Here is a first draft of Paul's first two paragraphs. Read these paragraphs aloud, paying particular attention to Paul's thesis.

Paul's First Draft

The Men's Movement

Since the formation of the women's movement, a great many changes have been demanded of men; among other things, they have been asked to be more sensitive to women's needs and more understanding and supportive of women. As a result, a variety of men's movements have developed, designed either to help men change or to defend the often-criticized male. One such movement, with which Robert Bly was associated, supports many of these changes but argues that modern man is not happy and must undergo greater transformations.

In 1990, Robert Bly wrote a book titled *Iron John,* which became known as a manifesto of the men's movement at that time. The story of Iron John involves a boy and his golden ball. While the boy is joyfully playing with the ball, he accidentally allows it to roll into the cage of Iron John, "a large man covered with hair from head to foot" who was found at the bottom of a pond. Throughout his life, the boy makes several attempts to get the ball back but is told by Iron John that he can only have it if he releases him from his cage. In order to set Iron John free, the boy has to steal the key to the cage from underneath his mother's pillow. The scenario of the boy and this bright beautiful ball represents the youthful innocence, inner harmony, and happiness that Bly believes all men lose early in life. *Iron John* is symbolic of the "Wild Man" that must be released for us to get back our "golden ball" and is associated with what has been called the "mythopoetic men's movement" (Wikipedia).

Reading Paul's first two paragraphs aloud will enable you to notice the absence of an explicit thesis statement. Because Paul has become so involved with retelling the story of *Iron John,* he has lost track of the prompt:

To what extent is this movement likely to be beneficial?

Note that Paul's first draft does not refer to the essay prompt at all and that he does not have an explicit thesis statement or central claim.

In his second draft, however, Paul refocused his material about *Iron John* so that its relevance to the question in the writing prompt was more apparent to the reader.

Paul's Second Draft

The Men's Movement

Since the formation of the women's movement, a great many changes have been demanded of men; among other things, they have been asked to be more sensitive to women's needs and more understanding and supportive of women. As a result, a variety of men's movements have developed, designed either to help men change or to enable men to reassert their rights. Among these men's movements are the men's liberation movement, profeminist men's movement, men's rights movement, and the mythopoetic men's movement. The mythopoetic movement, originating with Robert Bly's book, *Iron John* published in 1990, argues that the women's movement has had an emasculating effect on men, and therefore, modern men should seek to reestablish their lost masculinity by engaging in male oriented activities such as drumming and storytelling camps. This idea about reclaiming masculine energy through some type of ritual is unlikely to benefit men and certainly not women, because it is based on what is now considered a stereotypical view of men and values that will not result in cooperation between men and women. However, the mythopoetic movement also addresses other issues affecting men, such as male friendships, mentoring and the role of fathers. These will benefit society as a whole and should be the focus of a men's movement.

The "manifesto" of Bly's concept of a men's movement and which initiated the mythopoetic men's movement is a story told in *Iron John*. The story involves a boy who accidentally allows his favorite plaything, a golden ball, to roll into the cage of Iron John, "a large man covered with hair from head to foot" living at the bottom of a pond. As Bly recounts the story, the boy makes several attempts throughout his life to get the ball back but is told by Iron John that he can reclaim the ball only by releasing Iron John from his cage. Moreover, in order to do so, the boy must steal the key to the cage which is hidden underneath his mother's pillow. According to Bly, the scenario of the boy and this bright beautiful ball may be considered a metaphor for the condition of modern man, the golden ball representing the youthful innocence, inner harmony, and happiness which Bly believes all men lose early in life and which, he feels, can be reclaimed only by a men's movement. However, this tale addresses only one aspect of masculinity and does not discuss issues that should be the main focus of a men's movement.

In this second draft, Paul has included a clear thesis statement and placed greater emphasis on establishing the context for his ideas. When he refers to the story of *Iron John*, he does not simply retell the story, but links it to the issue he is addressing.

3. Check Your Essay for Adequate Support (LOGOS)

If the writing prompt requires that you have a clearly stated thesis, the revision process should begin with a focus on what you wish to say—your main point or purpose for writing. However, it is also important to examine your essay for adequate support. In particular, pay attention to the following:

- Credibility
  How have you established credibility?

Is this a topic in which personal experience is likely to be relevant? Have you included pertinent statements from authorities? Do they strengthen your position or have you simply quoted from outside material to fill in space?

- Reasoning
  Can you cite adequate reasons or supporting points for the thesis? Are these reasons based on sound assumptions?

- Evidence
  Have you supported your main points with compelling evidence?
  Do you need additional evidence or examples?
  Are statistics relevant to this topic? If so, have you spent sufficient time analyzing them?

- Elaboration

In writing early drafts, writers often leave out important information or give certain points only cursory attention, which means that the essay may require additional explanations, details, or examples. Actually, in revising your paper, you should **expect** that you will need to do at least some additional writing because in a first draft or even a second, third, or fourth, it is likely that you will have left out at least something. Also, remember that details are what makes your writing interesting, so in checking for adequate details, note whether you have included any that evoke sensory images—pictures, sounds, or feelings. Look for any representative anecdotes that can help your reader understand your ideas and hold your reader's attention as well.

4. Check Each Paragraph for Function and Connection to the Thesis

As you reread your essay, note the main point of each paragraph in the margin. Then see if you can find words or sentences within that paragraph that refer directly to the thesis. Often an essay will contain a number of good examples, but their relationship to the thesis is not well established. In Paul's first draft in his essay about the men's movement, for example, Paul discussed Robert Bly's book, *Iron John,* but he did not link that discussion to his main argument. Go through your essay paragraph by paragraph adding linking words or transitional sentences as needed.

5.   Note Arrangement and Structure

Examine the order of your paragraphs and consider the following questions:

Do your paragraphs lead naturally into another?
Have you addressed the opposing viewpoint?
Does the conclusion wrap things up adequately?
Would another arrangement be more effective?

6.   Read Your Essay Aloud, Paragraph by Paragraph, Checking for Sentence-Level Coherence, Fluency, and Correctness

Reading aloud is a useful strategy for all aspects of revision, but it is especially useful for detecting sentence level problems and areas where the text does not read smoothly. In reading for coherence, fluency, and correctness, think about the following questions:

Does one sentence lead naturally into another?
Are the sentences too short? Can these sentences be combined?
Is there a need for additional details?
Are your sentences too long? Can these be divided?
Have you checked for common mechanical errors such as subject-verb agreement, pronoun reference, or missing or extraneous commas?
Have your used your spell checker?

As you plan your revision, note the changes you would like to make. When Irene revises, she tends to scribble all over her first drafts, jotting down as many thoughts as possible before she loses them. Don't be afraid to write directly on your essay—remember that you can always print another copy. Finally, in thinking about revision, you should leave enough time to utilize whatever human resources you have available to you. If there is a writing lab or center at your school, ask a tutor to give you some feedback on your essay. Or let a friend read it, indicating areas that may not be clear. You don't always have to act on the recommendations of a tutor or a friend, but sometimes they might notice something that you, as the writer, may have overlooked.

Revision can be a tedious component of the writing process. It is so tempting to say to yourself, "the essay is probably fine as it is, so I don't have to spend any more time on it." However, even if you revise as you write, your essay will be better if you go through it, at least one more time. You will be glad you did.

13

CHAPTER

Narrative and Argument

"The most amazing thing happened today as I was walking to campus!"
"I can certainly understand, because I have had the same experience."
"Did you read about what happened in that country just yesterday? I would never go
    there for a vacation now."
"The dog ate my homework."

Telling stories is part of being human. Every day we recount experiences to our friends and family members, and many of our ideas, values, and world views are based on what we have experienced, read about, or been told. In fact, human reasoning is very often based on stories, because they enable us to understand how the world "works" and make judgments about what is or is not true or possible. We find some stories more compelling and believable than others because they are in accord with our sense of reality.

Stories, often referred to as "narratives," are also used in college writing. Argumentative essays may use a narrative example or perhaps several examples to support a main or subsidiary point, and a literacy narrative or autobiographical narrative may be based entirely on personal experiences. Narrative and argument are thus interrelated because both can be used to move a writer to say, "That experience is worth sharing." Or "That is an idea worth considering." This chapter, then, discusses strategies for writing an effective narrative, focusing particularly on the literacy narrative, a genre that is frequently assigned in college classes.

WHAT IS A NARRATIVE?

A narrative or story is a retelling of something that happened; it usually involves a connected sequence of events, and frequently includes a reflection on the significance of those events. It can be of varying lengths and can be based on personal experiences, which are recounted in order to have an impact on a reader. In an argumentative essay, a narrative may serve as an example to illustrate or support an idea. Narratives may be used to introduce or conclude an essay, and they can also be woven into the body of an essay. In a personal narrative, such as a literacy narrative, the entire essay may focus on personal experiences, describing what happened in the context of a main point or thesis. Often the thesis or main point in a narrative focuses on an understanding that the writer gained by overcoming a challenge, although that thesis may not be explicitly stated.

NARRATIVE AND ARGUMENT

To a certain extent, a narrative essay may be considered a type of argument that utilizes a sequential or chronological structure, beginning with what happened first, then second, etc. Its goal is to present the elements of a story as a means of supporting a main point, and it may incorporate elements often associated with fiction, such as character, dialogue, setting, point of view, and concrete details. Deciding where a narrative begins and ends is important, as is the question of whether it is necessary to include an explicitly stated thesis statement or whether the main purpose of the narrative is clear to the reader on its own.

FOR THINKING AND WRITING

Think about an experience you had on your college campus (some ideas: Meeting a roommate, registration, parking, the first day of class, locating a classroom, joining a club, buying books, trying out for a team). Then write a brief narrative of that experience that you might send to a friend. Can you find an underlying purpose or main idea in that story? Would you state that idea explicitly?

Then rewrite that narrative for someone in your family (perhaps your parents or other relatives). Did the narrative change? What differences can you note about the purpose, focus, or language choices between the two narratives?

THE NARRATIVE ARC

A narrative recounts or recalls a story or experience and usually begins by introducing the story in the introduction. The body, then, explains what happened, when it happened, why it happened, ultimately leading to a conclusion in which the writer explains how he or she met a challenge or learned from the experience. In terms of structure, many narratives utilize an organizational pattern that is often referred to as the "narrative arc," which is characterized by a rising conflict that builds to a crisis and then leads to a resolution. In a Literacy Narrative or Literacy Autobiography, a genre that is frequently assigned in composition classes, the writer recounts an experience or several experiences in which he or she has learned something that has to do with reading, writing, language, or becoming part of a group. Often the essay discusses how the writer overcame a challenge, such as being an outsider in a culture, school, or club. Below is a bare bones structure that exemplifies the narrative arc:

1. The Beginning of the Experience: Once I was—
2. But then—The writer feels uncertain or inadequate in some way.
3. And then—An event occurs in which the writer experiences more intense feelings of uncertainty and inadequacy. The tension builds to a climax!
4. But then—the writer takes an action toward improving the situation or encounters someone who helps the writer take the necessary action.
5. The writer struggles with the challenge but persists with great effort and the help of others.
6. Ultimately, the writer triumphs (the resolution). Or—the writer fails, but learns something.

FOR THINKING AND WRITING

Think about a personal challenge you have met and outline how you might present it in the structure of the narrative arc. Consider whether you would like to develop this narrative further and if so, what details you might wish to add.

FICTIONAL ELEMENTS IN A PERSONAL NARRATIVE

Concrete Detail

If you wish your intended reader to find your narrative compelling and meaningful, it is important to make the details as concrete and vivid as possible. Abstract language is rarely as moving as a specific detail that creates an image in the mind of your reader. Consider, then, what you see, hear, taste, touch, or smell when you reflect on an experience you might wish to narrate. If possible, locate pictures that can help you visualize details. Below are some examples of how details can make an abstract statement more vivid.

For example, if you wish to convey a sense of the bad weather you encountered when you first came to campus, you could say:

The weather was terrible when I arrived on campus. (abstract)

Or you could say,

As I stepped out of the car, a cold wind blew my hat into a ditch, and icy rain streamed down my face. (detail has been added)

Similarly, if you wish to convey that your English teacher made you welcome on your first day of class, you could say,

> Mr. Smith, the English teacher, made us welcome. (abstract)

Or you could say,

> With a friendly smile, Mr. Smith, the English teacher, greeted students one by one as they entered the classroom, shaking hands and asking about books and movies they liked.

FOR THINKING AND WRITING

Reflect on an experience you have had when you first came to your college or university. Then write two sentences about it: one using abstract language and the other using concrete detail. Share your work in small groups.

The Setting

Where your narrative takes place can be an important element in your story, so you may want to consider how much of the setting you want to include. In thinking about your story, what scenes come to your mind? What details about those scenes are important to the story? How do you feel about those scenes?

Characters

As in a short story or a novel, the use of people can play an important role. Which people do you want to include? How will you describe them? Is their physical appearance or how they dress important? How do these people contribute to the purpose of your narrative?

Dialogue

If you include people in your narrative, will you also include dialogue? If so, consider what you would have these people say that would contribute to your overall purpose? How would these people speak? Can you recall a conversation you have had with someone who has been important in your narrative?

FOR THINKING AND WRITING

Think about someone who has played a role in a narrative you plan to write. Write a physical description of this person, including the clothes they habitually wear. Then write a one-page dialogue between this person and yourself. What would be the focus of the conversation? Can that conversation be included in some way in your narrative?

AN EXAMPLE OF A LITERACY NARRATIVE

A literacy narrative is concerned with a writer's experience with some form of literacy—often it focuses on some form of school experience involved with reading or writing, or on learning a new language or culture. Literacy narratives are often assigned in writing classes as a means of helping students think about their relationship with reading, writing, language, and the cultures with which they are associated. Sometimes, students are assigned to read published essays that exemplify this genre, as does Lida's essay that is included later in this chapter. Two popular readings, available online, are "Mother Tongue," by Amy Tan, and "How to Tame a Wild Tongue," by Gloria Anzeldua.

Below is an example of a literacy narrative assignment:

> Write an autobiographical essay that recounts an experience you have had with literacy (reading, writing, language, becoming part of a culture). In developing your narrative, consider the situation in which your experience with literacy occurred, and, if appropriate, narrate how you were able to resolve that situation and indicate why this experience was significant.

Here are some possibilities:

A memory about writing and reading
Someone who helped you learn to read and write
A challenge about learning a new language
An experience with a book, language, or text of some sort that has made a difference in
     your life.

Below is an early draft of the essay Joanna wrote in response to this assignment:

Finding Friends Through Language

When I was seventeen years old, my parents and I immigrated to America from Poland, and when I first saw the apartment they had rented in Los Angeles, I thought I was living in paradise. The living room was modern and comfortable, I had my own room, and best of all, there was a pool and a Jacuzzi in the apartment complex. My parents and I spent that first summer exploring the neighborhood and visiting amusement parks, and I felt as if I was on an amazing, permanent vacation—that is, until I enrolled in high school for my senior year.

The local high school was Bedford Grand, and at first, I wasn't too worried about fitting in because I had studied English in my home country. But soon I discovered that although I could read and write English at least somewhat, I couldn't speak English very well—in fact, I was so frightened of all those American teenagers who already had so many friends, that I couldn't say anything at all. All I could do was observe the different groups, trying to figure out who they were by the way they were dressed. Each day, I sat alone in the cafeteria eating my lunch, looking with envy at the groups of girls who sat together, laughing and talking. One particular girl, Jennifer, was always surrounded by a group of other girls, and I wanted so much to be friends with her, but I knew that could never happen. One day, I overheard Jennifer (she was actually called, "Jen") talking about a party she was having, and of course, I didn't expect to receive an invitation, although I secretly prayed for one.

The next day, though, to my surprise, Jen handed me an invitation as I was leaving school, although, I have no idea why she had invited me since I had never spoken to her. Of course, I was very excited, but I was also totally freaked out. "What should I wear?" "How should I act?" I knew I was different from Jen and her friends, and I so wanted to fit in. But how could I do it?

During the week before the party, I could think of nothing else. But finally I decided that in order to make friends, I needed to at least LOOK like the rest of the teenagers. So I went shopping at the mall to buy new clothes from a store that I had heard some of the girls talking about. At least I could look like an American teenager and hoped that then maybe I would begin to fit in with the popular girls.

Finally, it was the night of the party. But when I stood outside the enormous house, I felt really nervous. "What was I doing at this party?" I thought. I can hardly speak a word of English. Eventually, I made myself walk into the house, where I recognized several girls from my school, all talking and laughing together. Loud music was coming from several of the many rooms, and disco lights were flashing in the entryway. Snacks were being passed around on trays and refreshing fruit drinks. Everything was just what I expected a party to be. But then I didn't know what to do. Should I eat something? Dance? Get a drink? Should I hold onto my purse or put it down somewhere? I didn't dare start a conversation with anyone because my English was so terrible. All I could say when someone spoke to me was "Please speak more slowly" or "Sorry, I don't understand." A few of the girls did try to talk to me, but then I could see that they got annoyed or bored and soon walked away.

After a while, I decided to leave the party, and all the way home, I kept saying to myself, "You are such a loser. You will never fit in." I felt like a complete failure and when I came home, I told my mother that I hated being in America and wish we had never come here.

But then, after several days, I decided that I would make more of an effort to become an American teenager. I watched TV trying to learn teenage slang and I practiced some of the expressions I heard in school. Also—I decided to attend an adult school program so that I could improve my vocabulary and learn to speak more fluently. At this school, I met other kids my age who were struggling to fit in with American teenage society, and it was there that I began to make friends. In fact, I learned that some of my new friends, Jane from Korea, Dana from Rwanda, and two girls from Iran, Farah and Mona, were also students at Bedford Grand high school. Soon, I didn't have to eat lunch alone anymore, because we all sat together trying out our English and eating American food.

Senior year passed quickly, and soon it was graduation day, and my friends and I all shouted for each other when our names were called. No longer did I feel alone because of my broken English, because I had friends who liked me in spite of it. We now understand that we are part of the American culture, and this semester, we are all enrolled in college, where we will continue to improve our English. Someday, I know, we will earn our degrees.

QUESTIONS FOR REVISING A NARRATIVE

The questions below can help you think about possibilities for revising a literacy narrative:

1. What is the purpose of this narrative?
2. What is the "shape" of this narrative? Does it have a narrative arc?
3. Where does this narrative begin? Should it begin elsewhere?
4. What are the most important events that took place?
5. Which sections are the most moving or compelling? Why?
6. Are there sections in the text that don't work as well as they should? If so, please identify them and suggest possibilities for helping the writer use them more effectively.
7. Does this narrative have a theme or agenda? If so, is it easily identifiable?
8. Is there additional information or elaboration that would improve this narrative?
9. Are there strategies in published works that you can adapt to your own narrative?

These revision questions can be very useful for revising a narrative, and when Joanna thought about them, she wrote the following responses:

1.   What is the purpose of this narrative?

Actually, now that I am thinking about it, I think the purpose of this narrative is to show that I managed to find good friends who were not in the popular group and didn't judge me because of my bad English. But I don't think I show that enough.

2.   What is the "shape" of this narrative? Does it have a narrative arc?

This narrative does have a narrative arc, but I get to the solution too quickly—like—okay, one day I decided to go the language classes and then all of a sudden I had good friends. It didn't really happen as quickly as that.

3.   Where does this narrative begin? Should it begin elsewhere?

I began the narrative with a description of my apartment. But maybe the apartment doesn't matter so much in my story. Maybe I should begin with a description of me sitting alone in the cafeteria and then summarize a little how I got there.

4.   What are the most important events that took place?

The loneliness in the cafeteria (need to show that more), the party, and the language classes.

5.   Which sections are the most moving or compelling? Why?

Sitting alone in the cafeteria and the party are moving. But I could also add that I yelled at my mother and blamed her for my situation.

6.   Are there sections in the text that don't work as well as they should? If so, please identify them and suggest possibilities for improving them.

The attendance at the language school doesn't work that well. It needs more detail.

7.   Does this narrative have a theme or agenda? If so, is it easily identifiable?

The theme is that you have to take charge of your own progress, not blame others, and not focus only on how you are dressed.

8.   Is there additional information or elaboration that would improve this literacy narrative?

More dialogue, a description of my English teacher and more information about the school.

9.   *Are there strategies in published works that you can adapt to your own narrative?*

In my English class, we read Mike Rose's *Lives on the Boundary* and maybe I should begin my narrative with my name, the way he does with "Laura." Here is the beginning of Mike Rose's book:

> Her name is Laura and she was born in the poor section of Tijuana, the Mexican border city directly south of San Diego. Her father was a food vendor, and her memories of him and his chipped white cart come back to her in easy recollection.
> **Rose, Mike. *Lives on the Boundary*. New York: Penguin Books, 1990. Print.**

After responding to these questions, Joanna decided to revise her literacy narrative. Below is a copy of her revision. Do you think it has been improved?

Finding Friends in America

My name is Joanna, and I am sitting next to my friend, Farah, in a first-year Composition class at State University. Farah and I registered for several of the same classes, and later on, we will be meeting other friends for lunch. I look around the classroom thinking that soon I will know some of these other students too, and that maybe some of them will become new friends. I also recall that last year at this time, I had no friends in America at all. In fact, last year, "lunch" for me meant sitting by myself in the high school cafeteria, trying to eat the sandwich that my mother had packed for me—the bits of bread scratching my throat like clumps of sand. Just a few tables away, I could see a group of girls dressed in tight jeans and colorful shirts, laughing and talking, and I so wanted be part of that group. But aside from the fact that I could barely speak English, I knew that my clothes were all wrong, and I thought that if I didn't have the right clothes, I could never be part of that group.

Right before my senior year in high school, my parents and I had immigrated to America from Poland, and when I first saw the apartment they had rented in Los Angeles, I thought I was living in paradise. The living room was modern and comfortable, with a cozy beige sofa, matching chairs, and a large television set. I had my own room, with a pretty blue and white comforter trimmed with lace, and best of all, there was a pool and a Jacuzzi in the apartment complex. "How bad could this be?" I thought. But then, at the end of August, I enrolled in the local high school, Bedford Grand, and realized how much of an outsider I was.

Actually, before I enrolled in classes, I didn't worry too much about fitting in, because I had studied English in my home country. But soon I discovered that although I could read and write English at least somewhat, I couldn't speak very well—in fact, I was so frightened of all those glamorous American teenagers who already had so many friends, that I couldn't say anything at all. All I could do was observe the different groups, trying to figure out who they were by the way they were dressed. Some of them had body piercings and wore mostly black, while others wore jeans with bright colored tops. Everyone looked so different from the kids I knew in Poland, where everyone wore a school uniform. "I need new clothes," I whined to my mother every day, "or I will never have any friends." But she kept telling me that what I needed to do was work on my English so that I could have conversations with other kids my age. "Having the right clothes is all very well," she said. "But you need to be able to speak," and whenever I complained that I had no friends, she would suggest a language school that I could attend. But I kept saying, "no" to her suggestion. "I don't want to hang out with people from other countries," I said. "I want American friends, like the girls in school."

So each day, I sat alone in the cafeteria trying to swallow my lunch, looking with envy at the popular girls having so much fun with one another. One particular girl, Jennifer, was so pretty—slim with long blond hair and beautiful clothes that fit her perfectly. She was always surrounded by a group of other girls, and I wanted so much to be friends with her, but I knew that could never happen. One day, I overheard Jennifer (she was actually called, "Jen") talking about a party she was having, and of course, I didn't expect to receive an invitation, although I secretly prayed for one.

The next day, though, to my surprise, Jen handed me an invitation as I was leaving school, although, I have no idea why she had invited me since I had never spoken to her. Of course, I was very excited, but I was also completely freaked out. "What should I wear?" "How should I act?" I knew I was different from Jen and her friends, and I so wanted to fit in. But how could I do it?

During the week before the party, I could think of nothing else and managed to talk my mother into letting me buy some new clothes for the occasion. So I put some gold streaks in my dull brown hair and went shopping at the mall to buy a pair of cool tight jeans and a bright red shirt from a store that I had heard some of the girls talking about. I figured that if the girls at school bought their clothes there, I should buy something there too. At least I could look like an American teenager and hoped that then maybe I would begin to fit in with the popular girls.

Finally, it was the night of the party, and although my parents gave me a funny look when I left the apartment in my new clothes, I thought I looked good enough. "Maybe tonight I would finally begin to fit in," I thought. However, when I stood outside the enormous yellow Spanish style house with a beautiful green lawn and low growing red and white flowers along the walkway, my heart began to pound, and I had to force my feet to move forward. "What was I doing at this party?" I thought, "I look okay, but I can hardly speak a word of English." Eventually, I made myself walk up the path and into the house, where I recognized several girls from my school, all talking and laughing together. Loud music was coming from several of the many rooms, and disco lights were flashing in the entryway. Snacks were being passed around on trays—little tacos, meatballs, guacamole, and chips—also cokes and refreshing fruit drinks. Everything was just what I expected a party to be. But then I didn't know what to do. Should I dance? Get a drink? Should I hold onto my purse or put it somewhere? I didn't dare start a conversation with anyone because my English was so terrible. At school, all I ever said when someone spoke to me was "Please, can you speak more slowly" or "Sorry, I don't understand." At the party, one of the girls did come over to say something to me, but when I said, "Sorry, I don't understand," she rolled her eyes and said, "Whatever," and walked away. I could see that she really didn't want to make any effort to talk to me, and neither did anyone else.

After standing around at the party clutching my purse for about a half hour, I began to feel so sad that I wanted to cry. In fact, I felt so uncomfortable and lonely that I decided to walk home, and all the way, I kept saying to myself, "You are such a loser. You will never fit in." I felt like a complete failure and when I came home, I told my mother that I hated being in America and wish we had never come here. Then I went up to my room and slammed the door.

After several days, though, I decided that I would make more of an effort to make friends, aside from buying American style clothes. I watched TV trying to learn teenage slang and I practiced some of the expressions I heard in school. And then, finally, about a week later, I told my mother that I would try going to the adult language school that she had recommended so often.

Fortunately, I was able to begin right away, so the following Monday, after my regular classes, I went to another part of the campus, where I was greeted by Mrs. Moore, the English Language teacher, who smiled and introduced me to several other girls, who were also struggling to fit in with American teenage society. Right away, I felt more comfortable as we all experimented with our new language, and it was there that I began to make friends. Mrs. Moore encouraged us to try speaking English to one another, and she made us feel so comfortable that soon we all began to improve. Soon, I didn't have to eat lunch by myself, because I had the company of Jane from Korea, Dana from Rwanda, and two girls from Iran, Farah and Mona. Every day, we sat together trying out our English and eating American food, such as pizza and hamburger, but sometimes we shared food from our own country too. On the weekend, we spent time shopping, going to the beach, going to sports events, and sleeping over at each other's houses. Our bond was that we were all immigrants, trying to become part of a new culture, but we talked about the traditions of our own cultures too.

Soon it was graduation day, and when my name was called, my friends screamed out loud for me and I screamed for them. No longer did I feel alone because of my broken English, because I had friends who liked me in spite of it and who were struggling to learn English too. Yes, we were all immigrants, and maybe we would never fit in with the girls at that awful party. But we now understand that we are also a part of the American culture, like so many people before us. Together we will attend our college classes, and someday, I know, we will all receive our degrees.

JOANNA'S REVISIONS

Compare Joanna's second draft with her first, noting differences between the two. Do you think that Joanna has improved her essay? Why or why not?

LIDA'S ESSAY

Below is another example of a literacy narrative, this one which requires the writer to use a conceptual lens to introduce an experience concerned with literacy. Here is the assignment:

Assignment Using a Conceptual Lens to Present a Personal Story
Assignment adapted from Joanna Wolfe, Barrie Olson, and Laura Wilder. "Knowing What We Know about Writing in the Disciplines: A New Approach to Teaching for Transfer in FYC." *The WAC Journal*, 25 (2014): 42–77.

Deborah Brandt argues that literacy sponsors, those who have been involved in fostering literacy acquisition, "set the terms for access to literacy and wield powerful incentives for compliance and loyalty" (166). Considering this idea, write a literacy narrative that describes the literacy sponsorship you received that ultimately led you to have a seat in this classroom. In other words, reflect on the writer/speaker/reader you are today and the role that literacy sponsors (positive or negative) played in creating you.

My Literacy Journey

By Lida Perez

When I was twenty-four years old, I came from Colombia to the United States, which I wanted to make my new home. The United States was a new and exciting place for me, a highly diverse culture, and most of all, people spoke another language—English. My fascination with distant places, cultures, and languages, to some extent, came from my father and my family's values, and once I came to the United States and enrolled in English classes, I had the good fortune to meet kind and encouraging teachers, who helped me conquer frustration and develop the strength to continue to learn. This is a narrative of my literacy journey and the "sponsors" who helped along the way.

When I was very young, my father would talk about countries and cities before I had ever heard of them in my Geography classes; he would show them to my younger sister, Pilar, and me in a World Atlas book. "The world is a big place," he would say, "and you need to be aware of what's going on because in the end it affects us all." He liked to travel and took us many places throughout Colombia—also to Ecuador and Venezuela. It was as if he knew that years later, I was going to live somewhere far away. My father emphasized the importance of being careful observers and adapting to our surroundings. His serious look would let us know that what he was saying was very important. We used to pretend that we spoke an exotic foreign language and babble on in nonsensical chatter.

Our parents would take us to Cerro de Monserrate, a famous destination that took tourists to the top of the mountain for some spectacular views and breathtaking scenery, and there we would hear tourists speaking many different languages. My sister and I would stand next to them giggling and trying to repeat their sounds—shua, shua, shua—It was fun—we were two little gringas for a few minutes, and even back then, it felt exciting to make new sounds, to witness there were other ways of communicating; Spanish was just one of many. The fresh and sweet evergreen fragrance of the Eucalyptus forest with its big trees and its gummy sap from the leaves sticking to our playful fingers is as vivid in my memory as this morning's breakfast. Going up in the teleferico (cable car) and hiking down from the Cerro Monserrate in Bogota, taking in the spectacular natural beauty and the foreign speech of gringo tourists is where my love affair with English began.

Fifteen years later, I was no longer that little girl playing with a foreign language as a game; instead, I was an adult, trying very hard to acquire and learn English. My first days here in the United States were full of ambivalence. I was very excited to be here, but sometimes despair took over—I felt lost, left out of the conversation and unable to communicate and understand the world around me. A simple daily activity like asking for directions or finding a product at the grocery store was such an elaborate process and such a daunting task. Answering the phone? Forget it! You couldn't get me anywhere near it! Foreign sounds, coming out so quickly from peoples' mouths made my head hurt—trying to concentrate to catch a sound—maybe.

On the other hand, I perceived English as a language full of potential; despite its confusing and contradictory rules of grammar and pronunciation; it was a rich language, replete with words of precision and description, and I found that extremely compelling. I was so grateful that my family had always encouraged me to pay attention to language, because I had always loved words: their sounds and their spellings, but mostly the meaning they convey, charged with power, emotion and association. It was pleasing to observe people's faces full of gestures and deliberate eye contact as they communicated with one another, because it gave me the hope that someday I would too speak in the natural and confident way of a native.

Rinaldi Adult School was the first place where my new adventure began. As it turned out, the beginner levels were full, so I was asked if I would sign up for the intermediate levels, and eager to learn, I agreed to do so. After enrolling (someone translated for me at the admission's office) in several English classes,

I found myself sitting in a classroom divided into four large wooden tables with seven students at each. The bright and colorful letters glued to the board on the back of the classroom, the world maps on one corner, and the poster filled with words separated into categories of parts of speech on the other reminded the students that we had entered a new language world, a world where we were all foreigners, unable to convey messages clearly and quickly, as we were used to in our primary languages. Needless to say, it was complicated. Right away, everything around me sounded something like shua shua, tind, tint, threst.

The class members had mastered the lesson on how to introduce themselves, and "glad—nice—a pleasure to meet you" greeting phrases were becoming easy to all of us along with a basic list of adjectives to describe ourselves and to talk about our favorite kinds of food. But as the days went by, the lessons became more complex. All of these words printed on a page! What was all of that? Words that didn't make any sense, and I know mine wasn't the only puzzled face—words that are spelled one way and pronounced another way. "Yes, I am sorry," the English instructor would say. "That word, or this word, 'Chevrolet,' for example, comes from French, so you don't pronounce the 't' at the end of the word." "What? Are you serious?" Frequent instances like this, different sets of rules, more exceptions than rules, were extremely frustrating. In the Spanish language, most words end in a vowel, unlike English where most words end in a consonant. As a result, Spanish speakers have the tendency to drop the last sound of the word.

I can smile now as I reflect on my many struggles and moments of confusion and frustration—frustration in its purest form. "I am never going to be able to learn English. It is too hard, and perhaps I am not smart enough; I don't have what it takes." "With practice, you will learn," my teacher would say again and again. But during those first classes, I felt great frustration and disappointment. Still, at the back of my mind, I kept hearing my father talking about the importance of being in a larger world and learning a new language, so one day, I went to the 99 cent store, bought a bunch of little notebooks, placed one in each bag or purse and started writing and making lists that consisted of four columns, sometimes five: Word, Meaning, Pronunciation, Translation, and Examples. I made a classroom out of every place I visited: the grocery store, the Colombian restaurant, the Italian restaurant, the Falafel Palace. I was determined to learn English, so the bank, the mall, the streets, and my very favorite place, the mountains—all of these became classrooms for me. With notebook and pen in hand, I opened my eyes widely and there they were—words and more words available for me to enter in my respective columns.

So that's how it all started to feel like I was finally having fun. An English-Spanish dictionary, a blue pen (I love blue) and my little notebook from the 99 cent store were my best companions. Two years later, in my diary entry, I would name them, "Instruments of Progress." But words were not as much fun as catching new phrases and idiomatic expressions. "Take it easy" and "I am not kidding you" were some of my first ones. If I was writing in those little notebooks and filling them from cover to cover, why not start a diary too? My most loyal friend—my diary, where I could express my deepest self, and I did so mostly in English.

Little by little, I started feeling like a rich woman; putting money in one's pocket feels good. I didn't have much money, but I felt wealthy putting words, phrases and paragraphs in my literacy bank. But I was also very fortunate to learn from kind and knowledgeable teachers. One English instructor that I am very fond of, even until this day, is Mrs. Powers. Her sweet blue eyes and her permanent half-way smile are what I remember when I think of ESL level six. She would dress in green on St. Patrick's Day, in orange during Thanksgiving week, and in red during Christmas. Her classic, yet casual style emphasized her enthusiastic and compassionate nature. She was always pleased to teach us a new word, a new expression—and she was always respectful toward all the students, even those resisting the English they were studying.

One afternoon, toward the end of the semester, I was on my way to the parking lot when Mrs. Powers caught up with me to tell me that I might like to listen to KCRW, which I could find on 89.9 FM radio. A few days before, I had asked her for any ideas of how to increase my vocabulary, not words found in the dictionary, but ideas, and full sentences. Being the caring and efficient educator she was, she thought of NPR news, warning me that at first I might not get much out of it, but that eventually it would be clear to me and that I would increase my vocabulary a great deal while becoming informed of the current issues. This was certainly one of the best and most practical pieces of advice I ever got from any of my instructors. Today, this is my favorite way to get the news and eventually, something really incredible happened. I gradually discovered that this second language, which I had, at least to a certain extent, mythicized and perceived as so different, was, indeed, more similar to Spanish than I had expected. I learned that as the world of English became more accessible to me, I could associate it with concepts or ideas I already had in my own language.

Some day, I hope to share my English acquisition experience with other adults who are struggling to learn English, to show my students that I understand how difficult it is to start from zero and regress to feeling like a child again. I still feel that I am an English Language learner, but I have had powerful sponsors who continue to help me learn—the people who provided the motivation and enthusiasm for learning a new language, as my father did, and the teachers who encouraged me, teachers like Mrs. Powers. These were my literacy sponsors, and one day, it is my goal to become a literacy sponsor myself.

FOR DISCUSSION

How is Lida's essay similar to and different from Joanna's?

EXAMPLES OF LITERACY NARRATIVES

Below are two additional examples of literacy narratives, one written by Enrique Solis and the other by Cesar Soto. Do you find these narratives compelling? Why or why not?

Delving into a New World: A Sellout or Success Story?

By Enrique Solis

In high school, I failed eight classes, took summer school every year, and barely graduated with a 2.1 GPA. And those are just my academic shortcomings. Don't forget the curfew tickets, truancy tickets, arrests, gang activity, and the two occasions I succeeded in evading police helicopters. The miscreant, the delinquent, statistic, society's worst nightmare—Me. Strangely, it took hindsight to see this person. At the time I thought of myself as the experiencer—one enthralled and beckoned by nature, the universe, music, humanity, and danger. I was the boy who shot out street lights to see the stars. I knocked on friends' windows at 3 a.m. to wander, talk, and trespass into deserted buildings and on school roofs before watching the sunrise. I climbed into my window at 6 a.m. to start my school day at 7:30 a.m.

What could high school offer this experiencer? Ideally a lot. But almost everything about my particular high school was cumbersome and lifeless. Good grades were the end all, be all. I saw no value in this system—I had already learned that getting an "A" had less to do with actually learning than passively completing busywork. My priorities consisted of testing my limitations—mentally and physically—and engaging with the world on multiple levels. It seemed that almost every class I attended strove to anchor me down to a rigid world where success was going through the motions and learning to do what you're told. I was bored. And quite frankly, I was frightened at the idea of becoming anything like the vapid, stiff teachers who kicked me out of class for sagging my pants, disagreeing with them, or questioning their authority in any other way. My school supplanted learning with character-shaping.

Until one day I entered a real classroom (real in the sense that learning took place daily). It was AP English: Rhetoric and Composition, and I failed it. This class blew my mind. I was thrust into the academic world: We grappled with the theoretical, historical, and philosophical; instead of vocabulary words, we had rhetorical terms; and we wrote essays constantly. The level of engagement with the texts and with my classmates was on another level. I participated daily and marveled at the knowledge of my teacher and the authors we read. Yet at the same time I was altogether unprepared to *pass* a class like this—I lacked the structure, discipline, and overall care for school, especially grades to really do what was necessary. I wish this could have been my turning point, but it's not easy to suddenly stop being the person you've always been.

Eventually, I got through high school, just barely, but completed nonetheless. Needless to say, I was apprehensive about entering the "real world," which my mom defined as a full-time job or full-time school—"not half this, part that. Commit to something." Eventually, I would commit fully as a college student. The semester after high school I earned straight A's. I felt like it was a mistake. Even my family was in shock. Academic counselors at my high school never even talked to me about college—I needed to focus on making up fails—so five A's when I got there was way beyond everyone's expectations, including my own. But I was there and doing well, which was when I decided to pursue a new major. I wanted to become a high school teacher and bring life, purpose, and learning into the classrooms that lacked so much of it. So everything was on track as I entered my first 200-level course in my new major, English.

The class was Major American writers from the late nineteenth century onward. At my community college the vast majority of students were minorities— Black and Hispanic—but as I entered this class there was a sudden demographic transformation. Even the professor noticed: "There are no black students in here, are there?" I raised my hand and answered "No", and there were about twelve movie posters all over the walls so I pointed out, "and there is only 1 on the walls." I pointed to a half-illuminated half-silhouetted image of Denzel Washington from *Remember the Titans*. Everyone looked around to check my findings and seemed to think it an odd observation. But after being there only five minutes, it was blatantly obvious to me—I had entered a different world, a secret community amongst my own consisting of readers, writers, and thinkers few of which were Black or Latino. The students began small talk about a show called *Dexter*, other English classes, and previous courses with this same instructor. My apprehension grew. These were not high school failures, nor were they any of those students who drop as soon as they get their financial aid. These students were readers. While I was breaking into buildings, they were reading *The Great Gatsby*; while I slept atop school roofs, they were delving into *1984*. Based partly on the literary references they made, and partly on the way they spoke in general, I quickly saw the literacy gap between them and me. I began regretting all those classes I ditched, books I never read, and papers I never wrote. I had read only 3 novels total before college. This was going to be my trial: could I really excel or even just survive in a field I had utterly failed in previously?

The process began. The first book assigned was *Adventures of Huckleberry Finn*. I had heard of this book but had no idea what it entailed, when it was written, where it was written, who had written it, or really anything about it other than it was American. The instructor asked difficult questions and coaxed intelligent answers from many of the students. When it came time to write our papers, we had to choose two opposing scholars on the subject we would discuss. I chose two scholars with differing perspectives on race and whether or not *Huck Finn* should be banned in certain schools. One scholar, Justin Kaplan, praised the book for its groundbreaking depiction of a black slave, Jim, as a character round with humanity. He emphasizes *Huck Finn's* relevance for young students today. Julius Lester takes a cutting and opposite approach. He states that the depiction of Jim is still fraught with stereotypical elements that can be damaging to young black readers who must try to identify with a slave. The instructor had no problem writing Lester off as a loon that didn't understand the book. For most of my schooling, minorities had ironically been the majority so racial discussions were usually very sensitive, possibly even suppressed. It was odd hearing my instructor say that "anyone who wants to ban *Huck Finn* is clearly illiterate and incompetent." I saw his position as radical and dismissive of social contexts other than our own so I decided to take it up in my paper. I followed all of this scholarly work and felt confident in my understanding of the material. I chose to use Lester's argument to show how the depiction of Jim could cause racial identity issues with modern black readers, especially because the story is told through the eyes of a young narrator (Huck) who struggles with the racism of his culture—I argued that *Huck Finn* was valued and more relevant to white audiences who struggle with racism at the expense of discomfort or uneasiness felt by black readers. I knew I had picked a controversial position, so I tried to back up my arguments as best I could. I found the task harder than I had imagined and I did not create the essay I originally envisioned. Nonetheless, I turned it in and waited anxiously for his response.

On that essay, I received a zero. Devastated, shocked, and totally embarrassed, I immediately stuffed it into my backpack—hiding my results as everyone critiqued each other's. I tried hard on that essay, thought I covered the material thoroughly, and even had fun with it. I was ready to quit. The instructor didn't agree with my position at all and demanded I rewrite it completely. For some reason, it hit me hard: my heart shot adrenaline though my system every few seconds, I stared at a fixed point of my desk, then the wall as tears almost surged forth in front of Denzel's poster. I honestly did not expect his reaction to be so violent. My paper addressed the discomfort felt by some young Black students when the word "nigger" is read out loud in class, especially by white students. He wrote on my paper, "It is of course, ok for blacks to call each other 'nigga' though. It's called being hypocritical." Somewhere along the academic process, the argument got brought down to this. I was shocked by his hatred of my paper. It was not *truly* a zero paper so he must have hated it so much he couldn't even grade it. I had obviously not been privy to certain rules of that literacy community. In his class, certain arguments are just plain off-limits. I climbed up the academic ladder, skipped a step, slipped, and came tumbling down.

So I rewrote the essay with turbulent emotions: a blend of embarrassment, anger, and determination. I took the opposite stance of my previous essay as proof that I understood the other argument but didn't agree with it. That rewrite process called upon every faculty I had as a writer (and is quite possibly when I became a writer). I brainstormed for like three days in order to gather the absolute strongest points, labored to find the perfect words, and then edited with a fury. It was exciting and almost easy because I thought of it as just refuting every claim in my previous essay. By presenting his strong perspective on the matter, my instructor, in a way, showed his hand. I knew exactly what the *right answer* was so to speak. It was then I realized that literature classes are not strictly about making a sound argument, they are about gathering all the information possible from the texts, then reading the instructor to figure out what *they* want gathered from it. When I turned that rewritten paper in, it was with smug confidence because I knew it was the best paper I could produce, yet I couldn't suppress the deep fear that my best was simply not enough and I just did not belong in that classroom.

The day the rewrite papers were returned was about as believable as the ending of an episode of *Full House*. Everyone got their papers but me. Instead the instructor had the nerve to read it to the class in its entirety! He said it was "A well-written, intelligent, even inspiring essay defending Twain and Huck," then he walked over and put it in my hands. I couldn't believe it. I felt like I had sold my soul to the devil. Never before had I been more ambivalent: I was incredibly proud of myself for actually pulling it off, yet deeply perturbed by the fact that I was basically being praised for fully embracing ideas that I didn't even necessarily agree with.

Some would call me a sellout, and the few people I told *did* call me a sellout. I saw it as proving I wasn't "illiterate" or "incompetent" just because I chose a difficult position to defend. I had been a social rebel, deviant, and dissenter all my life—I didn't have to prove that to anyone. If anything, rewriting that paper helped me prove to myself that I could get over my rebellious tendencies and pride in order to successfully enter this new world. I think most people would say that reading and writing about literature is an enriching experience; however, in order to enter this particular literary community, I had to first give up a huge part of myself. Now, as I grow and come to fruition as a writer, I feel encouraged to find a way to rediscover and utilize those passionate parts of myself that I previously worked so hard to suppress.

Wrath, or How I Learned to Read

By Cesar Soto

I couldn't go to Mexico because I'd been told by my mother that there were scorpions *everywhere*. I cringed, a seven year old boy, afraid to get stung. I associated Mexico, then, as a land of scorpions, waiting to sting you in cupboards and under benches, no place was free from their double-pronged poisonous attack. I reluctantly agreed to stay, while my mother and brother flew to Mexico to visit my dying grandmother. In retrospect, it was probably the cost and the fact that my older brother (Oscar) is and has always been a wild child that prompted my mother to take him. My four year old sister and I stayed behind, safe from scorpions but with a dull ache in our chests at seeing our mother leave us for three months. We stayed with our eldest brother Jaime and his new wife.

I missed my mother terribly, her physical presence, her words. She had long, jet-black hair and jutting cheekbones, a beautiful indigenous-looking woman, her brown almond-shaped eyes lit with intensity or crinkled with mirth depending on the tenor of the story. And she was beautiful because endless language spilled from her lips, like unraveling yarn. She'd begin: "In my village there was a little candy shop. One day . . . ." or with "They said the priest had fallen in love with *Teresita* . . ." my eyes widening, expectant, rapt with a sublime feeling in my chest that mounted as the story went on, knowing that it would surpass her last story, leaving me to consider its elements for days at a time.

After school, on the way to the supermarket, she'd spin a yarn about being a teenager in her hometown in Mexico and how proper she was brought up. She'd continue with her story through the produce aisles, my eyes never leaving her face which was imprinted in my mind; again, my mother meant life-force, language constantly streaming through her lips. Even before bed, I would seek her out for one more story . . . and she'd read us biblical stories, for she loved to read the Bible and theological texts. I listened closely, especially to the story of Jesus letting the children come unto him. Maybe in some ways my mother was kind of like Jesus, always telling parables and stories with a rustic flair and easily discerned bad and good characters.

In the dark lonely silence of my room, I yearned to hear a story. Hence the ache in my chest, no matter how much I laughed while swinging on the monkey bars on the playground or while watching The Gummi Bears cartoons; the ache deepened into a dark void . . . Unconsciously, perhaps, I realized that for me life was language and stories, and their absence, unhappiness, silence, lament.

One day, I got the idea that I'd write my mother a letter. This swelled my heart with joy and I ran all the way home, not stopping to say 'hi' to my friends on the street. Panting, I asked Jaime to teach me how to read in Spanish. He was more fluent in Spanish than in English anyway. He smiled and took out the Bible, and I smiled back thinking of my mother.

Soon enough, I made the thrilling discovery that letters could combine to make words and words sentences and sentences . . . ideas, not so much paragraphs since the Bible had verses. Verses were the linguistic unit after sentences. And what a discovery . . . "En...e-ee-ll...prin-cii-pioo..creo Dios..." : In the beginning God created the heavens and the earth. And the earth was without form . . . I strained and strained and my older brother looked nervously at me, as if maybe this was too much for me. But then I narrowed my eyes and recited the entire first verse of this huge book called the Bible that I'd seen only adults read, and I felt immense pride and joy wash over me. I said the verse again, this time with more confidence, feeling my voice deepen, resonating with the power of the words: "En el principio creo Dios los cielos y la tierra." I let out a happy yelp and jumped from my chair and clapped my hands. I told my brother, "I can read! I can read!" I'd forgotten that I wanted to learn how to read to write to my mother. In fact, I'd forgotten all about my mother and was wholly absorbed by my discovery of reading this story that was much grander than any my mother had ever told me: there was nothing, *void*, and God called forth the universe. My brother looked at me, again, worried, perhaps the intensity in my eyes uncharacteristic for someone so young. Later on that night, I plotted how I would read all of Genesis and Exodus before my mother came back.

One Saturday, my father, whom I saw only on the weekends, took me to the supermarket. He was quiet and gruff, though he would buy me whatever I wanted. I had been practicing writing in Spanish, now, for a month. As we passed the stationery section, I asked him nonchalantly if he could buy me a birthday card. He asked what for. I said for my mom, for her birthday when she came back. He said, "Pero ni puedes escribir, hijo." "Yes, I can," I shot back. He laughed, stroked his thick beard and said I was loco. When we got home, I wrote out in big block letters on the card: "Feliz cumpleaños, mama. Te amo y me haces falta." After I was done, I went up to my father and said, "Look." He looked at the open card and said, surprised, "Ah caray, si puedes leer." He asked me who had taught me. I said, "Nadie," while sharply folding the card shut. He kept stroking his beard, eyed the card but said nothing.

By the time my mother returned, I had read only up to chapter 13 of Genesis: I hadn't counted on the cognitive limitations of being a child: Though I could sound out the words and pronounce them correctly and could even look up the definitions of difficult words, I could not conceive of sex and adultery and murder and eye for an eye. But reading about these whetted my appetite: There was still yet another dimension to reading that I aimed to discover, a shadowy realm of deceit and terrible things that adults know about. I aimed to penetrate into this world by reading even more.

My mother showed up. My sister and I ran to her, crying, telling her we had missed her. She cried too, while our brother Oscar stood by smiling broadly. He had had a great time in Mexico. No scorpions had stung him. I said, "Mama, look what I got you." I gave her the card, and yet again, another adult was shocked at my literacy, which instilled in me an addiction to see that light of approval and amazement in all adults, and later on, in my teachers and professors. She looked confused. She said, "Who . . . who taught you how to read and write, son?" She seemed disappointed. I said, truthfully, "Jaime showed me a little. Now I just teach myself." She nodded and read it out loud, and then said, "Perfect. No mistakes." That night I couldn't wait to get to bed so I could read a Bible for children an older sister had given me. Though it had pictures, it still had a lot of text and the cover stated, "for ages 11–15." I was way younger than this age bracket, so I felt proud. I met my mother in the hallway on my way to the bathroom and she asked, with a bright smile, "A story?"

Something, then, rose inexplicably in my chest—and I could think of Jehovah asking Cain about his murdered brother, and the word *vengeance* flashed across my mind—and I said, quietly, "No, mama. I want to read my book now. In my room." I looked up at her, at her startled expression as if she'd been struck, eyes wide, a faint sadness seeping into her eyes (regret?). She stammered, blinked twice, but then shook her head as if to dispel a bad thought. She quickly said, "Ah, ok. Well . . . well, don't forget to say your prayers." She cleared her throat and then flashed me a weak smile, eyes glimmering.

I felt a satisfaction that I couldn't name. Yet, I somehow knew that though I still loved my mother's storytelling, her face had been the medium, the sole filter for life and reality, and now I knew that there were many, many other filters to tell me about life, other faces now, with text written across them. And they stayed with me through lonely nights. It was then too, that I began to feel, a little, a part of that adult world of unspoken things and feelings and destruction. I somehow understood vengeance and the wrath of the Lord at the wicked people of the earth who had forsaken his ways, and as a result, needed to be punished with a diluvial apocalypse.

CHAPTER

Evaluating Visual Texts

We live in a world in which we communicate visually a lot more than we used to, and increasingly, arguments are being presented through images. Actually, though, creating arguments using images is a genre that can be traced back to the early stages of all societies. A quick glance through history will show us that we have been using images to communicate all along. From the prehistoric cave paintings; to the mosaics in the Mediterranean region, to the complicated hieroglyphics found in several continents, images have always played a part in communicating ideas. With the advancement of technology, we can see a steady use of images, just think about how popular Apps like Instagram and Tumblr are, both depending specifically on how the user creates, or manipulates, an image. Although college argument tends to emphasize verbal elements—words, sentences, and paragraphs—increasingly, it is recognized that visual images or pictures can also be arguments and certainly can contribute to an argument. The advertisement that appeared at the beginning of this book can be viewed as a type of argument, although it did not employ the type of evidence that academic arguments require. Nevertheless, images can be extremely persuasive, often more convincing on an emotional level than a logically supported verbal argument. Many college writing classes now emphasize the importance of understanding "visual rhetoric," which is concerned with the relationship between images and writing and the way in which visual images communicate. This chapter discusses the role of the visual in constructing an argument, how to look for those elements that create a visual argument, how do these elements work together and how to use them effectively when creating your own visual argument.

THE POWER OF IMAGES

If the saying "a picture is worth a thousand words" is true, we would like to add that an image is not worth a thousand words, but also can be "an argument in disguise." Think about it for a second. When was the last time you read the words in an advertisement first? Most likely, you saw the images in the advertisement first and then move to the words in it. Also, notice that the relationship between the amount of words and images in any advertisement is likely to be disproportionate, with more images and fewer words. Yet those images work together to make a point, buy this, pay attention to this, or think about this.

Many of us believe that we can think beyond the power of an image and that we are not significantly influenced by advertisements. We view ourselves as savvy consumers, people who make rational decisions based on careful consideration and logic-based evidence. We may admit that we are moved emotionally by an image, but we claim that these feelings do not influence our ability to reason. Nevertheless, a glance around a college classroom or a restaurant parking lot will suggest that images have more impact on us than we may wish to believe. Why is it that so many of the students are wearing similar clothing, sometimes manufactured by the same company? Why are there so many SUVs in parking lots? No law required people to purchase these items, and no image *compelled* anyone to rush out and buy a particular pair of jeans or a popular car. However, the images in advertisements all around us promoted the *value* of these products. Perhaps they are associated with a particular style we think is "cool" or they suggest a lifestyle we view as desirable. Alternatively, we find the image aesthetically pleasing because it is so artfully designed. We may not be aware of these influences, but insidiously, images worked on our consciousness so that somehow, we began to want the product and then, before we knew it, we began to construct good "reasons" for why we must have that pair of jeans or drive an SUV.

It is impossible to withstand the power of the visual completely. However, if you understand how to analyze a visual text, you will gain insight into how it "works"—that is, how its various components function to promote a claim or argument. Below are strategies you can use to gain insight into visual elements so that you can decide whether to accept the idea they are promoting.

EXAMINING A VISUAL TEXT: LOOKING AT THE ELEMENTS

In order to understand how a visual argument works, we must be able to identify what elements are utilized in that particular visual argument. Most visual texts are composed of five elements: Image, text, size, color, and composition. By looking at each of these elements on their own, we will be able to see how they work together.

The Image

Visual arguments will not be visual if they do not include an image. This is the reason that we will begin with this particular element. Of course, images are not all created the same way and it should be the type of image we see that determines how we analyze that particular visual argument.

Drawings and Paintings

Until the invention of the photograph, drawings and paintings used to be the most common way to create an image to be used in a visual argument. These could range from simple sketches, to very complicated paintings. What drawings and paintings have in common is that they are not real. Think for example of some popular cartoons, like Bugs Bunny or Sponge-Bob. You are never going to run into them in the "real world" because they stem from the imagination of their creator. However, we can see that because they are cartoons, their features are exaggerated, and thus they are supposed to be comical. The same can be said about political cartoons. Although still exaggerated and funny, they are meant to communicate an opinion regarding a specific subject. Recognizing what kind of drawing you are looking at will help you understand what effect they are meant to have on the viewer. Even when we have a portrait, it can be argued that the painting does not represent the subject completely. A good example of this could be the Mona Lisa, where there are clear aspects of the painting that tells the viewer, that this is not an accurate portrait. At a first glance we see the image of this woman and think "Oh a detailed portrait of woman." However, when we take a closer look we see that the horizon is not even, the lines around the face are blurred and she has no eyebrows or eyelashes! The painter may have given the individual a better skin tone, added some features, or maybe even change the proportions. Both drawings and paintings show us things that may be "real," but we are never going to bump into them in the real world. What we need to keep in mind is that the creators of these images are already manipulating our perspective in order to get their point across.

Diagrams

Diagrams are closely related to drawings and paintings in that they are not necessarily a true representation of what is real, but the main difference is that they are informative. A clear example of how diagrams communicate can be found in instructions. Ever purchased a piece of furniture from IKEA? If you have, you will probably recall that the instructions do not use any words; they are all based on drawings that resemble the piece of furniture and show the various components. These drawings are intended to show the purchaser how to put that piece of furniture together and often do not use any words. color, or texture or photographs. Instead, they use drawings that inform you about what you need to do in order to put that brand new sofa or bed together. Another example of diagrams could be found in maps. Ever taken a train or a rail somewhere? Did you look up the stations? The metro diagram will show how to get to your destination, but most likely did not have pictures of the station or the trains you are boarding. Their job is not to give you a visual interpretation of your trip, but rather to inform you about where you are, where you want to go, and which train you need to take to get there. Remember that diagrams are meant to inform you, and thus they are a bit more reliable than a drawing or a painting.

Photographs

Photographs for the most part are often considered more reliable than drawings and paintings because until recently they were used to capture a moment in time. In the past, when you looked at a photograph, you were able to see exactly what the photographer saw when she/he was taking that picture. This is the reason many photographers became famous—they were able to capture the fine details and the majestic scenes that existed out there. Today, however, this presumption of accuracy is not always the case. When looking at photographs we need to ask ourselves "when was this taken?" With the invention of image manipulation software, a photograph can now be re-touched and manipulated to show something that is not real. We have examples of models and celebrities that have come out and spoke against publications changing their appearance in photographs. Therefore, when you look at a photograph, the older it is, the more reliable it may be.

Text

Text is the next element that visual arguments rely on to deliver their message. Text can be divided into two categories, the type of text being used and what the text actually says. When looking at the text we can see that the message sometimes relies on the type of font being used. Is it a big bold text, or a small cursive one? Does it look futuristic or more classical? By looking at the style of the text, we can begin to analyze the effect that the text will have on the viewer. Text can be one word, as in an advertisement for a particular company, but text could also be a slogan, where more than one word is being used. It can also be a phrase or set of instructions, perhaps telling you where you can buy something, or the price, or even what it is made out of. One thing to keep in mind is that as much as we need to pay attention to the text in the visual argument, we need to pay attention also to the lack of text. Why would the creator of the visual argument not use text? Is the image that powerful that it does not require text? By looking at the use, or lack of, text we can begin to focus on how the visual argument is created.

Size

Size is an important element that can also be divided into two components. One, how big is the visual argument, and two, how does size affect any of the images or text presented within that visual argument? Let us focus first on the size of the visual argument itself. How big is it? The size will tell us a lot about who the intended audience may be. Is it on a billboard? This would tell us that there is a bigger audience in mind. Is it on a postcard or a flyer? This will show us that the audience may be more specific. By looking at the size of the visual argument, we can find out a lot about its purpose. Now let us look at the size of the other elements. How big is the text used? Does it cover the entire visual argument? Are they tiny little letters hiding in one corner? Is the image big and bold, or maybe it is more about the text and the image is small, just to connect an idea or two? The element of size can play a great role when it comes to understanding what the argument in the visual may be.

Color

Color is one of the most important elements we have when analyzing a visual argument. Colors are usually associated with emotions; they have social weight to them, and can easily convey an idea. Let us look, for example, at the color red. Red can be used to define something that is hot, or dangerous, or something you are supposed to do, like stop at a crossing or a red light. It can also signify cheer and love. Think of some major holidays, like Christmas or Valentine's Day. These two holidays heavily rely on red to get their point across. Red is also a color that in some cultures can be seen as holy or sacred. So depending on the color(s) being used, the creator of the visual argument may want the viewer to understand certain arguments based on the interpretations of the color(s). On one hand, color can really give us a lot of information to use in order to begin our analysis; on the other hand, we can also face a visual argument that lacks color. Just as we did with the element of text, we need to figure out why a visual argument would lack color. In some instances, the lack of color may be done to bring us back to the past, where color was not used in visuals. It could also mean that we need to pay more attention to the image and the text and not worry about colors. In that instance you will need to focus a bit more on the other elements but always asking yourself why there is no color.

Composition

Composition is the last element we will discuss when it comes to visual arguments. Now composition in itself is not something as clear as text, or an image, but rather the combination of all the previous elements combined. Does the text overlap the image? Is the color consistent or does it change? Is the image sideways, or tilted? Is the text on the side, or at the bottom? By looking at the composition of the visual argument, we can really begin our analysis of the piece because we are not just looking at one element at a time, but combining them to see what the argument really is. Composition is important because it will show us the form that will give that visual argument a genre. For example when we look at a visual argument, do you see a product? A price? A specific image? Maybe you are looking at an advertisement and now we know that the main argument is that this particular product is good and you must buy it. Are you looking at a visual text with political images? Maybe the colors and text are bold and powerful? Maybe you are looking at a propaganda poster that is supposed to influence the way you think, or feel, about a particular group or nation. By looking at the composition, not only are we going to understand how the elements work, but we may also find out what genre the visual argument belongs to.

ANALYSIS OF A VISUAL ARGUMENT

Once we are able to identify the elements that create the visual argument, we can begin our analysis of the argument and really see what this visual argument is trying to do. In Chapter 2, we suggested a number of questions that you can use to gain insight into an article or book, and similar questions can be helpful when you examine a text that includes images. Following are several questions that pertain to both print and visual texts:

1. What is the subject of this text (image, advertisement, etc.)?
2. What do I already know about this subject?
3. Is there a controversy associated with this subject?
4. What do I know about the author or the source in which the image appears?
5. For whom is this text intended?
6. Does this image make a claim or argument? Is the claim or argument consistent with what I believe about the world?
7. Is this claim or argument supported by evidence?
8. What values or beliefs are being promoted?
9. How do the various elements in this visual text work to fulfill its overall purpose?

In responding to this question, it is necessary to consider the following components:

The central image?

Additional elements—What else is in the picture? Are different props being used? Is there more than one person or product in the picture? Why are they there?

The composition—Is this a single image? Or multiple images imposed on top of each other? What is given the greatest emphasis? How do the other elements contribute to that emphasis?

Colors, lights, shadows, designs, and background—How do these work to focus attention on the main purpose of the visual text?

Cultural or historical context—Does this image rely on your knowing something from the brand? Does it rely on another historical image, event, or idea?

Text and subtext—Is there any text in the advertisement? Is the text used for emphasis or does it just relay information? How does the text contribute to the main purpose of the image?

ANALYSIS OF THE HIBISCUS HAZE ADVERTISEMENT

Following are responses to the questions applied to the advertisement for Hibiscus Haze that began this book:

1. *What is the subject of this text (image, advertisement, etc.)?*

The subject of this advertisement is the product "Hibiscus Haze," which is a skin product.

2. *What do I already know about this subject?*

There are many products that claim to benefit the skin—some expensive, some not. But I do not know anything about this particular product so I may need to research it.

3. *Is there a controversy associated with this subject?*

Yes. Although there is general agreement about the importance of eating well and staying out of the sun to promote "younger-looking" skin and prevent dryness, people disagree about which products applied externally are best.

4. *What do I know about the author or the source in which the image appears?*

The advertisement appeared in a magazine that is usually purchased by women. But very little is said about the product itself. There is no author stated in the visual text, I may have to look that up.

5. *For whom is this text intended?*

This advertisement is presumably intended for women who would like to have skin like the young woman in the picture. Women who may be worried about older-looking skin are the likely target audience.

6. *Does this image make a claim or argument? Is the claim or argument consistent with what I believe about the world?*

The claim is that Hibiscus Haze will promote beautiful natural skin and that it is number 1. I tend to doubt claims of this type. But since no one really knows how to promote beautiful skin through any proven method, it might be worth a try.

7. *Is this claim or argument supported by evidence?*

No evidence is included.

8. *What values or beliefs are being promoted?*

This advertisement maintains that if the product is number 1, it must be good, and that the beauty of the woman in the picture is due to the product. It promotes the idea that youthful skin is associated with beauty.

9. How do the various elements in this visual text work to fulfill its overall purpose? In responding to this question, it is necessary to consider the following components:

The central image? The central image is the beautiful young woman with a hibiscus in her hair. She is natural and fresh looking, but not glamorous. It seems to indicate that beautiful skin is simple to get.

Additional images—What else is in the picture? Are different props being used? Is there more than one person or product in the picture? Why are they there?

The only other element in the picture is the hibiscus, which is a tropical flower, associated with warmth and sunny days.

10. The arrangement—Is this a single image? Or are multiple images imposed on top of each other? What is given the greatest emphasis? How do the other elements contribute to that emphasis?

The only image is the picture of the young woman with the hibiscus. In some ways, she looks like a painting. But she is not in the center of the visual text, she is to the right, and surrounded by text from all sides, except on the right. In addition, a frame seems to enclose all the elements together.

11. Colors, lights, shadows, designs and background—How do these work to focus attention on the main purpose of the visual text?

This is a black and white picture. Even the text is black, but we can see the use of shadows and light on the picture making her skin look either soft or shiny.

12. Cultural or historical context—Does this image rely on your knowing something about the brand? Does it rely on another historical image, event, or idea?

Some women may think that if they find the right skin cream, their skin will become beautiful. There is also the belief that what is "natural" is best. But the word *natural* is not defined.

13. Text and subtext—Is there any text in the advertisement? Is the text used for emphasis or does it just relay information? How does the text contribute to the main purpose of the image?

The statement makes the claim that this product will promote skin beauty and that many people think so. However, very little information is provided about how it was determined that this product is "Number 1," and the statement that the product promotes beautiful, natural skin is ambiguous. What is meant by "natural" or "natural ingredients"? Also the font used looks as if it was a type of calligraphy, thus reinforcing the idea of "natural." The name of the product is reemphasized by the text since the name is in a large font on the top, capitalized in the text on the left, and in bold at the bottom of the visual.

EVALUATING VISUAL ARGUMENTS

Developed by Emmanuel Sabaiz-Birdsill

When looking at visual arguments, we need to look at every single part of the argument in order to understand the connections that have been created. It is through this connection that the argument is being made. This is a two-part worksheet that will help you gather information and begin analyzing the arguments made in visual texts.

First Part

1. Where did you find the visual argument? Magazine, TV, Internet, side of a bus?
2. How big is it?
3. What is the company behind it?
4. What is the product/service or idea in the visual argument?
5. List all the images in the visual argument, from the main one, which is usually the main product, to the very small one.
6. Is there a background? If so, what is it? Can you tell if the image takes place outdoors/ indoors?
7. List the colors used in the visual argument, including the one used for the text.
8. Text: Does the visual argument have any text, and if so what kind and how big is it? Where is the visual argument? How much text is there in relation to the images?

Second Part

After you have listed all this information, here are a few questions you should be able to answer in order to start making the connection:

1. What is the main purpose of the visual argument? To sell something, to inform, to make a point?
2. Who is the intended audience? Men, women, teens, politicians?
3. Is this a new visual argument or an old visual argument? Can you date it? If so how?
4. Does it rely on your previous knowledge of the brand, product, ideas, or topic?
5. Is there a Website, phone number, or address where you can look up more information? If so, what is it?
6. If we were to remove certain images, or the text, would the visual argument be as effective? Explain.
7. Do you think the visual argument is successful at what it is supposed to do? If so, why?

APPENDIX

Using the Library and Documenting Sources

USING THE LIBRARY

The question "what is in a library?" once seemed obvious, even simpleminded, because everyone knew that libraries were places where one could find books. Today, however, although libraries do, indeed, have books, as well as magazines, journals, newspapers, and other information sources in paper form, most libraries are computerized and have a multitude of online information sources. In fact, upon entering a library, you might not immediately see any books at all, and to find the information you need, you may never have to enter a library building. Information from all over the world, on every subject one can imagine, exists in virtual form, and you can access it while sitting in sweats and using your home computer. This appendix provides an overview of how to find information in a library, both virtual and actual. It also discusses two systems of documentation: MLA and APA.

THE LIBRARIAN AS A RESOURCE

Have you been to the library at your college or university? Some students don't see the need to go, because they are able to access various resources on their own computer, which is certainly a comfortable way to do it. Nevertheless, we recommend actually going to the library on your campus, at least a few times. The librarians who sit at the "Help Desk" are experts in accessing and retrieving information and can unlock the mysteries of the library remarkably quickly; they are there to help you do so. Gone is the stereotypically genteel library lady who goes around saying "sssh." Today, librarians today are computer savvy detectives who understand how to locate all kinds of information and it will be very helpful for you to consult the librarian at all stages of your search.

Libraries, though, can seem intimidating, and students sometimes are reluctant to approach a librarian because they are afraid of asking a foolish question or of being a nuisance. We urge you to conquer this initial timidity, because librarians have heard questions of all sorts and are happy to provide assistance. Helping students is an important part of a librarian's job, so **don't be afraid to ask questions.** Even an experienced library user will find a new library unfamiliar and somewhat confusing, so you will save yourself a great deal of frustrating and fruitless searching by consulting the librarian rather than wandering around hoping you will be able to figure things out by yourself. Once a librarian understands the topic you are exploring, he or she can direct you to specific reference works that make your library time a great deal more efficient. Some libraries even have specialized librarians that deal with specific fields (history, science, religion, etc.) and may be aware of particular information or resources you might need. They may be able to direct you to specialized online resources, pull books from archives that are not available to the general public or request a book or document from other libraries. By asking them for help, not only will you save time but also have access to very specific information that will help you create a stronger essay.

THE ADVANTAGES OF BROWSING

Aside from the invaluable help you can obtain from a librarian, it is also useful to browse library shelves. When experienced library users search for a particular book, they often find other books that they didn't know anything about. When they locate a journal that has a particular article they need, they often find another article that is also helpful, or another issue of that journal may contain useful information as well. All of us lead busy lives these days, and our inclination is to locate what we need as quickly as possible and then move on to something else. But in a library, the opportunity to browse can lead to discovery, so keep your eyes open for new possibilities. With this in mind, make sure that you give yourself plenty of time to do your research. Do not go to the library during the fifteen minute break you may have between your classes. Give yourself time to ask questions and look at bookshelves and periodicals. You should plan to be there for a few hours, and although this may sound like too much time, you will find that if you devote a few good hours to your research, you are more likely to find the information you need. By doing this you will avoid endless trips to the library and dedicate more time to your writing process.

INFORMATION RETRIEVAL SYSTEMS

To access information at universities today, you will use a computerized catalogue to access information in the library catalogue, which will include books, journals, and a variety of databases. The beginning screen at most libraries usually presents the option of searching for books, articles, and databases in a variety of ways—by title, author, subject, periodical title, etc. The opening screen at our university, for example, enables a user to search for information either by keyword, title, author, or subject. It also provides access to periodicals, databases, reserves, and the opportunity to consult a librarian. The opening screen can also be an efficient source of information about whether something you are looking for is in the library itself or if it can be accessed online (many articles are now in electronic form, enabling you to access them and print them out). So if you already know the title or author of a book you wish to find, the opening screen is the place to find its call number, learn whether it is readily available or on loan to someone else, or download it to your own computer.

The Right Search Terms or Descriptors

When you do not know the titles of specific books or articles, you can search for material under the heading "subject," which involves inputting the right search terms, sometimes referred to as *keywords* or *descriptors* (at my library, they are called *keywords*). The opening screen of the library may explain a keyword search as follows:

> A keyword search looks for words in the title, author, subject, and note fields. Multiple words are searched together as one phrase. You may use the Boolean operators AND, OR, NOT to expand or narrow search results. Use an asterisk (*) to search word variations.

For example:

- gender and media
- college or university
- government and not federal

Figuring out the right descriptors is sometimes obvious, but at other times it requires a bit of imagination, and this is another aspect of the search process with which a librarian will be able to help. If you find that a particular term yields no listings, do not give up and assume that the library doesn't have what you are looking for. Try a few more related terms. And if these don't work, consult a librarian. The librarian can also help you narrow your search if you find that the term you entered yields five thousand entries. Often, combining two or more terms will narrow the field sufficiently, giving you a more manageable number of possibilities.

Related Search Terms

When you input search terms, in addition to listing books and articles on the topic, the computer will often suggest additional terms you can use for subsequent searches. For example, one student, Peter, was using the library to search for articles on the subject of requiring school uniforms for urban high school students, so he used the search terms "school uniforms." The computer returned a list of twenty-seven articles concerned with these terms, but it also suggested other terms he could use to expand his search, such as "urban youth—crimes against," "school children clothing," "uniforms, laws, regulations," and "children's clothing—appreciation." These additional search terms provided Peter with many other possibilities for conducting searches and enabled him to expand his perspective on the topic. Do not dismiss these suggestions. Different libraries use different systems and not all databases use the same search parameters. Make a note of these suggested terms in case you may need to search more than one database or go to a different library; you will have more terms to use and find the information you are looking for.

Recording Information During a Search

Computerized library facilities usually enable students to print, e-mail, or text what they wish to investigate further. However, it is always advisable to copy down the information you need. Pay particular attention to call numbers because it is very easy to make a mistake.

USING DATABASES

For college essays, you may wish to find articles from periodicals (journals or magazines), newspapers, or databases that focus on a particular type of information or subject. Our library includes several databases that are particularly appropriate for college arguments. These include Academic Search Elite (EBSCO), which provides abstracts to 3,000 journals (over 1,500 peer-reviewed journals), with full text to more than 2,000 of the journals; JSTOR, which is a comprehensive archive of back issues of core scholarly journals in the arts, business, humanities, sciences, and social sciences; and LexisNexis Academic, which is a full-text database containing news, legal, business, and medical information. In searching these databases, be sure that you narrow the search to a manageable number of articles.

ENCYCLOPEDIAS AND ABSTRACTS

Most libraries also have online general and specialized encyclopedias, such as Britannica Online, which enables you to search the contents of the Encyclopedia Britannica; CQ Researcher, which explores a single hot issue in the news in depth each week on topics ranging from social and teen issues to environment, health, education, and science and technology;

and Readers' Guide Full Text, which provides full text of about 215 journals (from 1994 on) including abstracts (from 1984 on) and indexing of over 400 periodicals.

GENERAL TIPS FOR USING THE LIBRARY

Getting acquainted with the library at your college or university is an important part of being a successful student. So don't delay your visit because of apprehension. Push open those imposing looking doors, find a computer, and note where the information librarian's desk is located. Then, as you engage in your search, keep these tips in mind:

1. Do not give up, even when you are having difficulty finding what you need.
2. When in doubt, ask the librarian.
3. Leave enough time to explore related topics.
4. Keep careful records of what you have found.
5. Browse.

Today's technology offers infinite possibilities for discovering all sorts of exciting information, but in the beginning, you may find it difficult to navigate. However, if you leave time for exploration, you are likely to make discoveries that will lead you in many new directions. If you keep these tips in mind, the library will provide you with material you will be able use for your essay.

CITING AND DOCUMENTING SOURCES

When you write a college argument, you will probably include information from secondary sources either in the form of direct quotes, summary, or paraphrase, and it is important that you cite your sources and document them correctly according to the documentation system required by your instructor. Citing and documenting correctly involves paying attention to many details, and it is beyond the scope of this book to provide information about all the possibilities you might need. However, the Purdue University OWL (On-line Writing Lab) provides a great deal of easily understood information about documentation in both MLA (Modern Language Association) and APA (American Psychological Association) form. You can also look at the MLA and APA Websites.

THE MLA SYSTEM
PARENTHETICAL REFERENCE AND A "WORKS CITED" PAGE

According to the MLA system, information from secondary sources must be acknowledged by parenthetical reference within the body of your paper and through a "Works Cited" page at the end. The parenthetical reference is meant to provide enough information so that your reader can locate the full reference in the "Works Cited."

A parenthetical reference consists of the author's name (or an abbreviated title if the author's name is missing) and a page number. Here is an example:

> Rosenberg says that television "warps our sense of reality because it perpetuates racial stereotypes" (46).

Note that since Rosenberg's name appears in the sentence it does not need to be repeated in the parentheses with the page number. Your readers have enough information here to locate Rosenberg in the "Works Cited" section if they desired to peruse Rosenberg's article themselves. Note also the placement of the quotation marks, the parentheses, and the period. The period goes at the very end, after the parentheses, not inside the quote (this is a common mistake). Think of it this way: The period indicates that the sentence is ending. If you were to place the period inside the quotes, then the information in the parenthesis seems to be just floating around in-between sentences. Remember that you are telling your reader, "this is who said this, this is what he/she said, and this is where you can find it." All that has to be part of your sentence and thus the period must go after the parenthesis. Follow these conventions correctly or you will annoy and confuse your reader.

If you do not include the name of your source in the course of your sentence, then it is necessary to include the name and page number in the parentheses:

> It is now commonly acknowledged that television "warps our sense of reality because it perpetuates racial stereotypes" (Rosenberg 46).

Note that there is no comma between the name of the author and the page number.

Sometimes you may have two sources by the same author. In this case, in order to allow your reader to locate the source within the "Works Cited" section, you would have to include the title of the work along with the author's name in the parentheses. For example:

> It is now commonly acknowledged that television "warps our sense of reality because it perpetuates racial stereotypes" (Rosenberg, "Medium's Influence" 46).

If the work you are referring to is a book, then the title is italicized. If it is an essay or an article, the title is put in quotation marks.

LONG QUOTATIONS

For quotations that are more than four typed lines (not in the source but in your paper) writers use "block quotations," in which the quote is indented one inch from the left margin and double spaced. The parenthetical reference should be placed after the punctuation at the end of the block. Notice also that quotation marks are omitted. Here is an example:

In "Fenimore Cooper's Literary Offenses" Mark Twain criticizes Cooper for his lack of realism:

> Another stage property he pulled out of his box pretty frequently was his broken twig. He prized his broken twig above all the rest of his effects, and worked it the hardest. It is a restful chapter in any book of his when somebody doesn't step on a dry twig and alarm all the reds and whites for two hundred yards around. Every time a Cooper person is in peril, and absolute silence is worth four dollars a minute, he is sure to step on a dry twig. There may be a hundred handier things to step on, but Cooper requires him to turn out and find a dry twig; and if he can't do it, go and borrow one. (Twain 524)

THE MLA SYSTEM: THE WORKS CITED PAGE

References on the Works Cited page consist of the author, title, the publication information (city, publisher, and publication date), and the medium (print, web, DVD, film, etc.). The items are arranged in alphabetical order by the last name of the author. If no author is listed, use the first significant word of the title. Each citation begins at the left margin and additional lines in each citation should be indented five spaces. Double space between each line and between each citation. The title "Works Cited" should be placed one inch down from the top of the page. Then double space between the title and the first citation.

MLA suggests the general following scheme (with variations) for including information in a Works Cited page (note that 1, 3, 8, and 11 are required):

1. Author
2. Chapter or part of a book
3. Title of the book
4. Editor, translator, or compiler
5. Edition
6. Number of volumes
7. Name of the series
8. Place, publisher, and date
9. Volume number of this book
10. Page numbers
11. Medium of publication

Here are some examples you can use as models:

A Book with One Author

Rose, Kathleen. *Socialization and the Inner City.* Los Angeles: Embassy Press, 1991. Print.

Two or More Books by the Same Author

Rose, Kathleen. *Dropping Out: Alternatives to Academic Careers.* New York: Leisure Press, 1992. Print.

---. *Socialization and the Inner City.* Los Angeles: Embassy Press, 1991. Print.

A Book by Two Authors

Johnson, William, and Marilyn Reid. *Emancipating Your Children.* Berkeley: Dome Press, 1987. Print.

A Book with Three Authors

Agassi, Arnold, Jerome Connors, and Malcolm McEnroe. *Tennis Etiquette.* London: Hillman, 1989. Print.

A Book with Four or More Authors

Dessing, Harmond, et al. *The Fear of Intimacy.* Los Angeles: Coward Press, 1987. Print.

You can also list all the names.

A Book with a Translator or Editor

Ulysses, Stephen. *The Agony of the Artist.* Trans. Buck Mulligan. Dublin: Whiner Press, 1985. Print.

If there is an editor, write Ed. instead of Trans.

A Chapter Which is Part of an Anthology or Collection

Stearns, Eliot. "Can Notes Elucidate Meaning?" *Understanding Poetry.* Ed. Edward Pound. 3rd ed. London: Cryptic Books, 1982. Print.

An Introduction, Preface, Foreward, or Afterword

Simpson, Bart. Introduction. *Life is Unfair.* By Homer Simpson. Los Angeles: Larson Books, 1991. i–ix. Print.

THE WORKS CITED PAGE: PERIODICALS

In general, the MLA suggests the following sequence for listing references to periodicals on the Works Cited page.

1. Author
2. Title of article
3. Name of periodical
4. Volume and issue
5. Year
6. Page number
7. Medium of publication

Enter the author's last name at the margin, followed by a comma, then the author's first name, followed by a period. The title of the article should be enclosed in quotation marks followed by a period placed inside the closing quotation marks. The name of the periodical is then italicized with no following punctuation. Scholarly publication citations should reference both volume and issue number followed by year of publication and page number. All citations should end with the medium of publication.

JOURNALS (SCHOLARLY SOURCES)

For journal entries, you should include the volume number, the issue number (if any), the year within a parenthesis, followed by a colon, inclusive page numbers, and the medium. Separate the volume number from the issue number with a period.

Here is an example:

Phorney, Bill. "Extracting Canine Incisors: Pros and Cons." *Journal of American Dentistry* 9.6 (1988): 9–12. Print.

MAGAZINES

Citations for magazines differ slightly from journals. For magazines, omit the volume number and provide a month or even a specific day in the case of weekly publications. Here are some examples:

Magazine (monthly)

Hoss, Dirk. "How Old is Too Young?" *Maturity* May 1990: 21–23. Print.

Magazine (weekly)

Joseph, James. "Hands-On Experience." *Volunteer* 6 Sept. 1982: 19–23. Print.

There is no mark of punctuation between the name of the magazine and the date. Also note that if the magazine does not indicate the name of the author, begin with the title of the article as shown:

"Economy in Chaos." *Time* 11 Mar. 1991: 60–61. Print.

Note also that Arabic, not Roman numerals are used.

NEWSPAPER

For newspaper entries, provide the author's name, the title of the article, the name of the newspaper as it appears on the front page (*New York Times* not *The New York Times*) and the complete date (day, month, year). Page numbers are listed according to how they actually appear on the page. If the article does not continue on the next page, that is, if it is not printed consecutively, write only the first page number and add a + sign. Thus, if the article begins on page four and continues on page twenty-one, you should write 4+.

Here is an example of a newspaper citation:

Reid, Anne. "Dining Out Will Save Your Marriage." *San Francisco Chronicle* 22 Jan. 1989: 23. Print.

ELECTRONIC SOURCES

As much of the following information as possible should be recorded before citing electronic sources: (1) author and/or editor names; (2) name of database, or title of project, book, article; (3) any version numbers available; (4) date of version, revision, or posting; (5) publisher information; (6) date material was accessed; and (7) medium (Web). If the citation information cannot be easily found, then an URL should be included. Additionally, for an online scholarly journal, (1) if no publisher name appears on the Website, include N.p. for no publisher given; (2) if a site omits a date of publication, write n.d. for no date; and (3) for online journals that appear only online, or for databases that do not provide pagination, write n.pag. for no pagination.

Following are some examples you can use for models.

An Entire Website

The basic format for an entire Website is the name of the site, the date of posting/revision, name of the institution/organization affiliated with the site, and date that you accessed the site. The URL is included only if the Web page is not easily found. Here is an example.

> Mothers Against Drunk Driving. *MADD*. Mothers Against Drunk Driving, 2009. Web.
> 20 Aug. 2009.

Note: The URL is not included because this Web site is easily found. Additionally, if there is no publication date, the abbreviation n.d. should be included.

A Page on a Website

> "Underage Drinking." *MADD*. Mothers Against Drunk Driving, n.d. Web. 21 Aug.
> 2009. <http://www.madd.org/Parents/UnderageDrinking.aspx>

Note: This webpage would not be easily found so the URL is included.

Online Periodicals

A citation to an online periodical includes both the name of the Website and the Website publisher. If no publisher is listed, use N.p. to denote no publisher name was given. The citation also includes the date of publication, medium, and the date of access.

> Buckley, Nick. "Government Will End Clunker Program Early." *New York Times*. New
> York Times, 20 Aug. 2009. Web. 21 Aug. 2009.
> Chen, Stephanie. "When a Parent Goes to War, Military Kids Grow Up Fast." *CNN.
> com*. CNN, 20 Aug. 2009. Web. 21 Aug. 2009.

Online Database (Scholarly) Journal Article

Citations to journal articles obtained from an online database generally follow the same format as a citation to an article from a print journal. However, the name of the database is included in italics, the medium of the publication is listed as Web, and the date of access is included.

Here is an example:

> Coll, Jose E., Patrick R. Draves, and Mary E. Major. "An Examination of Underage
> Drinking in a Sample of Private University Students." *College Student Journal* 42.4
> (2008): 982–985. *Academic Search Elite*. Web. 6 June 2009.

Online-only Publication

For articles that only appear in an online-only journal format or in databases that do not provide page numbers, use the abbreviation n.pag. for no pagination.
Here is an example:

Warner, Allison Brovey. "Constructing a Tool for Assessing Scholarly Webtexts." *Kairos*
12.1 (2007): n.pag. Web. 20 Aug. 2009.

E-mail or Other Personal Communication

The general format for a citation to an e-mail is author of the e-mail, title of the message if any, "message to [the person's name]," and date of the message, followed by the medium.
Here is an example:

Doe, John. "Breaking Up." Message to Susan Smith. 14 Feb. 2009. E-mail.

OTHER ELECTRONIC SOURCES

A Tweet

For messages conveyed via Tweets, start the citation with the user's name (last name, first name) followed by the related Twitter username in parenthesis, followed by a period. Next, place the whole tweet in quotations, including a period after the message and within the quotation marks. Include the date and time of posting, using the time zone related to the reader; separate the date and time with a comma and end with a period. Finish the citation with the word "Tweet" afterwards and end with a period.

Brokaw, Tom (tombrokaw). "SC demonstrated why all the debates are the engines of
this campaign." 22 Jan. 2012, 3:06 a.m. Tweet.

YouTube Videos

A general way to cite sources from YouTube follows, although at the moment there is not a prescribed style of writing these citations. Begin your citation with the author or poster's username, followed by the title of image or video, media type, the name of the Website and the publishing information for that website. Include the date of posting, the medium, and the date the video was retrieved.

Shimabukuro, Jake. "Ukulele Weeps by Jake Shimabukuro." Online video clip. *YouTube*.
YouTube, 22. Apr. 2006. Web. 9 Sept. 2010.

OTHER TYPES OF SOURCES

Some sources are neither books nor periodicals. Here are some other possibilities:

An Interview

An interview or personal letter follows the same format as an e-mail. However, if the interview is published, treat it as a work in a collection: Here is an example:

> Bly, Robert. Interview. *Interviews With Robert Bly.* By John Schaffer. Chicago: Westwood Press, 1988. Print.

A Broadcast Interview

> "Alice Sebold's Dark Tale Moves to the Silver Screen." *FreshAir.* Host David Bianculli. Natl. Public Radio, 11 Dec. 2009. Radio

Material from a Computer Service

> "Civil Disobedience." *Grolier's On-Line Encyclopedia.* 1988. Web. 20 Aug. 2009.

THE APA SYSTEM

Parenthetical Citation

In the APA system, you should refer to outside sources within the body of your text and include enough information so that the reader will be able to locate the source in the References page at the end of your paper. In the APA system, the year of publication is included in parentheses immediately after mention of the author's name. If you do not mention the author by name in the sentence in which you are referring to his or her work, then you should include the author's name (or a short title if the author's name is missing) and the year of publication, separated by a comma enclosed in parentheses at the end of the sentence. If you quote from your source, you must also add the page number in your parentheses, with "p" preceding the page number. For example:

> Harding (1993) insists that "proposed budget cuts in our universities threaten the quality of undergraduate education" (p. 6).

Like the MLA system, in the APA system you do not need to include Harding's name in the parentheses because it already appears in the text. Thus, the reader is already aware of the author's name and would be able to find the rest of the information about the source in the References section. Note also the placement of the quotation marks, the parentheses, and the period.

In the example that follows, Harding's name is not mentioned in the course of the sentence. Therefore, it is necessary to include her name as well as the page number within the parentheses:

> Administrators overlook the fact that "proposed budget cuts in our universities threaten the quality of undergraduate education" (Harding, 1993, p. 6).

A Work with Two or More Authors

If a work has two authors, refer to both within the text. For example:

> In a recent study of single mothers (Kelly & Rose, 1991), it was discovered that . . .
>
> or
>
> Kelly and Rose (1991) discovered that . . .

Note that the "&" sign is used only in parentheses.

If a work has several authors (fewer than six) they should be mentioned in the first reference:

> Kelly, Rose, Mangan, Burgess, and Dyer (1991) argue that . . .

However, in subsequent references, you can use "et al." ("and the rest"):

> Kelly et al. (1991) argue that . . .

THE APA SYSTEM: THE REFERENCES PAGE

Similar to the Works Cited page in the MLA System, there are also three main components in the References page—the author, title, and publication information (city, publisher, and publication date). Again, the sources are arranged in alphabetical order by the last name of the author. If no author is listed, use the first significant word of the title. Each citation begins at the left margin and additional lines in each citation are indented three spaces. Double space between each line and double space between each citation. One space follows a period, one space follows a comma, semi-colon, or colon. The title "References" is placed one-and-one-half inches down from the top of the page. Double space between the title and the first citation.

Below are some of the major differences between APA and MLA style:

1. Initials, instead of full first names, are used for authors.
2. Titles of books and articles do not use capital letters, except for the first word.
3. Titles of articles do not use quotation marks.
4. There is a greater emphasis on the year of publication.

Here are some examples you can use as models:

A Book with One Author

Rose, K. (1991). *Socialization and the inner city.* Los Angeles: Embassy Press.

Notice that the author's first name is indicated by an initial and that only the first word of the title is capitalized.

Two or More Books by the Same Author

Rose, K. (1991). *Socialization and the inner city.* Los Angeles: Embassy Press.
Rose, K. (1992). *Dropping out: Alternative to academic careers.* New York: Leisure Press.

Notice that two or more books by the same author are listed in chronological order.

A Book with Two Authors

Reverse all authors' names and separate them with commas. Use an ampersand (&) before the last author.

Johnson, W., & Reid, M. (1987). *Emancipating your children.* Berkeley: Dome Press.

A Book with a Translator or Editor

Ulysses, S. (1985). *The agony of the artist.* (B. Mulligan, Trans.) Dublin: Whiner Press.

A Chapter Which is Part of an Anthology or Collection

When you list the pages of an essay or chapter after a book title, use "pp." before the numbers. This abbreviation does not appear before the page numbers in periodical references, except for newspapers.

Stearns, E. (1982). Can notes elucidate meaning? In E. Pound (Ed.), *Understanding poetry* (pp. 56–71). London: Cryptic Books.

APA STYLE PERIODICALS

Article in a journal with continuous pagination:

Hoss, D. (1990). How old is too young? *Maturity, 12,* 21–23.

The number following the title of the journal is the volume number. Note that commas separate the journal title, volume number, and page numbers.

Article in a journal paginated separately in each issue:

Joseph, J. (1982). Hands-on experience. *Volunteer, 6* (12), 19–23.

In the previous case, you follow the volume number "6" with the issue number (12), which is placed in parenthesis.

If the journal does not indicate the name of the author, begin with the title of the article as shown:

Economy in chaos. (1991, Mar. 11). *Time,* 60–61.

General Interest Magazines

General interest magazines are usually published either monthly or weekly and often cite the date of publication rather than the volume number. For example:

Tripper, J. (1989, April). Dogs that chew too much. *The Canine Courier,* 262–269.

Newspapers

If you are citing a newspaper article, provide the author's name, the title of the article, the name of the newspaper as it appears on the front page (*San Francisco Chronicle,* not *The San Francisco Chronicle*) and the complete date (day, month, year). Page numbers are listed according to how they actually appear on the page. For example:

Reid, A. (1989, Jan. 22). Dining out will save your marriage. *San Francisco Chronicle,*
p. 23.

OTHER TYPES OF SOURCES USING APA

Interviews, E-mail, and Other Personal Communication

In the APA system personal communication is not included in the reference list but is cited in the body of the paper. Below is an example of how to incorporate a personal interview into your text. Note that the parenthetical information is placed at the end of the sentence so as not to interrupt its flow.

John Gaunt indicated that . . . (personal communication, June 21, 1990)

However, instructors in college writing classes usually prefer to include a citation about an interview on the References page. Here is how you would cite it:

Gaunt, J. (1990, June 21) [Personal Interview].

Published interviews are cited as works in a book or periodical:

Keidis, A. (1987, July). Censorship in the nineties. (Interview). *Rolling Stone*, 4–7.

ELECTRONIC SOURCES APA

Article from an Online Periodical

Online articles follow the same guidelines as printed articles. Include all information the online host makes available. A retrieval date is only provided if the information is likely to be updated or changed at a later date (i.e., blogs).

Warner, A. (2007). Constructing a tool for assessing scholarly webtexts. *Kairos*, 12 (1). Retrieved from http://kairos.technorhetoric.net/12.1/binder.html?topoi/warner/index.html

Article from an Online Scholarly Journal

APA recommends providing a Digital Object Identifier (DOI), when it is available, as opposed to the URL. Generally the DOI is located on the first page of the document and consists of a long alphanumeric code. Online scholarly journal articles without a DOI require a URL but do not require a retrieval date. If the article appears as a printed version as well, the URL is not required. Therefore, the URL is only required for an online journal.

Coll, J. E., Draves, P. R., & Major, M. E. (2008). An examination of underage drinking in a sample of private university students. *College Student Journal*, 42 (4), 982–985.

Article from a Database

Articles retrieved from an online database are cited just like a print citation. If the article is easily located, you need not include the database. The retrieval date is necessary only if the source could change, as in the case of wikis.

> Shafer, G. (2001). Tests that fail democracy. *The Humanist,* 61 (3), 14–19. Retrieved March 15, 2009, http://www.americanhumanist.org.

Online Encyclopedia or Dictionaries

Since encyclopedias and dictionaries don't generally have authors for entries, the entry name begins the citation. Provide the publication date if present or specify (n.d.) if no publication date is present. The retrieval date and the URL (to the entire link from the encyclopedia or dictionary) should be included. Here is an example.

> Feminism. (n.d.) In *Encyclopedia Britannica online.* Retrieved from http://www. brittanica.com/EBchecked/topic/724633/feminism

If the examples provided do not provide enough information, consult a style manual. Finally, it is important to remember the following:

1. Acknowledge *all* secondary source material. Do not risk plagiarizing either deliberately or inadvertently.
2. Ask your instructor which style of documentation to use or look at journals in your discipline to see which style is preferred.
3. Do not *guess* the correct form when documenting sources—keep a set of citation conventions handy. Make sure that spacing and punctuation are accurate. Since documentation is detailed, it can be time consuming, so leave plenty of time to do it correctly.

INDEX

CPSIA information can be obtained
at www.ICGtesting.com
Printed in the USA
LVHW052327150721
692755LV00001B/1